RELIGIOUS ACCOMMODATION AND ITS LIMITS

When does religious accommodation undermine the autonomy of others? On what grounds should religious accommodation claims be limited? This book offers an original model of religious accommodation which can be applied in practice in secular liberal democracies where religious diversity continues to pose various challenges. Firstly, the book makes a case for religious accommodation by addressing the key normative challenges raised by religious claims. Secondly, it offers a typology of how religious claims can be managed and limited through the careful balancing of competing interests. The author draws on case study examples from jurisdictions subject to the European Court of Human Rights and the European Union's Court of Justice such as the UK, Germany and France.

The result is a timely contribution to the debate on how a legal duty or policy approach in favour of religious accommodation can be applied in practice. Moreover, the proposed model offers criteria that can be used to guide the implementation of equality policies in contexts such as employment and education. The book will be of interest to academics, legal practitioners and policy-makers.

Religious Accommodation and its Limits

Farrah Raza

•HART•

OXFORD • LONDON • NEW YORK • NEW DELHI • SYDNEY

HART PUBLISHING

Bloomsbury Publishing Plc

Kemp House, Chawley Park, Cumnor Hill, Oxford, OX2 9PH, UK

1385 Broadway, New York, NY 10018, USA

29 Earlsfort Terrace, Dublin 2, Ireland

HART PUBLISHING, the Hart/Stag logo, BLOOMSBURY and the Diana logo are
trademarks of Bloomsbury Publishing Plc

First published in Great Britain 2023

A catalogue record for this book is available from the British Library.

A catalogue record for this book is available from the Library of Congress.

Library of Congress Control Number: 2022951403

ISBN: HB: 978-1-50993-710-3
        ePDF: 978-1-50993-712-7
        ePub: 978-1-50993-711-0

Typeset by Compuscript Ltd, Shannon

To find out more about our authors and books visit www.hartpublishing.co.uk.
Here you will find extracts, author information, details of forthcoming events
and the option to sign up for our newsletters.

For Rukshanda

FOREWORD

It is surely the case that some freedoms are easier to handle than others. If one seeks to avoid difficulties with implementation, it is best not to choose to deal with the freedom of religion and belief. Not only because so much has already been written on the subject, but also because it is probably the freedom that sows the deepest division among the many authors who have addressed the question. Some even go so far as to call into question whether it is advisable to maintain it in the contemporary era.

However, to take such a position would be to underestimate the author of this work, who has not shied away from taking on this enormous challenge. Dr Farrah Raza has taken the trouble not only to read first-hand and seek a correct understanding of a substantial number of authors who have published in English – more or less recently – on the topic of the protection of the freedom of religion and belief, but to give each of them their due by summarising their thought and arguments without taking sides. She has done this in a very clear and accessible manner. That exercise in itself is worthwhile and will be very useful for teaching about the urgent issue of the raison d'être of a highly controversial freedom.

But for Farrah Raza, the study of the literature is but a first step in a process that seeks to go further and offer a working instrument for anyone who, in the practice of law, is confronted with concrete cases of religious freedom. They cannot afford to simply stop at the observation that they are faced with a conflict of interest that is difficult to reconcile, but must, come what may, find a legal solution to conflicts.

For anyone interested in the questions relating to freedom of religion and its protection in the context of a contemporary democratic (and liberal) society, chapters 5 and 6 will be the most compelling, for it is in those two chapters that the reader will learn more about the method that Farrah Raza proposes to take vis-à-vis the conflicts, in all their complexity, that arise in connection not only with religion but also with other beliefs that seek to be treated with respect. The author makes no false promises when, in the introduction to Chapter 5, she speaks of '... an original model of religious accommodation'. She speaks of a model, and specifies how it differs from other proposals made or suggested in the past: '... the model I propose differs from the [earlier models] in that it systematises various kinds of harm and introduces definite evaluative criteria to determine when harm should be considered a strong enough reason for non-accommodation'.

Deeply inspired by the work of Joseph Raz, albeit without limiting herself to him, and most importantly without letting herself be discouraged by the difficulties he himself evoked in his writings, Farrah Raza develops her own model of accommodation of religious and philosophical diversity around the criterion of harm caused to others: '... the harm principle requires supplementary criteria or "mediating maxims", she writes, an observation that is both obvious and yet eminently ambitious.

Given the topic addressed, one could, of course, fear that there will be repetition rather than originality. The criterion of 'harm caused to others' has indeed been used more or less consistently in jurisprudence; it is relied on when defining the contours of the scope of various rights and freedoms covered, all under the protective umbrella of human rights, and is therefore nothing new. The difficulties accompanying this approach are also well known, from field experience, legal theory and case law. The criterion of harm is most certainly a textbook example of a concept that is difficult to define concretely, not to mention that it acquires meaning only when applied to individual situations. It requires in each case a scrupulous weighing of the scope of the harm caused, on grounds of the protection of freedom of religion and belief, to any person who may have to suffer the consequences: one and the same behaviour risks causing harm to one person, whereas another person will see the situation entirely differently and downplay its significance or find no problem with it at all. The harm may be objective and material or it may be subjective – which does not make it any less real.

Weighing up what constitutes harm on one side or the other, and how to remedy it, is therefore a most perilous exercise. Farrah Raza does not allow herself to be discouraged by these obstacles: 'My model is meant to act as an analytical guide to the task of determining the limits of religious claims by applying a normative consistent method', she writes in her introduction to Chapter 5. And she keeps her promise, by distributing her analysis over several concrete cases whose common denominator is that they have all been drawn from legal practice, which renders the model both more tangible and hence all the more convincing: education, health care, the enormous field of supply and demand in the service sector, whether in the private or the public sector, to name but a few examples. Raza proposes, moreover, to pose frank questions about the usefulness of maintaining the distinction between public services and the private sector, a bold suggestion that is justified by means of illustrations that the readers can analyse and assess for themselves.

Farrah Raza convincingly demonstrates that, despite its open-ended and therefore uncertain nature, the criterion of harm to others can serve as a sufficiently solid basis for the legal technique of reasonable accommodation to be able to adjudicate questions touching upon freedom of religion and belief and its protection in a profoundly divided society. At the very least, she has the courage to draw up a very concrete, perfectly comprehensible model. With great conviction she writes: '[T]he need for supplementary criteria does not render the harm principle useless in and of itself'. This is a phrase that accompanies the bulk of the argument, across chapters 5 and 6.

Chapter 5 clearly distinguishes four categories of harm: we might consider that what the author calls 'categories' are as many constellations of situations which, in practice, will no doubt overlap at least in part. But that is not the issue. The aim is to enable the reader to see the criterion of harm playing out from the perspective of four clearly different angles: harm to health and safety; harm flowing from denying access to rights, goods and services; violations of dignity; and excessive practical costs. For each of the four categories or constellations, Farrah Raza offers several suggestions ('guidelines'), which are essentially targeted questions aimed at helping decision-makers faced with freedom of religion-related conflicts of interest to undertake a contextual analysis of the different interests invoked and to assess, as objectively as possible, the harms as these are defined by each of the parties concerned.

In the final chapter (Chapter 6) Dr Raza analyses a number of what she refers to as 'hard cases' that prove that it is unrealistic to expect law and its techniques to offer an adequate solution in every single case. Law has its limits. Chapter 6 provides a very honest conclusion to Dr Raza's work, reminding the reader that any intellectual attempt, no matter how voluntaristic, must avoid losing touch with reality. Hard cases are in a sense to be regarded as an invitation to remain keenly aware that, particularly where the questions at issue are sensitive and play an emblematic role, touching as they do on the internal equilibrium of society and its cohesion, law takes on a political dimension: 'Hard cases demonstrate the limits of relying on a notion of harm when trying to resolve conflicts, and bring to the fore the challenge of regulating religion through legal techniques alone'. The challenge in such cases exceeds any attempt to design, as the author does, a model for managing conflicts that, while no doubt making it easier on a daily basis to find solutions in recurring situations, also has its limits. The intellectual honesty with which Farrah Raza acknowledges this observation adds in no small measure to the value of her work; namely, that she also recognizes its limits.

One could wish to more frequently be given the opportunity to read works like this one, which, on a question as delicate as the freedom of religion and belief and its protection, takes a decisive stand, while at the same time remaining within the bounds of what the author feels authorized to hope from purely legal solutions. The unique combination of in-depth knowledge of the literature, complemented with an explicit wish on the part of the author to contribute to the quest for practicable solutions while remaining clear-eyed on the limitations to the process, is what gives Farrah Raza's work its originality. It has earned its right to be included among the list of supremely courageous works that address the urgent question of religious freedom and belief and its protection, and it distinguishes itself from so many by its merits: it is clearly written, respectful of the existing literature, offers concrete proposals but remains honest as to their limits. With all these qualities, there is no doubt that this work is a veritable pearl.

Professor Marie-Claire Foblets
Halle (Saale), Germany, 2022

ACKNOWLEDGEMENTS

Thank you to my mother and father for everything.

This book is an updated version of my PhD thesis. Therefore, I would like to first thank my PhD supervisors Professor Maleiha Malik and Professor Robert Wintemute for their kind supervision, support, and encouragement during the course of my doctoral thesis and thereafter. I am also very grateful to Professor Marie-Claire Foblets for her kind supervision during my post-doctoral period and for the generous foreword that she contributed to this book.

I would also like to thank my academic colleagues at different stages of my career. In particular, I am forever grateful to Professor Robert Blackburn, Professor Satvinder Juss, Professor Peter Leyland, Professor Rebecca Williams, Professor Ariel Ezrachi, Professor Sandra Fredman, and Professor James Neuberger, and the Revd Dr Andrew Teal for their advice, support, and critical engagement with my work. I also thank the members of the Oxford Human Rights Hub for their insightful comments on earlier drafts.

The PhD and book manuscript would not have come to fruition without the support and careful reading of the text by Matthias Freidank.

Thank you to Professor Justin Jones and Charlotte de Cabral for their comments on draft chapters. I would also like to extend my gratitude to Dr Maja Beisenherz, Ruksana Chowdhory, Yonique McQueen, Hena Sial, Tasneem Bint Ghazi, Dr Jacob Wiebel, Dr Jenny Prüfe, Knut Fournier, Dr Emily Dawes, Isobel Williams, Oriane Froguel, Dr Maknun Hashmi, Dina Begum, Naheed Azar, Saima Raza, Sarah and Andre Sarvarian, Farheen Raza, and also Haidar Ali, Anaya and Amara.

Finally, thank you to Sinead Moloney, Sasha Jawed, and Tom Adams and the rest of the editorial team at Hart Publishing.

CONTENTS

ABBREVIATIONS

ACA   Patient Protection and Affordable Care Act of 2010

BMA   British Medical Association

CJEU   Court of Justice of the European Union

ECHR   European Convention for the Protection of Human Rights and Fundamental Freedoms 1950

ECtHR   European Court of Human Rights

FBO   faith-based organisation

FORB   freedom of religion or belief

FGM   female genital mutilation

HRA 1998   Human Rights Act 1998

HSS   US Department of Health and Human Services

ICCPR   International Convention on Civil and Political Rights 1966

RFRA   Religious Freedom Restoration Act of 1993

TFL   Transport for London

UDHR   Universal Declaration of Human Rights 1948

UN AIDS   United Nations Programme on HIV/AIDS

UN CRC   UN Convention on the Rights of the Child 1989

WHO   World Health Organization

TABLE OF CASES

The Court of Justice of the European Union

NATIONAL COURTS

Canada

France

Germany

India

Scotland

TABLE OF LEGISLATION

Introduction: Realising
Religious Freedom

World-wide interest in ensuring the right to freedom of thought, conscience and religion stems from the realization that this right is of primary importance. In the past,
its denial has led not only to untold misery, but also to persecutions directed against
entire groups of people. Wars have been waged in the name of religion or belief, either
with the aim of imposing upon the vanquished the faith of the victor or as a pretext
for extending economic or political domination.[1]

Arcot Krishnaswami

The words of Arcot Krishnaswami, the former Special Rapporteur of the
Sub-Commission on Prevention of Discrimination and Protection of Minorities,
ring as true today as they did when he made this statement more than 60 years ago.
His words poignantly capture the tension explored in this book: namely, that the
denial of religious freedom can lead to immeasurable suffering, whilst the exercise of religious freedom can cause, at the same time, harm to others. Religious
freedom is a complex right both philosophically[2] and in practice. It continues to
be a vulnerable fundamental human right under attack in all parts of the world.
Yet, it is undeniable that religion is often weaponised as a tool for the oppression of women and minorities and is invoked to limit the rights and freedoms of
others. Thus, it can be said that the exercise of the right to Freedom of Religion or
Belief (FORB) is 'Janus faced' – it frequently pulls in different directions. This book
argues that the tension can be resolved, or at least softened, by acknowledging that
the answer to the complex questions posed by the realisation of religious freedom
must lie somewhere in the middle.

Throughout the world today, religion continues to raise complex questions
for liberal and non-liberal states alike. The last two decades have witnessed an
accelerating process of 'constitutionalisation' and 'juridification' of the right to
FORB[3] as is evident from the increase of high-profile litigation concerning a wide

---

[1] Arcot Krishnaswami, Special Rapporteur of the Sub-Commission on Prevention of Discrimination
and Protection of Minorities, 'Study in the Matter of Religious Rights and Practices' (1960), E/CN.4/Sub.2/
200/Rev. 1.
[2] See H Bielefeldt, 'Misperceptions of Freedom of Religion or Belief' (2013) 35 *Human Rights
Quarterly* 33.
[3] R Hirschl, *Constitutional Theocracy* (Cambridge, Harvard University Press, 2010).

range of issues including abortion;[4] the display of religious symbols;[5] and conflicts between religious rights and the rights of LGBTQ+ individuals and groups.[6] In addition, the proper scope of secularism as a constitutional principle remains a highly controversial issue.[7] The increase of religious litigation has demonstrated that religion is not simply 'privatised' under conditions of secularism or 'modernisation'; rather, religion continues to pose a diverse set of constitutional challenges for the liberal secular state. One of the key challenges is to simultaneously protect moral pluralism, the right to FORB, and the rights of other citizens. The boundaries between these interests are not always clear-cut and are, therefore, subject to deep disagreement(s) and open to fierce contestation. For some, the secular state is under serious threat[8] from the global resurgence of faith-based movements and religious identity politics that are perceived to undermine liberal democratic polities that have assigned a limited or carefully regulated role to religion in the public sphere. Indeed, liberal democracies find themselves today under growing pressure internally, not least due to the demands for recognition and accommodation of diverse religious beliefs and practices made by a range of faith-based groups and organisations, as well as a persistence of incoherent approaches to limitations of the right to FORB. The various approaches are often based on different normative principles and understandings of religion. Courts have adopted various approaches that sometimes are in conflict. And although secularism as a constitutional principle is supposed to organise religion-state relations and provide the necessary, foundational condition for the right to FORB, alone is insufficient for delineating this right's precise boundaries.

This book defends an expansive interpretation of the right to FORB whilst outlining a model of religious accommodation that could be implemented in practice. International human rights law requires states to 'respect', 'protect' and 'fulfil' their human rights obligations.[9] Although international human rights law provides general principles and standards, it does not *in and of itself* offer a fully developed account of the right to FORB. The right to FORB can generate conflict between religious beliefs and non-religious ideologies. Disputes arise when religious freedom conflicts with the fundamental rights of others or emerge from inter-religious disagreements that are the result of divergent interpretations of religious doctrine. Since religion itself is not a monolithic phenomenon but is instead characterised by diversity and heterogeneity, calls for religious accommodation

---

[4] *Dobbs v Jackson Women's Health Organization*, No 19-1392, 597 U.S. ___ (2022).

[5] *SAS v France* App no 43835/11 [2014] ECHR 695 (GC Judgment, 1 July 2014), and *Eweida and others v UK* App nos 48420/10, 59842/10, 51671/10, 36516/10 (ECtHR, 15 January 2013).

[6] *Masterpiece Cakeshop, Ltd v Colorado Civil Rights Commission* Case no 16-111, US Supreme Court (4 June 2018).

[7] *Lautsi v Italy* App no 30814/06 (ECtHR, 18 March 2011) Grand Chamber.

[8] R Bhargava, 'Rehabilitating Secularism' in C Calhoun, M Juergensmeyer and J VanAntwerpen (eds) *Rethinking Secularism* (Oxford, Oxford University Press, 2011) 92.

[9] H Bielefeldt, N Ghanea and M Wiener, *Freedom of Religion or Belief: An International Law Commentary* (Oxford, Oxford University Press, 2016) 33.

are often accompanied by intense debate and controversy. Proponents of religious accommodation argue that religious freedom requires the liberal state to take positive action in order to ensure better protection of the right to FORB beyond the minimum level of protection.

Realising religious freedom entails clarifying how the values of the liberal state can be implemented. General principles such as secularism, neutrality, equality and autonomy are in need of further, detailed elaboration. On the one hand, there is a need for flexible principles whilst, on the other, general consistency in application has to be ensured across a wide range of different cases. Protecting personal choices and autonomy is central to upholding the right to FORB since it covers a range of practices.

The preservation of the conditions necessary for enabling individuals to make choices about their deeply held commitments and beliefs is essential in liberal societies. Those conditions are realised at various levels: in the workplace, in educational institutions and in access to goods and services, to name but the core areas of everyday life. It is the choices of both religious and non-religious individuals that need to be protected. That is not to say that the right to FORB should be framed in a simplistic or dichotomous way (religion v nonreligion). Religious freedom encompasses a wide spectrum of beliefs given the diverse range of religious and ethical beliefs; moreover, it must account for the fact that people's convictions and commitments often change during the course of their lifetime. Thus, the right to FORB represents something fundamental but also fluid and ever-changing. Accordingly, this book argues that personal autonomy should be a central concern when determining the limits of the right to FORB. This seems particularly crucial in an age where personal autonomy is undermined in multiple ways, either through state or non-state interference. For instance, lack of economic opportunities, the ubiquity of 'fake news' that can stoke tensions between different groups, growing prejudice and increasingly complex forms of discrimination – all of these impinge on and circumscribe the individual's autonomy.[10] Thus, religious accommodation is one important tool that can help to uphold key liberal values such as personal autonomy and substantive equality, which are ever more important in an era of growing wealth inequalities and the surge of anti-liberal policies even in North America and Western Europe.[11] The realisation of individual freedom requires more than 'lip service' being paid to the ideals of the liberal state. There is a need for concrete human rights frameworks that can be implemented in practice. Yet, some pressing questions remain unanswered: is there a principled way to accommodate religion? On what grounds should religious claims be limited? When do

---

[10] See S Hänold, 'Profiling and Automated Decision-Making: Legal Implications and Shortcomings' in M Corrales et al (eds), *Robotics, AI and the Future of Law* (Springer Nature, Singapore Pte Ltd, 2018).

[11] For the UK, see 'OECD Economic Surveys: United Kingdom' (OECD, October 2020), available at www.oecd.org/economy/surveys/United-Kingdom-2020-OECD-economic-survey-overview.pdf.

religious claims cause harm to others? This book will address these questions and offer a model of religious accommodation that includes guidelines to be implemented in liberal secular states where the problem of managing pluralism persists and dealing with religious diversity continues to pose vexing challenges.

I. The Problem of Pluralism in a Changing Landscape

A liberal vision of the right to FORB is intimately tied to the need to protect moral pluralism, that is, the existence of numerous conflicting worldviews and conceptions of the good life. The importance of moral pluralism was emphasised by the European Court of Human Rights in the leading case of *Kokkinakis v Greece* where it stated:

> As enshrined in Article 9, freedom of thought, conscience and religion is one of the foundations of a 'democratic society' within the meaning of the Convention. It is, in its religious dimension, one of the most vital elements that go to make up the identity of believers and of their conception of life, but it is also a precious asset for atheists, agnostics, sceptics and the unconcerned. The pluralism indissociable from a democratic society, which has been dearly won over the centuries, depends on it.[12]

It is one thing, however, to uphold the ideal of pluralism; it is quite another to manage incommensurable conceptions of the good where they conflict in specific situations in practice. The reality of increasing pluralism in secular liberal states is generally accepted as a 'social fact'.[13] How exactly to manage this pluralism is contested. Theories of secularisation that were taken to provide a sufficient framework for modern responses to religion had been, primarily, grounded in the work of Max Weber who, outlining the relationship between modern societies and religion, assumed that processes of secularisation would eventually diminish the salience of religion in society. It has become necessary to revisit these assumptions in light of recent global events that confirm that religion continues to be influential not only in the Global South but also in the public life and the spheres of politics and law of modern, liberal states in Europe and North America. This reality has generated various normative accounts by political theorists and sociologists as to how pluralism should be regulated. For instance, John Rawls' influential theory of political liberalism, which proposes a set of principles that are designed to ensure that all citizens are treated equally,[14] as well as the theory of secularisation

---

[12] *Kokkinakis v Greece* App no 14307/88 (1994) 17 EHRR 397, para 31.
[13] See the studies cited in P Weller et al, *Religion, Belief or Discrimination and Equality: Britain in Global Contexts* (London and New York, Bloomsbury Academic, 2013) 65–82. For global trends on religion see Pew Forum, 'The Future of World Religion' at www.globalreligiousfutures.org.
[14] J Rawls, *Political Liberalism* (New York, Columbia University Press, 1993, 1996) xxi–xxii.

by sociologist Peter Berger[15] remain key points of reference for scholars working on the legal accommodation of religion. As historical experience has shown, the constitutional entrenchment of religious freedom in national constitutions does not mean that the right to FORB is automatically guaranteed and can be taken for granted.

The role of religion in the public domain in European liberal states has garnered renewed interest in recent years. The concept of a 'post-metaphysical state',[16] that is, a state not rooted in moral legitimacy, has opened up the possibility of *new* forms of religious and ethical pluralism. The work on secularism by Charles Taylor, for instance, has drawn attention to the fact that even the most 'devout religious person' cannot avoid engaging with the external doubts to his faith because of increasing pluralism.[17] There are no longer moral certainties in our secular age. Taylor asks 'why was it virtually impossible not to believe in God in, say, 1500 in our Western society, while in 2000 many of us find this (non-belief) not only easy, but even inescapable?'[18] Taylor observes that:

> ... when a naturalistic materialism is not only on offer, but presents itself as the only view compatible with the most prestigious institution of the modern world, viz., science; it is quite conceivable that one's doubts about one's own faith, about one's ability to be transformed, or one's sense of how one's own faith is indeed, childish and inadequate, could mesh with this powerful ideology, and send one off along the path of unbelief, even though with regret and nostalgia.[19]

Certainty of belief in God, a higher power, or a transcendent legitimating source is, then, no longer to be taken for granted. Taylor has conceptualised the transformation from a pre-modern 'enchanted' world to secularized modernity in the following terms:

> The key difference we're looking at ... is a shift in the understanding of what I called 'fullness', between a condition in which our highest spiritual and moral aspirations point us inescapably to God, one might say, make no sense without God, to one in which they can be related to a host of different sources.[20]

The plurality of sources of legitimacy is a reality of the post-secular condition: God is no longer the ultimate or only source of moral legitimacy and agency. For Taylor, 'One of the big differences between us and them [our ancestors] is that we live with a much firmer sense of the boundary between self and other'.[21]

---

[15] P Berger, 'Second Thoughts on Substantive and Functional Definitions of Religion' (1974) 13 *Journal for the Scientific Study of Religion* 125.
[16] See J Habermas, 'Religion in the Public Sphere' (2006) 14 *European Journal of Philosophy* 1.
[17] C Taylor, *A Secular Age* (Cambridge, MA, Harvard University Press, 2007) 28.
[18] ibid 25.
[19] ibid 28.
[20] ibid 26.
[21] C Taylor, 'Buffered and Porous Selves', available at tif.ssrc.org/2008/09/02/buffered-and-porous-selves.

People today understand themselves as capable of making sense of their identity themselves and without recourse to an 'external' higher power, whereas, for the premoderns the mindbody distinction was 'porous'. Taylor outlines key transformations over the course of the past centuries that have shaped the conditions that have led to the unsettling of old, established beliefs and that made room for 'unbelief' or new beliefs. Jane Bennett challenges the assumption that modern life is 'without enchantment',[22] arguing that the conditions of modernity open new possibilities for fulfilment.[23] Recent decades have witnessed both the emergence of 'new' belief systems as well as reinterpretations of established religions. The conditions for new possibilities have resulted in the emergence of *new* belief systems or worldviews. According to Danièle Hervieu-Leger, 'at least some of the modern developments such as new religious movements are in fact vehicles of an *alternative rationality* which is as much in harmony with modernity, as it is in contrast with it'.[24]

As Taylor outlines, the role of religion in the public sphere and in the life of individuals in liberal secular states has undergone radical transformations. The shift to a 'less religious public', which includes decoupling political structures from religion, is not explained simply by 'calculating' how many people still believe in God. These social changes raise questions for constitutional law, since it is necessary to determine the scope of the role of religious reasons in secular, liberal public reason.[25] It is also necessary to adopt a definition of religion in order to decide whether a particular belief can or cannot be accommodated in law. In other words, there are deep normative disagreements about what the role of religion *should* be in liberal states. For instance, to what extent does the reshaping of the public sphere and the loss of 'religion' in many parts of public life influence our understandings of religious freedom? Is religion merely a secondary concern or

---

[22] The notion of 'enchantment' is often traced back to Max Weber's argument that the modern world is no longer mysterious and can be explained in scientific, rational and materialistic terms which means that knowledge is no longer constituted by mystery or magic and accordingly, disenchantment entails a new epistemology. Charles Taylor's idea of enchantment is by no means simplistic or straightforward. Enchantment relates to sources of 'transcendental legitimacy' and the source of 'meaning making'. For Taylor, disenchantment entails not merely a new dominant epistemology, but also, with this, a shift in the social and cosmic imaginaries – how individuals understand themselves, or their place, in relation to the social world and the cosmos, respectively (C Taylor, *Modern Social Imaginaries* (London, Duke University Press, 2004) 156) as quoted in G Watts, 'Recovering Enchantment: Addiction, Spirituality, and Charles Taylor's Malaise of Modernity' (2019) 34 *Journal of Contemporary Religion* 39. Likewise, Marcel Gauchet's work on enchantment offers a complex analysis of the processes of secularisation: 'Religion's demise is not to be ascertained by declining belief', Gauchet argued, 'but by the extent of the human-social universe's restructuring' in M Gauchet, *The Disenchantment of the World: A Political History of Religion* (Princeton, Princeton University Press, 1999) 4.

[23] J Bennet, *The Enchantment of Modern Life* (Princeton, Princeton University Press, 2001).

[24] D Hervieu-Leger, 'Religion and Modernity in the French Context: For a New Approach to Secularization' (1990) 51 *Sociological Analysis* 15, 22.

[25] See R Audi and N Wolterstorff, *Religion in the Public Square: The Place of Religious Convictions in Political Debate* (Washington, DC, Rowman & Littlefield, 1996).

is it a part of the need to protect a range of moral and ethical views that now also must include non-belief and new beliefs?

Given the pluralisation of beliefs, the question that remains central for the liberal state is how religious diversity should be managed. Jürgen Habermas maintains that the secular normativity and the legitimisation of the liberal state must be grounded in non-transcendental reasons.[26] That is, the liberal state should not compromise its secular normative foundations, although room has to be made for religious beliefs and practices to be accommodated. Accordingly, the normative core of the liberal state is secular. Yet, this in and of itself does not offer an answer as to *how* secularism should be formally, or informally, codified in the constitution. Whilst some forms of secularism are compatible with comprehensive conceptions of the good, the liberal state should not favour any particular conception of the good. However, whilst the importance of secularism is undisputed, the meaning, scope and application of secularism is. A substantial body of scholarship in 'critical secular studies' has emerged in recent years, including the work of Craig Calhoun, Talal Asad, Saba Mahmood, Akeel Bilgrami and Rajeev Bhargava. These scholars have challenged the view that processes of secularisation inevitably lead to the demise of religion or that secularism and religion are binary opposites. Talal Asad's genealogical study of secularism highlights that the secular is intimately tied to religion itself.[27] Asad challenges the notion that definitions of the secular and of religion are value-neutral and historically unchanging. This has consequences for the legal definition of religion. Ultimately, the way definitional boundaries are drawn determines which groups and organisations are entitled to the legal privileges and protections that inclusion in the category of recognised religion bestows. There is an urgent need for an approach to religious pluralism that is both liberal and inclusive of as many religious beliefs as possible so that secularism is not used as a tool for exclusion. Asad's scholarship undermines claims about there being a strict distinction between the 'secular' and the 'religious'. Rather, there are multiple meanings of the secular. Asad distances himself from the over-simplified claim that secularism is in fact a religion or is merely a construct of the 'West'. He explicitly states: 'I do not claim that if one stripped appearances one would see that some apparently secular institutions were *really* religious. I assume, on the contrary, that there is nothing *essentially* religious, nor any universal essence that defines "sacred language" or "sacred experience".'[28] Critical secular studies thus have established that there are different versions of secularism and that some forms of secularism and religion are not necessarily binary opposites, but rather, form a complex relationship.

---

[26] Habermas (n 16).
[27] T Asad, *Formations of the Secular: Christianity, Islam, Modernity* (Stanford, Stanford University Press, 2003).
[28] ibid 25.

Cécile Laborde's book *Liberalism's Religion* is a timely and important contribution to this debate as it addresses religious claims within the nexus of political theory, secularism and law. Laborde defends liberal secular states from the criticisms advanced by critical secular studies. She engages with Asad's critique of secularism in addition to various arguments that fall under what she labels the 'Protestant critique', which essentially claims that 'liberal law favours individualistic forms of religion based on belief-reason, thought-action and mind-body distinctions'.[29] Accordingly, the liberal state favours some religions over others.

However, whilst genealogical studies of secular formations (per Asad) are useful in highlighting the lack of neutrality and the exlusionary effects of secularism for certain minority and religious groups, there are limitations to such a critique. As Sarah Shortall argues, 'Christianity has also been reshaped by its encounter with the secular', and whilst secular concepts 'may well have Christian roots, but it does not follow that they remain in any meaningful sense bound to Christianity or that their current uses are a function of these roots'. She further notes that 'such accounts of the relationship between Christianity and the secular frequently elide crucial differences between the Protestant, Catholic, and Orthodox traditions'.[30]

Yet, even if the 'Protestant critique' does not provide a full account of secularism, it makes a meaningful contribution to the field to the extent that it highlights the problem of assuming that secularism is simply and necessarily an aspect of state neutrality. Secularism is in fact a varied and complex requirement. Critical secular studies have highlighted the inequities sometimes produced by the secular/religious and the belief/manifestation distinction. For instance, there has been a general failure on part of the European Court of Human Rights (ECtHR) to adopt a more accommodative approach towards *non-Christian* religious practices. This compares unfavourably with the judgments that have been handed down in cases that involved Christian minorities such as Jehovah's Witnesses, who have generally fared much better in the courts. Critical religious scholarship is relevant to the case law analysis to the extent that it highlights deficiencies in the current approaches to the limitations to the right to FORB.

Whilst a commitment to a minimum secular normativity is a necessary condition of the liberal state, its scope is widely disputed. Critical engagement with secularism does not undermine secularism per se, but rather should lead to the realisation of the values that both secularism and the right to FORB should protect – that is, the values of personal autonomy and equality. Craig Calhoun has encouraged a reflective attitude towards the concept of secularism; in particular,

---

[29] C Laborde, *Liberalism's Religion* (Cambridge, MA, Harvard University Press, 2017) 21.
[30] S Shortall, 'Beyond a Christian Genealogy of the Secular' *SSRN The Immanent Frame* (6 September 2017), available at tif.ssrc.org/2017/09/06/history-and-theorizing-the-secular.

he argues that secularism is 'something that is shaped' by the choices we make.[31] Likewise, the liberal state's solution to religious pluralism is not simply given, but it is shaped in part by the way in which the core constitutional principles are interpreted. Calhoun thus strips secularism of its neutral covering. In fact, secularism is not to be equated with neutrality in all cases. In a similar vein, Lorenzo Zucca proposes a version of secularism that is both more 'robust and inclusive' and that better facilitates the protection of minority religions.[32] The role of secularism in the constitution and in defining the scope of religious freedom presents a diverse set of normative choices for the liberal state. Whereas some interpretations of secularism are hostile towards religion, an interpretation of secularism that supports personal autonomy is more successful in safeguarding the foundational values of a liberal state. A duty of religious accommodation situated within an appropriate secular liberal framework is achievable.

II. Law and Religion: Current Controversies

The right to FORB continues to be an important and controversial human right globally. The increase of religious pluralism has been accompanied by the escalation of religious disputes and conflicts, incidents of religious violence, the expansion of religious networks across borders,[33] and the rise of litigation across jurisdictions. In fact, religious conflicts will continue to be part of a complex global reality for the foreseeable future. However, as a recent UN Report argues, it is essential not to overestimate the role of religion both as a cause of conflict and as an element in post-conflict peacebuilding.[34] Addressing the nexus of political conflict and religious identity requires sensitivity and caution. Controversial issues include Jihadi terrorism and sectarianism in the Middle East; increasing Islamophobia in Europe, India and beyond;[35] as well as the child sex abuse

---

[31] S Ferrari (ed), *Routledge Handbook of Law and Religion* (London, Routledge, 2015).

[32] L Zucca and C Ungureanu (eds), *Law, State and Religion and in the New Europe* (Oxford, Oxford University Press, 2012).

[33] B Christerson and R Flory, *The Rise of Network Christianity: How Independent Leaders Are Changing the Religious Landscape* (Oxford, Oxford University Press, 2017). Brad Christerson and Richard Flory discern 'the beginning of a shift in the way that religious "goods" are produced and distributed, which will change the way people experience and practice religion in the future'. Their book specifically assesses Independent Network Charismatic (INC) Christianity as a subset of neo-Charismatic Christian groups whilst making some observations that are of more general import. Globalisation, they argue, 'has created an unstable religious marketplace in which multiple worldviews and beliefs are encountered on a daily basis, increasing the state of flux in patterns of religious belief and making many religious groups much more open to reconfiguration', at 147–49.

[34] A/HRC/49/44: Rights of persons belonging to religious or belief minorities in situations of conflict or insecurity – Report of the Special Rapporteur on freedom of religion or belief (2 March 2022).

[35] A Kunnummal, 'Islamophobia Studies in India: Problems and Prospects' (2022) 7 *Islamophobia Studies Journal* 25.

scandals that involved members of the Catholic Church.[36] Islam in particular has attracted negative attention from conservative and right-wing politicians and media pundits who have highlighted its alleged incompatibility with the core values of Western societies. As the world's fastest growing religion, Islam has won rising numbers of converts in North America and Western Europe.[37] The growing visibility of Islam in the public sphere – a visibility that has manifested itself in the rising demand for halal foods, the construction of new mosques and the controversies surrounding the wearing of the hijab – has led to an increase in litigation in a number of European states, Canada, and more recently, in India.[38] A 'conflicts of rights' scenario has now become all too frequent. The right to FORB has frequently been pitted against minority or women's rights. Moreover, religion generally has been considered to be a challenge to the secular public order. High profile cases concerning religious symbols in different contexts include the European Union's Court of Justice (CJEU) rulings on Islamic head-scarves in *Achbita v G4S Secure Solutions*[39] and *Bougnaoui v Micropole SA*,[40] as well as the leading ECtHR cases of *SAS v France*[41] and *Lautsi v Italy*.[42] The clash between religious freedom and LGBTQ+ rights was at issue in *Eweida and others v UK*.[43] In that context, the relationship between religious freedom, anti-discrimination law and the right to freedom of expression was litigated in the US case of *Masterpiece*[44] and the UK case of *Lee v Ashers Baking Company Ltd*.[45] Moreover, religious freedom in the context of family law has been no less controversial, as demonstrated, for instance, by the 2017 CJEU ruling on private Islamic divorce[46] and by the 2017 landmark Indian Supreme Court ban of the practice of unilateral Islamic divorce.[47] The US Supreme Court case of *Burwell v Hobby Lobby Stores, Inc* concerned whether three Christian closely held *for-profit* corporations could be exempt from providing health-insurance coverage that included access for its female employees to a range of contraceptives, some of which were considered by the owners to be a violation of their sincerely held

---

[36] M Keenan, Child Sexual Abuse and the Catholic Church: Gender, Power, and Organizational Culture (Oxford, Oxford University Press, 2013).

[37] See www.pewresearch.org/religion/2017/11/29/the-growth-of-germanys-muslim-population-2/#:~:text=Between%202010%20and%202016%2C%20the,77.1%20million%20to%2076.5%20million.

[38] *Smt Resham and another vs State of Karnataka and others* 10.02.2022 WP NO. 2347/2022.

[39] Case C-157/15 *Samira Achbita, Centrum voor gelijkheid van kansen en voor racismebestrijding v G4S Secure Solutions NV* EU:C:2017:203.

[40] Case C-188/15 *Asma Bougnaoui, Association de défense des droits de l'homme (ADDH) v Micropole SA, formerly Micropole Univers SA* EU:C:2017:204.

[41] *SAS v France* (n 5).

[42] See *Lautsi* (n 7).

[43] *Eweida and others* (n 5).

[44] *Masterpiece Cakeshop, Ltd v Colorado Civil Rights Commission*, 138 S Ct 1719 (2018).

[45] *Lee v Ashers Baking Company Ltd and others* [2018] UKSC 49.

[46] Case C-372/16 *Soha Sahyouni v Raja Mamisch* EU:C:2017:988.

[47] *Shayara Bano v Union of India*, etc (Supreme Court of India): Judgment on Constitutionalism of Triple Talaq (2017)1438.

religious beliefs.[48] The aforementioned cases concerned a number of areas of law such as employment law and family law and raised multiple complex issues ranging from the display of religious symbols in different contexts to the rights of religious businesses. The high-profile nature of these cases demonstrates that the right to FORB continues to be a sensitive and deeply politicised human right.

Moreover, a string of 'conscience claims' have generated ongoing debates about the very *nature* of some religious claims.[49] The kinds of beliefs or organisations that should fall within the scope of religious freedom is subject to dispute, as discussed in chapter two. These conflicts must be contextualised within the wider political, global context which is currently fraught with identity-based tensions or within what has become known as the new 'culture wars'. As Ronald Dworkin argues:

> The new religious wars are now really culture wars. They are not just about scientific history – about what best accounts for the development of the human species, for instance – but more fundamentally about the meaning of human life and what living well means.[50]

The cases cited above are centrally concerned with the *limitations* of the right to FORB. These cases pose a diverse set of challenges for the liberal secular state. In particular, they raise questions about what should be tolerated[51] and how to properly balance the relationship between different constitutional principles such as secularism, neutrality and equality. The developing case law on religion, as cited above, points to the urgent need for a normatively sound and consistent method of resolving the issues raised by religious pluralism. This book develops the core argument that religious accommodation is not only justifiable and desirable but also possible to achieve without unduly elevating certain religious beliefs or political and ideological preferences. I propose a model of religious accommodation that is both normatively sound and flexible, and which seeks to manage religious claims in a clear and consistent way, whilst upholding liberal values that include minimum secular normativity and human rights.

III. The Purpose and Scope of this Book

This book offers a model of religious accommodation and provides guidelines for decision-makers on how to decide on limitations to the right to FORB. The difficulty of implementing a legal duty or policy approach in favour of religious

---

[48] *Burwell v Hobby Lobby Stores, Inc* 573 US __ (2014).
[49] See S Mancini and M Rosenfeld (eds), *Conscientious Objection or Culture Wars?* (Cambridge, Cambridge University Press, 2018).
[50] R Dworkin, *Religion without God* (Cambridge, MA, Harvard University Press, 2013) 9.
[51] S Fredman, 'Tolerating the Intolerant: Religious Freedom, Complicity, and the Right to Equality' (2020) 9 *Oxford Journal of Law and Religion* 305.

accommodation, which would impose obligations on institutions and employers to aim to accommodate religious claims, lies in defining the *limits* of the right to FORB. A key argument against religious accommodation maintains that the rule of law is undermined if religious individuals are granted exemptions from generally applicable laws. For some, such a system would open the 'flood gates' and create problems for managing religious diversity. However, the accommodation of religious claims does not necessarily have to be unmanageable. Suppressing religious diversity is unhelpful and reductive. Rather, there is a pressing need for a unified and consistent approach to religious accommodation as the current case law on the right to FORB in liberal states shows. Religious accommodation is workable in practice if the limits of accommodation are managed by implementing an approach that is normatively sound, and yet, at the same time, flexible.

The case law across liberal jurisdictions is riddled with arguments about the limits of the right to FORB. In many cases, courts engage with the various harms that are caused by a religious claim. Whilst there are different approaches to limitations, I argue that an approach that focuses on the harms to the autonomy of others is preferable. The strengths of the harm principle are that it is a non-paternalistic principle that has a regulatory function by which religious claims that 'over-reach' and negatively affect the rights and interests of others can be limited. Ultimately, by drawing on the harm principle as an overarching framework for secular liberal states, the proposed model seeks to uphold individual choice whilst, at the same time, permitting the state to place limits on personal autonomy wherever it infringes the rights of others. The exercise of the right to FORB can harm the autonomy of others in a number of ways. My model of religious accommodation identifies four categories of harm to the autonomy of others. An approach based on the harm principle does not permit state interference with personal autonomy in every circumstance; instead, limits to personal autonomy must be clearly justified and subject to periodic review.

IV. An Outline of the Chapters

This book straddles constitutional and human rights law and offers a model of religious accommodation that can be applied in secular liberal states. The geographical and jurisdictional focus rests primarily on Western Europe, and this book draws heavily on the case law of the European Court of Human Rights and the European Union's Court of Justice. These courts have often limited the right to FORB by using harm-based arguments either implicitly or explicitly. But when exactly does a religious practice cause harm to others? Joel Feinberg notes: 'The word "harm" is both vague and ambiguous, so if we are to use the harm principle to good effect, we must specify more clearly how harm (harmed condition) is to be understood.'[52] In the context of religious freedom, this means clarifying when exactly the right to FORB negatively affects and harms others. We can understand and define harm in narrow or broad terms. I suggest we focus on how religious claims affect others. Thus, a value-based judgement about a belief or practice in and of itself is unnecessary. Rather, the focus shifts to evaluating just how religious claims affect the interests, rights, and actions of others. My model groups the various arguments of harm into four broad categories of harm to include harms that (i) endanger the health and safety of others; (ii) impede access to rights, goods and services; (iii) constitute violations of dignity; and (iv) pose excessive practical costs. The purpose of this is to simplify the complex and multi-faceted harm-based arguments found in the ever-expanding case law. Obviously, freedom from harm is not the only value being protected in religious freedom cases; limitations to the right to FORB, however, often concern the negative, over-reaching, and harmful consequences of a religious claim. To what extent are such limitations based on genuine harms? How do we identify harms that should matter? Could the various harms be interpreted in a consistent and flexible manner? My model of religious accommodation contextualises harm, outlines the problems raised by different sets of cases, and offers a number of guidelines as a way forward.

This book does not seek to offer a comprehensive normative theory of religious accommodation, although it is true that religious accommodation can be conceptualised in a number of ways.[53] For example, religious accommodation can be understood as 'state-centred' by either protecting or prioritising the state's interests or by focusing on the perspective of religious believers and their needs. For some religious accommodation is problematic for reasons of principle[54] or for pragmatic reasons.[55] Rather, this book proposes a model that pulls together multi-faceted, complex arguments found in both the literature on law and religion and in case law in liberal states in order to offer an overarching framework of religious accommodation. More specifically, my model of religious accommodation is neither state-centric nor geared towards protecting religious interests *per se*. My model, instead, adopts a positive and balanced approach to religious accommodation by systematising the various categories of harm to the autonomy of others.

---

[52] J Feinberg, *The Moral Limits of the Criminal Law Volume 1: Harm to Others* (Oxford, Oxford University Press, 1984) 31.

[53] BG Scharffs, 'Conceptualising reasonable accommodation' in PT Babie et al (eds), *Freedom of Religion or Belief: Creating the Constitutional Space for Fundamental Freedoms* (Cheltenham, Edward Elgar Publishing, 2020) 59: For Scharffs accommodation can mean: (i) state accommodation of religious exemptions; (ii) individual adaptation to the state; or (iii) accommodation as a place of safety wherein the state's and individual's perspective are closer together.

[54] See BM Barry, *Culture and Equality: An Egalitarian Critique of Multiculturalism* (Cambridge, Polity Press, 2001) and Y Nehushtan, *Conscientious Objection and Equality Laws: Why the Content of the Conscience Matters* (2019) 38 Law and Philosophy 227.

[55] JN Szymalak, *Expanding Public Employee Religious Accommodation and Its Threat to Administrative Legitimacy* (Cham, Palgrave Macmillan, 2019). Szymalak argues that expansion of religious accommodation in the workplace harms bureaucratic legitimacy.

The model is useful for decision-makers and for the balancing stage of the proportionality test.

This book is divided into two parts. The first part addresses the key theoretical questions raised by the right to FORB including arguments against religious accommodation and the 'exemptions debate'.

Chapter one outlines the challenge of religious accommodation. It identifies key legal sources of protection for the right to FORB and sets out why there is a need for normative clarity on deciding its limitations. The chapter argues that the right to FORB is a fundamental human right worthy of legal protection – notwithstanding the difficulties with the definitions and scope of this right. In order to ensure that religious freedom is meaningful, the right to FORB should have *practical* value. This means that the state or an institution should take positive steps to accommodate religious beliefs. The chapter, ultimately, argues in favour of religious accommodation on the basis that it is necessary to protect identity-forming commitments, personal autonomy, and substantive equality.

Chapter two intervenes in the debate on whether 'religion is special' by addressing the complexities raised by religious exemptions. Specifically, three sub-arguments are addressed: 'the preference-choice argument'; 'the intensity-cost argument' and 'the equality-rule of law argument'. The 'exemptions debate' concerns a range of normative theories about the nature of the distinction between religious and non-religious/secular beliefs. I argue that it is not necessary to offer answers to the vexing 'definitional question', nor is it possible to 'prove' that religion is distinct or special given that much depends on the starting premise and assumptions made about religion as a category itself. The question of religious accommodation can be framed and understood in another way. Conscientious exemptions are only one form of religious accommodation, albeit a very important one. Instead, the workability of exemptions is more appropriately understood within a general framework of religious accommodation.

Chapter three critically analyses four current dominant approaches to limitations to the right to FORB which include: (i) practices deemed to be against the liberal democratic order; (ii) practices that breach the duty of neutrality; (iii) practices that do not constitute a core religious belief; and (iv) the choice of alternative options. Appeals to neutrality, I argue, have often concealed the real normative disagreements raised by key cases such as *Lautsi v Italy*.[56] This has, in turn, often led to only a weak protection of the right to FORB. Yet, the focus on neutrality as the key criterion in deciding limitations continues to persist. Current approaches to the right to FORB have led to inconsistency, uncertainty and confusing outcomes. Therefore, there is a need for an alternative model and guidelines on limitations.

Part II of this book offers such a model of religious accommodation by proposing a categorisation of four key harms to the autonomy of others. The aim

---

[56] *Lautsi* (n 7).

is not to provide a mathematical formula for how cases ought to be decided but rather to maximise the autonomy of all parties. In particular, I will offer practical guidelines that are especially relevant to the proportionality/balancing stage.

Chapter four sets out the groundwork for the model by outlining its normative justification. The theoretical framework of my model of religious accommodation is discussed so as to include a critical analysis of the core constitutional principles relevant to the right to FORB.[57] Secularism can be considered a constitutional norm, but much is still left to debate about its interpretation. I argue in favour of substantive secularism that upholds personal autonomy and an approach to religion based on a version of the harm principle. The harm principle works as a regulatory principle that polices actions or religious practices that 'overreach'.[58] Ultimately, the harm principle seeks to uphold personal autonomy and choice whilst permitting the state to place limits on actions and practices that negatively affect others.

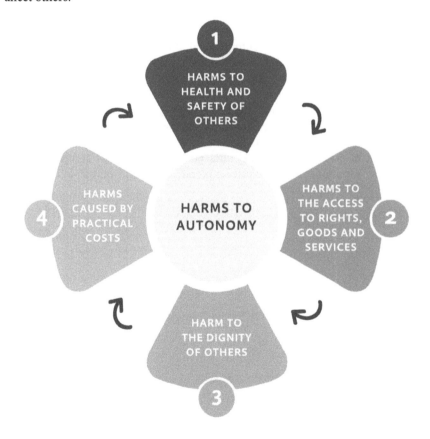

[57] J Raz, *The Morality of Freedom* (Oxford, Oxford University Press, 1986) 413.
[58] F Raza, 'Limitations to the Right to Religious Freedom: Rethinking Key Approaches' (2020) 9 *Oxford Journal of Law and Religion* 435.

In chapter five, I set out my model of religious accommodation in detail. The model outlines four broad categories of harm to include harms that (i) endanger the health and safety of others; (ii) impede access to rights, goods and services; (iii) constitute violations of dignity; and (iv) pose excessive practical costs. The different categories of harm are then applied to the case law of various jurisdictions, including the ECtHR and the CJEU, in addition to case law from the UK, France and Germany as well as the US and Canada.

Finally, chapter six engages with the conceptions of harm and their limits in a number of hard cases such as (i) those arising in the medical context; (ii) those involving children; and (iii) those concerning religious organisations. The chapter acknowledges that harm is a dynamic, social and moral construct with various dimensions. It is also ever-changing, as will be highlighted in the context of the rights of children and religious freedom. Thus, although governments in liberal states must sometimes decide on what constitutes harm through an exercise of state sovereignty, this should always be subject to scrutiny by the courts.

In conclusion, this book discusses the pressing question of the extent to which religious claims can be accommodated in liberal states, and, more specifically, it offers a workable solution as the proposed model narrows the range of *legitimate reasons* for limiting religious claims whilst, at the same time, respecting the personal autonomy of others. The aim of my model is to uphold the autonomy of *both* religious individuals and those affected by religious claims by offering an analytical guide. The following figure outlines the four harms, in the form of a hierarchy, and demonstrates visually how a model of religious accommodation could work in practice. The model does not ascribe religious accommodation unqualified importance, but it creates a hierarchy of principles and harms that must ultimately be balanced.

PART I

The Conceptual Dimensions of Religious Accommodation

1

The Case for Religious Accommodation*

This book addresses the challenge of determining the scope of religious free-dom as a fundamental human right by proposing a solution by way of a model of religious accommodation which offers normative criteria that can guide decision-making in religious disputes. When are limitations to the right to FORB necessary and justifiable? This chapter argues that religious accommodation is the preferable method for realising the importance of the right to FORB. Section I sets out three key challenges of the right to FORB as a multi-faceted right that often conflicts with other fundamental human rights and which includes the right to freedom *from* religion. Section II identifies the key sources of law that protect the right to FORB at the international, regional and national levels. Next, the chapter high-lights why there is a need for further guidance on how to interpret these legal sources. Section III makes a robust case for accommodation by tying together various arguments made in favour of accommodation. The chapter concludes that the difficulty with religious accommodation is related to the need to justify the limits of the right to FORB and can be overcome through adopting a clear approach.

I. The Challenge of the Right to FORB

Since religion itself is a complex, contested and evolving phenomenon, the right to FORB continues to pose a distinct set of challenges for the liberal state. The right to FORB is not a 'self-contained' right that exists within a set of defined boundaries or parameters. Rather, the exercise of religious freedom can entail detrimental consequences for the rights of others. The purpose of this section is to identify the key issues at stake as a preliminary to developing an overall case in support of religious accommodation. The right to FORB is challenging precisely because it is inherently complex, tends to conflict with others' rights, and raises difficult questions about its limitations.

Recent human rights reports highlight that religious discrimination and persecution continue to be an ongoing problem in many parts of the world.[1]

---

* I would like to thank Philine Dellbrügge for her assistance with this chapter.
[1] European Parliament Intergroup on Freedom of Religion or Belief and Religious Tolerance, *Report on Freedom of Religion or Belief and Religious Tolerance* (2017), available at www.religiousfreedom.eu/wp-content/uploads/2018/09/RS_report_v6_digital.pdf.

The 2022 UN Report entitled 'Rights of persons belonging to religious or belief minorities in situations of conflict or insecurity' emphasises the increased vulnerability of minorities and religious groups.[2] For example, the 2018 UN Report of the Independent International Fact Finding Mission on Myanmar found evidence of systematic oppression and persecution of the Rohingya Muslim community.[3] Similarly, the 2017 Report by the European Parliamentary Intergroup on Freedom of Religion or Belief drew attention to human rights violations committed against religious minorities in several countries, including Yemen, Saudi Arabia and Myanmar,[4] while urging the European Union to do more to protect religious freedom globally.[5] It is evident that the right to FORB needs to be protected at the national, regional and international levels and that efforts must be coordinated to enhance protection.

However, the pressing need to protect religious freedom is accompanied by the need to ensure that religious claims do not infringe on the rights of others. Achieving the correct balance and defining the scope of limitations are tasks that are far from straightforward. Heiner Bielefeldt, the former UN Special Rapporteur on Freedom of Religion or Belief, points out that the right to FORB is subject to numerous misconceptions.[6] Whilst international human rights law and regional treaties lay down the minimum standards for the protection of religious freedom, the extent to which these standards implement protection of religious freedom varies considerably across jurisdictions. The strength of protection of the right to FORB depends on a number of factors, including the formal constitutional relationship between church and state, the existence of political hostility towards minority religions, and the enforcement of anti-discrimination and equality laws.

A. A Multi-faceted Right

The significance of religion globally has grown over the past few decades, a fact that has challenged earlier theories of secularisation developed by influential scholars such as Max Weber and Peter Berger.[7] In fact, layers of complexity have

---

[2] Human Rights Council, *Rights of persons belonging to religious or belief minorities in situations of conflict or insecurity – Report of the Special Rapporteur on freedom of religion or belief*, A/HRC/49/44 (2 March 2022).

[3] Human Rights Council, *Report of the Independent International Fact-Finding Mission on Myanmar*, A/HRC/39/64 (10–28 September 2018).

[4] European Parliament Intergroup on Freedom of Religion or Belief and Religious Tolerance (n 1) 31–34, 39, 40.

[5] ibid 14.

[6] H Bielefeldt, 'Freedom of Religion or Belief – A Human Right under Pressure' (2012) 1 *Oxford Journal of Law and Religion* 15, 35.

[7] G Thuswaldner, 'A Conversation with Peter L. Berger "How My Views Have Changed"' (2014) 77/3 *The Cresset* 16 and see also D Reaves, 'Peter Berger and the Rise and Fall of the Theory of Secularization' (2012) 11 *Denison Journal of Religion* 3.

been added to the right to FORB because religion has come to play an increasingly prominent role in the civil societies of Europe and North America over the course of the past decades, and continues to be relevant in a number of positive and negative ways. In its positive dimension, religion can enrich the identity, culture, and ways of life of individuals. In its negative dimension, religious freedom can at times result in discrimination against minorities, fuel oppressive political movements, and lead to violent conflicts. The UN Special Rapporteur on freedom of religion or belief has recently reported that a number of conflicts globally have religious dimensions.[8] Therefore, given the multiple dimensions of the right to FORB, it remains a conceptually problematic and controversial right. Even though the right to FORB is considered to be one of the core universal human rights, recent attempts to undermine its importance and conceptual coherence have meant that its status as a fundamental classical right has been questioned.[9]

In theory, international human rights law requires states to be responsible for securing the right to FORB for all, although in practice states are often complicit in promoting one religion and its interests over others. This might be through preferential treatment in law realised by official constitutional recognition or by official codification in national constitutions. Many governments have also implemented policies to promote the principle of religious freedom. Most notably, the US and the EU have both made religious freedom an important foreign policy aim. For example, the US International Religious Freedom Act of 1998 established an Office on International Religious Freedom in the State Department.[10] Moreover, the EU's Parliamentary working group has adopted several resolutions including resolutions addressing the persecution of Christians or Ahmidiyya Muslims in Pakistan.[11] However, the European Parliament has also criticised specific minority religious practices. For example, the European Parliament endorsed a position that argues a need to limit or regulate ritual male circumcision – a view that is considered deeply offensive and unacceptable to members of the Jewish and Muslim communities.[12] Ritual slaughter of animals has also come under scrutiny in the European context. The CJEU has now heard

---

[8] Human Rights Council (n 2).

[9] H Bielefeldt, 'Misperceptions of Freedom of Religion or Belief' (2013) 35 *Human Rights Quarterly* 33.

[10] The Act established the Office of International Religious Freedom at the Department of State. See www.state.gov/bureaus-offices/under-secretary-for-civilian-security-democracy-and-human-rights/office-of-international-religious-freedom.

[11] See C de Jong, 'The Contribution of the European Parliament to the Protection of FORB through the External Relations of the EU' in M Evans et al (eds), *The Changing Nature of Religious Rights under International Law* (New York, Oxford University Press, 2015).

[12] European Parliament (ed), 'Citizens' Rights and Constitutional Affairs: Religious Practice and Observance in the EU Member States' (2013), available at www.europarl.europa.eu/RegData/etudes/etudes/join/2013/474399/IPOL-LIBE_ET(2013)474399_EN.pdf.

cases concerning ritual slaughter including *Liga van Moskeeen en Islamitische Organisaties Provincie Antwerpen VZW and Others*.[13] In the CJEU case of *Centraal Israëlitisch Consistorie van België and Others* the Court permitted EU Member States to place limitations on the methods to be used in the context of religious slaughter.[14] These cases highlight the need for clarity, guidelines and dialogue.[15]

State-backed promotion of the right to FORB has been problematic too. For example, one of the narratives used to justify military intervention in non-western countries such as in Afghanistan was, as one critic put it, the alleged need to 'rescue Muslim women from their (overly religious) male oppressors through moral and religious reform'. In this way, 'Religion was construed as both the problem and the solution' and the US sought to transform Muslim women into 'tolerant, free Muslim women'.[16] Yet, singling out religion in this way is simplistic. Religion, particularly as a category in law, usually captures a limited aspect of a complex broader picture. Elizabeth Shakman-Hurd points to the pitfalls of using religion as an 'over-inclusive general category'. Hurd argues that 'The discourse of religious freedom describes, and legally defines, individuals and groups in religious or sectarian terms rather than on the basis of other affinities and relations – for example, as groups based on political affinities, historical or geographical ties, neighborhood or occupational affiliations, kinship networks, generational ties, or socio-economic status'.[17] Hurd's scholarship highlights that religious identity does not exist in isolation as the causes of religious disputes are often multi-faceted.

Moreover, whilst religion has been used as a pretext to legitimise violence, its role in the public sphere remains diverse. Talal Asad, in his writings on secularism, challenges the assumption that religious violence is somehow distinct in nature as compared to secular regimes that have also legitimated violence; rather, he demonstrates that both secular and religious states and groups can be violent. In that sense, fears about Islam in Europe should be subject to more nuanced policy approaches. Asad points out that Islam, in particular, has been singled out for its purported failure to embrace secularism and enter into modernity.[18] These narratives have made their way into the legal debates about the limits to the right to FORB in several European countries. In France in particular, highly

---

[13] Case C-426/16 *Liga van Moskeeen en Islamitische Organisaties Provincie Antwerpen VZW and Others* EU:C:2018:335.
[14] Case C-336/19 *Centraal Israëlitisch Consistorie van België ea and Others* EU:C:2020:1031.
[15] F Raza, 'Accommodating Religious Slaughter in the UK and Germany: Competing Interests in Carving Out Legal Exemptions' (2018) 191 *Max Planck Institute for Social Anthropology Working Papers* 1.
[16] ES Hurd, *Beyond Religious Freedom: The New Global Politics of Religion* (Princeton, Princeton University Press, 2015) 25.
[17] ibid 39.
[18] T Asad, *Formations of the Secular: Christianity, Islam, Modernity*, Cultural Memory in the Present (Stanford, Stanford University Press, 2003) 10.

publicised events such as the terrorist attacks on the office of *Charlie Hebdo*,[19] the decades-long hijab debate, the application of the French version of secularism known as *laïcité* as discussed in the *Statsi Commission's Report*,[20] the case of *SAS v France* concerning the ban of face coverings in public,[21] and the so-called 'burkini' incident have raised questions about the correct relationship between the secular liberal state and religion(s).[22] These issues have heightened the ideological tensions between a 'muscular secularism' on the one hand, and more accommodative, multi-culturalist policies, on the other.[23] More recently, a new law in France specifically designed to protect republican values and prevent 'separatism' has served to highlight that the debates around the hotly contested right to FORB are far from having been resolved.[24] The examples above demonstrate how the right to FORB can be pulled in different directions: it can be a tool both for protecting individuals and minorities *and* also by states to support specific policy objectives that promote the interests of certain religious groups or practices over others. Given this multi-faceted nature of the right to FORB, a balanced approach to limitations is required.

B. Conflicts with Other Fundamental Rights

The right to FORB often conflicts with other fundamental rights and constitutional principles. Religious beliefs sometimes clash with the rights of women or those identifying as lesbian, gay, bi-sexual and transgender (LGBTQ+) or with the rights of religious minorities. Accordingly, the realisation of the right to FORB in practice can undermine the constitutional principles of equality, non-discrimination, neutrality, and secularism. More recently, the right to FORB and the right to freedom of expression have come into sharp conflict as can be seen in *Ashers* and *Masterpiece*.[25]

---

[19] For a critical analysis see SS Juss, 'Burqa-bashing and the Charlie Hebdo Cartoons' (2016) 26 *King's Law Journal* 27.

[20] B Stasi, 'Commission de réflexion sur l'application du principe de laïcité dans la République: Rapport au Président de la République' (11 December 2003), available at www.vie-publique.fr/rapport/26626-commission-de-reflexion-sur-application-du-principe-de-laicite. The report has also been published in book form as B Stasi, *Laïcité et République: Rapport au Président de la République* (Paris, La Documentation française, 2004).

[21] *SAS v France* App no 43835/11 ECHR 2014-III, 351.

[22] The incident was widely reported: see A Chrisafis, 'French Burkini Ban Row Escalates after Clothing Incident at Nice Beach' *The Guardian* (25 August 2016) www.theguardian.com/world/2016/aug/24/french-burkini-ban-row-escalates-clothing-incident-woman-police-nice-beach.

[23] T Modood and T Sealy, 'Concept Paper: Secularism and the Governance of Religious Diversity' (GREASE Project, May 2019).

[24] On 12 April 2021, the French Senate, with a majority of 208 votes for and 109 against, voted on the bill 'to uphold the principles of the Republic', see www.amnesty.org/en/documents/eur21/3912/2021/en.

[25] *Lee v Ashers Baking Company Ltd and others* [2018] UKSC 49, [2020] AC 413 and *Masterpiece Cakeshop Ltd v Colorado Civil Rights Commission* 138 S Ct 419 (2017).

Cases concerning a conflict of rights have been litigated in a series of high-profile cases in courts across the world. Religious symbols have been particularly controversial in secular liberal states. For example, in *Lautsi v Italy*, the parents of children attending a state school challenged the display of a crucifix in a classroom.[26] At the core of the dispute lay different normative accounts about the content of secularism. Moreover, the leading ECtHR case of *Eweida and others v UK* concerned the accommodation claims of four Christian claimants, two of which concerned religious symbols, and the other two concerned conflicts between religious freedom and the rights of others not to be discriminated against on the basis of their sexual orientation.[27] Another leading ECtHR case was *SAS v France*, which concerned the French ban on face veils that negatively and disproportionately affects a minority of Muslim women.[28] *Lautsi, Eweida* and *SAS* sparked public debates about the accommodation of religious symbols in public and, more broadly, the role of religion in European states.

Similarly, in the US, the case of *Hobby Lobby* was controversial as the Supreme Court held that regulations promulgated by the US Department of Health and Human Services (HSS) under the Patient Protection and Affordable Care Act of 2010 (ACA) that required employers to provide their employees with health-insurance coverage for access to a range of contraceptives violated the religious beliefs of owners of three Christian closely held for-profit corporations. The owners of the for-profit corporations argued that their sincerely held belief that life begins at conception meant that facilitating access to contraception and drugs after that point would violate their religious conscience. Specifically, the owners argued that four approved contraceptives that may operate after the fertilisation of an egg violated their religious beliefs.[29] The HSS had already exempted certain *religious non-profit* organisations. The HSS argued that the aforementioned companies and their owners could not be exempt. In contrast, the Religious Freedom Restoration Act of 1993 (RFRA) which applies to Federal laws prohibits the 'Government from substantially burdening a person's exercise of religion even if the burden results from a rule of general applicability' unless the Government can demonstrate that two conditions are met: (1) that the burden pursues a compelling governmental interest and (2) is the least restrictive means of doing so.[30] Could the claims made by the for-profit corporations fall within the scope of the RFRA and benefit from an exemption from the regulations?

The majority of the US Supreme Court held that the HSS regulations imposing the contraceptive mandate violated the RFRA as applied to closely held corporations. The majority emphasised that they did not consider that the consequences

---

[26] *Lautsi v Italy* (2010) 50 EHRR 42 (30814/06).
[27] *Eweida and others v UK* App nos 48420/10, 59842/10, 51671/10 and 36516/10 [2013] ECHR 37 (ECtHR, 15 January 2013).
[28] *SAS* (n 21) 351.
[29] *Burwell v Hobby Lobby Stores, Inc*, 134 S Ct 2751 (2014).
[30] ibid.

of their decision were far-reaching so as to enable corporations to have 'free reign to take steps that impose disadvantages on others'.[31] The Court held that the regulations constituted a substantial burden and the sincerity of the beliefs of the owners were not questioned. The Court also held that HSS did not pursue the least restrictive means of furthering the compelling interest because 'The most straightforward way ... would be for the Government to assume the cost of providing the four contraceptives at issue to any women who are unable to obtain them under their health-insurance policies due to their employers' religious objections'.[32]

Commentators disagree about whether *Hobby Lobby* is a step too far in favour of religious believers and is to the detriment of others, as in this case, female employees. It is debatable whether for-profit organisations should be granted a conscience-based legal exemption in this particular context. Justice Ginsburg's dissenting opinion was highly critical of the majority judgment. She framed the question in the following way: 'Is the "burden" on the religious beliefs of a corporation's owners "substantial" if a female employee uses one of the four religiously objectionable contraceptives?'[33] For Justice Ginsburg the link between the beliefs of the owners of the corporations and the potential results of the use of contraception was too weak to constitute a substantial burden on the religious beliefs of the owners of the organisations.[34] Andrew Koppelman and Frederick Gedicks argue that the Court's interpretation means that religious believers can harm non-adherents merely to protect the religious exercise of others.[35]

Some commentators raise the question of whether the owners of the corporations would also feel morally responsible for any pregnancy-related conditions or deaths that could have been prevented by use of the four religiously objectionable birth-control methods.[36] Some commentators argue that *Hobby Lobby* was decided correctly in that it helped protect religious liberty in the commercial sphere.[37] For others, *Hobby Lobby*, arguably, favoured 'religious commercial freedom' – an important dimension of religious freedom in light of the expansion of religiously inspired businesses and services[38] – over women's rights

---

[31] ibid, p 3.

[32] The Court found it unnecessary to adjudicate on the issue of whether HSS pursued a compelling interest (of promoting public health and gender equality) and went on to assume that for the purposes of RFRA the guaranteeing of cost-free access to the four challenged contraceptive methods was a compelling government interest (ibid 40).

[33] *Burwell* (n 29) p 23. The four religiously objectionable contraceptives include those 'that may have the effect of preventing an already fertilized egg from developing any further by inhibiting its attachment to the uterus'.

[34] ibid.

[35] A Koppelman and FM Gedicks, 'Hobby Lobby and Religious Liberty' in CW Durham et al (eds), *Law, Religion and Freedom: Conceptualizing a Common Right* (London and New York, Routledge, 2021).

[36] GJ Annas, T Ruger and JP Ruger, 'Money, Sex, and Religion – The Supreme Court's ACA Sequel' (2014) Faculty Scholarship Paper 1474, 865.

[37] P Horowitz, 'The Hobby Lobby Moment' (2014) 128 *Harvard Law Review* 154.

[38] See J Lever and M Miele, 'The Growth of Halal Meat Markets in Europe: An Exploration of the Supply Side Theory of Religion' (2012) 28 *Journal of Rural Studies* 528.

and universal healthcare policies. However, Jennifer Denbow argues that 'the Court imposed market-oriented logic on religious expression and in the process "spiritualized" economic activity', thereby 'securing neoliberal values through the empowerment of employers'.[39] The different readings of the *Hobby Lobby* case are underpinned by different conceptual understandings of the right to FORB. How far should the right to FORB extend in the context of women's rights and religious organisations?

The question about the limits of religion was also at stake in conflicts between the rights of LGBTQ+ persons and Christian business owners as in the UK case of *Lee v McArthur*[40] and the US case of *Masterpiece Cakeshop Ltd v Colorado Civil Rights Commission*.[41] These cases also concerned the right to freedom of expression because in both cases Christian bakers refused to embellish their cakes with a pro-gay marriage message. Equal treatment, it was held, was not the same as requiring a business owner to print a particular expression or message.[42] For some, *Masterpiece* protects offensive and bigoted behaviour, but that is considered to be necessary to protect freedom of expression.[43]

The cases cited above are all high-profile cases that arose in different contexts and areas of law. Some of the cases concerned religious symbols, others concerned access to services and private goods, and a number of them involved a conflict of fundamental rights. The unifying feature of the cases is that in all of them the *limits* of religious freedom are disputed. The wide scope for litigation highlights the need for a principled approach to setting limits to the right to FORB. The discussion above demonstrates that religious accommodation raises a number of challenges and that there is a need for workable solutions to religious claims in a pluralistic European (and global) context. The challenge is, then, to find an approach to religious claims that is generous and principled but at the same time constitutes a liberal solution to the conflicts created by the right to FORB. This book provides a solution to managing religious claims by offering an original model of religious accommodation that focuses on its *limits*.

C. Freedom *from* Religion

The jurisprudence on the right to FORB includes an 'emerging' right to freedom *from* religion. In one sense, freedom *from* religion is neither new nor surprising.

[39] JM Denbow, 'The Problem with *Hobby Lobby*: Neoliberal Jurisprudence and Neoconservative Values' (2017) 25 *Feminist Legal Studies* 165.

[40] *Lee v McArthur and others* [2016] NICA 39.

[41] *Masterpiece* (n 25).

[42] See www.theguardian.com/commentisfree/2018/may/06/gake-cake-fight-why-bakers-had-right-to-refuse-order.

[43] J Hart, 'When the First Amendment Compels an Offensive Result: Masterpiece Cakeshop, Ltd. v. Colorado Civil Rights Commission' (2018) 79 *Louisiana Law Review* 419.

It makes sense that, given the centrality of religious freedom, the right to be free from religious interference is equally important. The right not to be coerced or be subject to forced conversion has been long recognised as a fundamental aspect of the right to FORB and freedom of conscience. Article 18 of the Universal Declaration of Human Rights 1948 (UDHR) protects the freedom to change one's beliefs. Article 18(2) of the International Convention on Civil and Political Rights 1966 (ICCPR) states 'No one shall be subject to coercion which would impair his freedom to have or to adopt a religion or belief of his choice'. However, given that both the cultural and political conditions have changed since the enactment of the UDHR and ICCPR to include a wider range of religious and ethical beliefs, and coupled with a shift towards centring individual autonomy, the right to FORB has arguably taken on a renewed significance. This is best demonstrated in the case of *Lautsi v Italy* in which it was argued that the display of a crucifix in a classroom of a state school constituted an interference with the rights of non-religious pupils.[44] Thus, the right to FORB can conflict with the right to freedom *from* religion.

The right to freedom *from* religion now has several new dimensions. What counts as religious imposition or interference affecting the freedom of others is increasingly complicated not only because of the potentially wide scope of religious freedom, but also because the 'cross-fertilisation' of religions, beliefs and cultures creates more room for conflicts. For some, religious extremism and terrorism means that the right to FORB must be restricted and closely policed to protect national security.[45] Moreover, the right to wear religious symbols might be limited in favour of a policy that upholds ideological neutrality at the workplace.[46] However, the right to freedom *from* religion should not be equated with secularism. For example, Judge Bonello in the Grand Chamber in *Lautsi v Italy* (*Lautsi II*) emphatically opined:

> 2.5 ... Freedom of religion is *not* secularism. Freedom of religion is *not* the separation of Church and State. Freedom of religion is *not* religious equidistance – all seductive notions, but of which no one has so far appointed this Court to be the custodian. In Europe, secularism is optional, freedom of religion is not.

> 2.6 Freedom of religion, and freedom from religion, in substance, consist in the rights to profess freely any religion of the individual's choice, the right to freely change one's religion, the right not to embrace any religion at all, and the right to manifest one's religion by means of belief, worship, teaching and observance. Here the Convention catalogue grinds to a halt, well short of the promotion of any State secularism.[47]

---

[44] *Lautsi* (n 26).
[45] AN Guiora, *Freedom from Religion: Rights and National Security*, 2nd edn (New York, Oxford University Press, 2013).
[46] See Case C-157/15 *Samira Achbita and Centrum voor gelijkheid van kansen en voor racismebestrijding v G4S Secure Solutions NV* EU:C:2017:203 and Case C-188/15 *Asma Bougnaoui and Association de d fense des droits de l'homme (ADDH) v Micropole SA, formerly Micropole SA* EU:C:2017:204.
[47] *Lautsi v Italy* App 30814/06 (18 March 2011) Grand Chamber, p 40.

The right to practise one's religion and freedom *from* religion are both important aspects of a coherent and holistic conceptualisation of the right to FORB. Heiner Bielefeldt, Nazila Ghanea and Michael Wiener argue that:

> Taking freedom seriously implies equal concern for what has been termed 'positive' freedom and 'negative' freedom. These are two sides of the same coin. No one can be free to do something unless he or she is also free not to do it, and vice versa. That is why freedom of religion or belief also covers freedom not to profess a religion or belief, not to attend worship or just not to care about religious or philosophical issues etc. There is no hierarchy between positive and negative freedom. Indeed, any attempt to establish such a hierarchy would finally obscure the liberating essence of freedom of religion or belief in general.[48]

Therefore, the right to FORB does not suffer from internal conceptual incoherence. The right to FORB is not *a priori* in conflict with freedom *from* religion. Rather, if the right to FORB is inherently instable then it is because religion is continually evolving and due to the changing nature of religious claims (how religion is defined, what it ought to include, etc). This means that we can expect religious claims to continue to raise questions about their nature and scope, and, accordingly, the right to freedom from religion will inevitably be fashioned in relation to how those questions are answered.

II. The Scope of the Right to Freedom of Religion or Belief

The scope of the right to FORB is contested across jurisdictions. In liberal states there are several sources of law, constitutional norms, and principles relevant to the interpretation of the right to FORB. An overview of the key sources at the international level is a useful starting point because it lays down the minimum standards that states ought to meet. The 'core minimum' of the right to FORB, nevertheless, varies considerably across states, and part of the problem is that limitations are too easily granted.

A. The Sources of Law Protecting the Right to Freedom of Religion or Belief

The right to FORB is recognised in international law and the national constitutions of most countries. Such clauses are sometimes referred to as 'granting clauses'.[49]

---

[48] H Bielefeldt, N Ghanea and M Wiener, *Freedom of Religion or Belief: An International Law Commentary* (Oxford, Oxford University Press, 2016) 21.

[49] JT Gunn, 'Permissible Limitations on the Freedom of Religion or Belief' in J Witte and MC Green (eds), *Religion and Human Rights: An Introduction* (Oxford, Oxford University Press, 2012) 254–55.

There are various specific legal instruments that protect religious freedom at the international, regional and national level. The enforcement and level of protection of these instruments depends on various factors as outlined below. Any approach to religious accommodation must take into account these multiple layers.

i. The International Human Rights Framework

At the international level, the starting points are the UDHR and the ICCPR. International human rights law requires states to take positive steps to 'respect', 'protect', and 'fulfil' their human rights obligations.[50] The first basic step to realising these obligations is enacting laws that enshrine the importance of the right to FORB and constitutionally entrench religious freedom as a fundamental right. Article 18 of the UDHR reads:

> Everyone has the right to freedom of thought, conscience and religion; this right includes freedom to change his religion or belief, and freedom, either alone or in community with others and in public or private, to manifest his religion or belief in teaching, practice, worship and observance.

Similarly, Article 18 of the ICCPR protects the right to freedom of thought, conscience and religion:

1. Everyone shall have the right to freedom of thought, conscience and religion. This right shall include freedom to have or to adopt a religion or belief of his choice, and freedom, either individually or in community with others and in public or private, to manifest his religion or belief in worship, observance, practice and teaching.
2. No one shall be subject to coercion which would impair his freedom to have or to adopt a religion or belief of his choice.
3. Freedom to manifest one's religion or beliefs may be subject only to such limitations as are prescribed by law and are necessary to protect public safety, order, health, or morals or the fundamental rights and freedoms of others.
4. The States Parties to the present Covenant undertake to have respect for the liberty of parents and, when applicable, legal guardians to ensure the religious and moral education of their children in conformity with their own convictions.

Moreover, the Declaration on the Elimination of All Forms of Intolerance and of Discrimination Based on Religion or Belief 1981[51] emphasises the need for protection against religious discrimination:

> Article 2
> 1. No one shall be subject to discrimination by any State, institution, group of persons, or person on the grounds of religion or belief.

---

[50] H Bielefeldt et al, *Freedom of Religion or Belief: An International Law Commentary* (Oxford, Oxford University Press, 2016) 33.

[51] Declaration on the Elimination of All Forms of Intolerance and of Discrimination Based on Religion or Belief General Assembly Resolution 36/55 New York, 25 November 1981.

2. For the purposes of the present Declaration, the expression 'intolerance and discrimination based on religion or belief' means any distinction, exclusion, restriction or preference based on religion or belief and having as its purpose or as its effect nullification or impairment of the recognition, enjoyment or exercise of human rights and fundamental freedoms on an equal basis.

The right to FORB is also a qualified right in international human rights law. This means that states can legitimately limit religious freedom. However, the option to limit the right should be strictly interpreted and not be abused by states. Accordingly, limitations must be 'prescribed by law', based on 'a legitimate interest' such as 'public safety' be 'necessary' and 'proportionate'. However, as Jeremy Gunn argues, 'To the extent that limitations clauses impose practical limits on states actions, the "legitimate purpose" requirement is the weakest prong'.[52] This means that most laws and restrictions can meet this hurdle; a restriction is usually considered to be based on a justifiable reason in the very broad sense. In other words, the threshold for adducing a 'legitimate purpose' is generally low. The Human Rights Committee General Comment no 22 states:

> Para 8: Article 18.3 permits restrictions on the freedom to manifest religion or belief only if limitations are prescribed by law and are necessary to protect public safety, order, health or morals, or the fundamental rights and freedoms of others. The freedom from coercion to have or to adopt a religion or belief and the liberty of parents and guardians to ensure religious and moral education cannot be restricted. … Limitations imposed must be established by law and must not be applied in a manner that would vitiate the rights guaranteed in article 18. … Limitations may be applied only for those purposes for which they were prescribed and must be directly related and proportionate to the specific need on which they are predicated. Restrictions may not be imposed for discriminatory purposes or applied in a discriminatory manner.[53]

Since limitations can be based on the need to protect public morality, it is important that public morality itself is based on an open and pluralistic understanding which is not exclusionary. The Committee encourages states to adopt a pluralistic approach when interpreting limitations justified in reference to the need to protect public morality since morality is subject to interpretation, and the dominance of one interpretation of public morality can have exclusionary outcomes:

> Para. 8. The Committee observes that the concept of morals derives from many social, philosophical and religious traditions; consequently, limitations on the freedom to manifest a religion or belief for the purpose of protecting morals must be based on principles not deriving exclusively from a single tradition. …

Thus, the justification of public morality should not be used as a 'sword' to prevent other religious and secular, ethical beliefs from being practised or accommodated.

---

[52] Gunn (n 49) 261–62.
[53] Human Rights Committee General Comment no 22: The right to freedom of thought, conscience and religion (Art 18): 30 July 1993, CCPR/C/21/Rev.1/Add.4.

Normative pluralism is inherent within the human rights framework and the value of pluralism is enshrined in regional and national legal instruments. As Joseph Raz argues, the existence of moral pluralism – that is, the existence of numerous conflicting comprehensive conceptions of the good life – is essential for individuals to achieve personal autonomy.[54] This is so because without moral pluralism and the option of choice, personal autonomy would be limited due to the lack of opportunity to decide rationally between different options. Pluralism is important to developing an understanding of how the scope of the right to FORB should be realised and interpreted.

ii. The Regional Human Rights Frameworks

There are several legal instruments that protect the right to FORB at the regional level. The right to FORB is protected by the African Charter on Human and Peoples' Rights 1981:

> Article 8
>
> Freedom of conscience, the profession and free practice of religion shall be guaranteed. No one may, subject to law and order, be submitted to measures restricting the exercise of these freedoms.[55]

It is important to note that the limitation clause set out in Article 8 is drafted in a broad manner and does not specify the specific justifications or grounds for limitations. Similarly, Article 12 of the American Convention on Human Rights[56] protects freedom of conscience and religion and so does Article 30 of the Arab Charter.[57]

At the European supra-national level, there are two key instruments that protect the right to FORB and two distinct institutions that uphold it through different legal techniques. The first is the Council of Europe, which was responsible for drafting the European Convention for the Protection of Human Rights and Fundamental Freedoms 1950 (ECHR).[58] The ECHR opened for signature in Rome on 4 November 1950 and came into force on 3 September 1953, and currently has 47 signatories.[59]

---

[54] J Raz, *The Morality of Freedom* (Oxford, Oxford University Press, 1988).
[55] African Charter on Human and Peoples' Rights (Banjul Charter), adopted by the Organization of African Unity on 27 June 1981 and entered into force on 21 October 1986 (1982) 21 ILM 58.
[56] American Convention on Human Rights (Pact of San José), adopted by the Organization of American States on 22 November 1969 and entered into force on 18 July 1978 (OAS Treaty Series No 36, reprinted in *Basic Documents Pertaining to Human Rights in Inter-American System*, OEA/Ser L V/II.82 doc.6 rev.1 at 25 (1992)).
[57] Arab Charter on Human Rights (Arab Charter), adopted by the League of Arab States on 22 May 2004 and entered into force on 15 March 2008 76.
[58] European Convention for the Protection of Human Rights and Fundamental Freedoms, adopted by the Council of Europe on 4 November 1950 and entered into force on 3 September 1953 (ETS 5).
[59] See www.coe.int/en/web/tbilisi/the-coe/objectives-and-missions.

The second institution is the European Union which currently has 27 Member States and has enacted a range of laws.[60] The European Union's Employment Equality Directive (Directive 2000/78/EC) is a landmark achievement because it established a general legal framework for equal treatment in employment and occupation with respect to religion or belief, disability, age, and sexual orientation.[61] The two key European supra-national courts, the European Court of Human Rights (ECtHR) and the Court of Justice of the European Union (CJEU) respectively, are influential because they set the *minimum* applicable standards required for signatory states and establish a precedent that state parties should follow.

iii. The Convention for the Protection of Human Rights and Fundamental Freedoms

Article 9 of the ECHR is applicable in states that are members of the Council of Europe and addresses the right to FORB in the following terms:

Freedom of thought, conscience and religion

1.   Everyone has the right to freedom of thought, conscience and religion; this right includes freedom to change his religion or belief and freedom, either alone or in community with others and in public or private, to manifest his religion or belief, in worship, teaching, practice and observance.

2.   Freedom to manifest one's religion or beliefs shall be subject only to such limitations as are prescribed by law and are necessary in a democratic society in the interests of public safety, for the protection of public order, health or morals, or for the protection of the rights and freedoms of others.

Article 9(2) of the ECHR provides that the right to religion, belief, or conscience can be limited when the freedom of others is curtailed. Article 9 draws a distinction between the internal aspects of religious beliefs (the *forum internum*) and its external manifestation (the *forum externum*), where manifestations of belief are subject to certain limitations prescribed by law. The right to hold any belief is absolute.[62] Arguably, regulating an individual's internal private belief is impossible. Nevertheless, the absolute right to hold any belief has value in practical terms because it prohibits coercion and protects conversion.[63] However, the manifestation of religious beliefs can be limited under Article 9(2) of the ECHR. Limitations to religious belief must be prescribed by law; justified with reference to specific grounds as listed in Article 9(2); considered necessary in a democratic society;

---

[60] The European Union currently has 27 Members: https://european-union.europa.eu/principles-countries-history/country-profiles_en#tab-0-1.

[61] Council Directive 2000/78/EC of 27 November 2000 establishing a general framework for equal treatment in employment and occupation [2000] OJ L303/16.

[62] *Eweida and others* (n 27).

[63] P Dijk et al, *Theory and Practice of the European Convention on Human Rights* (Intersentia, 2006) 752.

and meet the proportionality test in the strict sense. This structured analysis allows for improved decision-making as the decision-maker must conduct a step-by-step analysis. However, the proportionality test leaves room for discretion, as will be discussed later. This discretion could benefit from further guidance to make decisions on religious claims more consistent.

Moreover, Article 14 of the ECHR also provides protection to the right to FORB. Article 14 states:

Prohibition of discrimination

The enjoyment of the rights and freedoms set forth in this Convention shall be secured without discrimination on any ground such as sex, race, colour, language, religion, political or other opinion, national or social origin, association with a national minority, property, birth or other status.

Article 14 of the ECHR thus shields individuals from discrimination on the grounds of certain protected characteristics, which include religious belief. Article 14 of the ECHR, however, is not 'a freestanding right' and can only be invoked when another substantive article of the ECHR is engaged.[64] This limitation has had the effect of weakening the non-discrimination principle.[65] Luzius Wildhaber argues that 'the accessory nature of Article 14 reduces its potential to be interpreted in line with a more activist and political understanding of discrimination'.[66] For some, this approach would be undesirable; however, non-discrimination should be considered as a dynamic right which is subject to development.

The jurisprudence of the ECtHR places both negative and positive obligations on the state.[67] The jurisprudence on positive obligations has the potential to develop a generous interpretation of Article 9 of the ECHR that could be applied rigorously to state institutions and employers which are currently not under a duty to take positive steps to accommodate religion. The ECtHR has held that the Convention should be considered to be 'a living instrument', which should be

---

[64] The court has shifted away from requiring there to be a breach of another Article before Article 14 could be relied upon. However, the court has endorsed an interpretation of the text that requires a case to fall within the ambit of a substantive right. See S Fredman, 'Emerging from the Shadows: Substantive Equality and Article 14 of the European Convention on Human Rights' (2016) 16 *Human Rights Law Review* 273. See also Council of Europe, Protocol 12 to the European Convention on Human Rights and Fundamental Freedoms on the Prohibition of Discrimination (adopted on 4 November 2000, entered into force 1 April 2005) ETS 177.

[65] See R Wintemute, '"Within the Ambit": How Big is the "Gap" in Article 14 European Convention on Human Rights? Part 1' (2004) 4 *European Human Rights Law Review* 366 and A Baker, 'The Enjoyment of Rights and Freedoms: A New Conception of the "Ambit" under Article 14 ECHR' (2006) 69 *Modern Law Review* 714.

[66] L Wildhaber, 'Protection against Discrimination under the European Convention on Human Rights: A Second-Class Guarantee?' in I Ziemele (ed), *Baltic Yearbook of International Law*, vol 2 (Springer, 2002) 71, 82.

[67] See *Osman v UK* Case no 87/1997/871/1083 (2000) 29 EHRR 245, paras 106–07.

interpreted in light of present-day conditions,[68] but the Court has generally shied away from developing a duty of reasonable accommodation of religion, although there is evidence of the need to do so in the face of increasing pluralism. Pluralism is also a key principle that informs the jurisprudence of Article 9, as emphasised in *Handyside v UK* where the court held that 'freedom of expression, pluralism, tolerance and broadmindedness are the foundations of democracy'.[69] The principle of pluralism was cited in the subsequent cases of *Kjeldsen v Denmark*,[70] *Kokkinakis v Greece*[71] and *Otto-Preminger-Institut v Austria*.[72] Thus, pluralism is a centrally important principle.

Julie Ringelheim identifies three additional key principles relevant to Article 9 of the ECHR: 'the right to autonomy of religious communities; state neutrality; and the necessity of the secularity of the legal order's foundations'.[73] These principles are inter-related and the complex balancing process between them poses a vexing challenge for the courts. The ECtHR has developed a 'vision of religious freedom'[74] that focuses on the individual and is based on the distinction between internal and external aspects of belief.[75] In *Kokkinakis v Greece*, for instance, the ECtHR emphasised that 'article 9 is one of the foundations of a plural democratic society that protects the identity of religious believers and others such as atheists and agnostics'.[76] However, the fact that there are different interpretations of the key principles underlying Article 9, as outlined above, is problematic since religious minorities have not benefitted from adequate protection under the Convention in some areas.

Moreover, the ECtHR's application of the belief/manifestation dichotomy can be problematic as it rests on a public/private distinction,[77] which does not always map neatly onto people's lived experiences of religious life.[78] Some individuals consider the manifestation of their belief to be an *extension* of their belief or even consider it as *more* important than holding an abstract belief. Roger Trigg argues that the ECtHR has defined religion very narrowly.[79] In addition, the Court has

---

[68] *Tyrer v UK* App no 5856/72 (1978) 2 EHRR 1, para 31.

[69] *Handyside v UK* App no 5493/72 (1976) 1 EHRR 737, para 49.

[70] *Kjeldsen, Busk Madsen and Pedersen v Denmark* App nos 5095/71; 5920/72; 5926/72 (1979–80) 1 EHRR 711, para 50.

[71] *Kokkinakis v Greece* App no 14307/88 (1994) 17 EHRR 397, para 31.

[72] *Otto-preminger-institut v Austria* App no 13470/87 (1994) 19 EHRR 34, para 49.

[73] J Ringelheim, 'Rights, Religion and the Public Sphere' in L Zucca and C Ungureanu (eds), *Law, State and Religion in the New Europe* (Cambridge, Cambridge University Press, 2012) 284.

[74] ibid 283.

[75] ibid 284.

[76] *Kokkinakis* (n 71) para 31.

[77] R Ahdar and I Leigh, *Religious Freedom in the Liberal State* (Oxford, Oxford University Press, 2005).

[78] See Hurd (n 16) on how legal definitions of religion do not necessarily reflect lived experiences of religious groups.

[79] R Trigg, 'Is Religious Freedom Special?' (Religious Freedom Project, Berkley Center, Georgetown University, Washington DC), available at https://s3.amazonaws.com/berkley-center/121120TriggIs ReligiousFreedomSpecial.pdf.

interpreted Article 9(2) of the ECHR narrowly, thus allowing for limitations to religious claims to be easily justified. In other words, the threshold for justifying limitations to religious claims is too low. There are several shortcomings of an approach that aims to limit the scope of religious freedom since it leads to a reduction of the rights of individuals, the side-lining of religious diversity, and, ultimately, failure to achieve substantive equality.

iv. The Charter of Fundamental Rights of the European Union

The second key institution that protects the right to FORB at the European level is the European Union. In particular, Article 10 of the Charter of Fundamental Rights of the European Union provides for freedom of thought, conscience and religion:

> Freedom of thought, conscience and religion
>
> 1. Everyone has the right to freedom of thought, conscience and religion. This right includes freedom to change religion or belief and freedom, either alone or in community with others and in public or in private, to manifest religion or belief, in worship, teaching, practice and observance.
> 2. The right to conscientious objection is recognised, in accordance with the national laws governing the exercise of this right.[80]

Freedom from discrimination on the grounds of religion or belief is protected by the Employment Equality Directive, which established a general framework for equal treatment in employment and occupation. The CJEU's development of anti-discrimination norms has been progressive in particular in the areas of sex discrimination and pregnancy.[81] EU anti-discrimination law offers individuals protection in key areas such as the workplace. It guarantees individuals freedom from discrimination on the grounds of religion or belief,[82] and prohibits both direct and indirect discrimination. Direct discrimination is found where 'one person is treated less favourably than another is, has been or would be treated in a comparable situation'.[83] Indirect discrimination is found where a neutral provision, criterion or practice puts persons of a particular religion or belief at

---

[80] Charter of Fundamental Rights of the European Union, proclaimed by the European Parliament, the Council of Ministers, and the European Commission on 7 December 2000 and entered into force on 1 December 2009 (2012/C 326/02).

[81] Case C-177/88 *Dekker* EU:C:1990:383 and see R Wintemute, 'Goodbye EU Anti-Discrimination Law? Hello Repeal of the Equality Act 2010?' (2016) 27 *King's Law Journal* 387.

[82] EU discrimination law expanded considerably from the regulation of equal pay between men and women, through to the Race Equality Directive (Council Directive 2000/43/EC of 29 June 2000 implementing the principle of equal treatment between persons irrespective of racial or ethnic origin [2000] OJ L180/22) and the Employment Equality Directive (Directive 2000/78/EC), which extended legal protection to include the grounds of religion and belief.

[83] Directive 2000/78/EC, Art 2(a).

a disadvantage vis-à-vis other persons.[84] Together, the concepts of direct and indirect discrimination can provide robust legal techniques to protect individual rights. The Employment Equality Directive sets out minimum requirements, leaving the option for EU Member States to provide more favourable protections to individuals.[85]

The CJEU has recently begun to develop its governing principles on the right to religious freedom. In 2017, the CJEU issued two rulings on Islamic headscarves worn at the workplace as well as a ruling on the legality of unilateral Islamic divorce in a private setting in a non-EU state,[86] whilst in 2018 it handed down a decision on religious slaughter of animals.[87] However, the CJEU has seemed to follow the trend established by many national courts of relying on the principle of neutrality to resolve complex cases on religion. Neutrality, as will be argued in chapter three, has been used as a default principle by courts and law-makers to manage religious claims. The constitutional principle of neutrality is, however, more complex than many decision-makers tend to assume. Cécile Laborde has pointed out that there are various subsets of neutrality.[88] Used as a blunt instrument by decision-makers, recourse to neutrality has led to the implementation of rather weak forms of protection of religious freedom. For instance, the CJEU's rulings on headscarves permit neutrality policies at work, thus reinforcing the point that neutrality continues to be problematic in religious freedom cases because it is often used to justify lower levels of protection.

The use of discrimination law to protect religious freedom has a number of limitations. First, discrimination law is limited by the scope of its application which depends on the specific legislation and jurisdiction. For example, the Employment Equality Directive is limited to employment, services and occupation. Second, the concept of indirect discrimination relies on the need for a comparator to demonstrate 'less favourable treatment'. The requirement for a comparator can be a restrictive requirement which limits protection.[89] Third, it may be possible for indirect discrimination to be objectively justified, and the weight of the justification will depend on how the courts balance the interests of the parties involved when conducting the proportionality analysis.[90] Isabelle Rorive has argued that the CJEU, through its implementation of EU law, could potentially develop a

---

[84] Directive 2000/78/EC, Article 2(b).

[85] Recital 28 of the Preamble to Directive 2000/78/EC.

[86] Case C-372/16 *Soha Sahyouni v Raja Mamisch, Judgment of the Court* EU:C:2017:988.

[87] Case C-426/16 *Liga van Moskeeen en Islamitische Organisaties Provincie Antwerpen VZW* (n 13).

[88] C Laborde, *Liberalism's Religion* (Cambridge, MA, Harvard University Press, 2017).

[89] See Directive 2000/78/EC, Art 2(b)(i). Direct or indirect discrimination are not completely distinct and the concept of indirect discrimination has also raised questions about individual and group disadvantage, see L Vickers, 'Indirect Discrimination and Individual Belief: *Eweida v British Airways Plc*' (2009) 11 *Ecclesiastical Law Journal* 197.

[90] See E Bribosia et al, 'Reasonable Accommodation for Religious Minorities: A Promising Concept for European Antidiscrimination Law?' (2010) 17 *Maastricht Journal of European & Comparative Law* 137, 157–58.

better jurisprudence on religious rights at the workplace than the ECtHR.[91] There was hope that EU anti-discrimination law might lead to better results for religious freedom, especially for minorities, as compared to the protection afforded by the ECHR. Article 10 of the Charter of the Fundamental Rights of the European Union ('the Charter') which protects religious freedom, was, for example, invoked in the recent CJEU ruling on religious slaughter of animals.[92]

However, the CJEU recent rulings have not paved the way for a stronger protection of religious freedom. A rather limited approach has characterised the recent Islamic headscarf rulings in the cases of *Samira Achbita v G4S Secure Solutions NV*[93] and *Asma Bougnaoui, Association de Defense des Droits de l'Homme (ADDH) v Micropole Univers SA.*[94] In 2017, the CJEU presided over these religious discrimination cases, which concerned Muslim women who had been dismissed from their employment because they wore the Islamic headscarf. In *Achbita* the applicant was an employee in Belgium for G4S (a multinational security services company). The company had an unwritten rule that prohibited employees from displaying visible signs of 'political, philosophical and religious' beliefs. This rule was later codified as a written rule that led to Achbita's dismissal. The relevant questions for the CJEU in *Achbita* were the following: 'Is a private employer permitted to prohibit a headscarf in the workplace? And is that employer permitted to dismiss her if she refuses to remove the headscarf at work?'[95] The CJEU did not find an instance of direct discrimination, instead approaching the case through the lens of indirect discrimination. However, since indirect discrimination can be objectively justified, the approach taken by the court led to a rather weak outcome from the perspective of enhancing religious freedom.

In *Bougnaoui* the applicant was an employee in France, working at the IT company Micropole, who was told that her headscarf could 'upset customers'.[96] The question for the CJEU was whether the wishes of customers not to see the headscarf could constitute 'a genuine and determining occupational requirement' ('the exemption').[97] The CJEU concluded that 'the willingness of an employer to take account of the wishes of a customer no longer to have the services of that employer provided by a worker wearing an Islamic headscarf cannot be considered a genuine and determining occupational requirement within the meaning of the directive'.[98]

The opinions of the two Advocate Generals (AGs) of the CJEU in *Bougnaoui* were very dissimilar and led to different outcomes. On the one hand, AG Eleanor Sharpston opined that a company policy that requires an employee to remove

---

[91] I Rorive, 'Religious Symbols in the Public Space' (2008–2009) 30 *Cardozo Law Review* 2669.
[92] *Liga van Moskeeen en Islamitische Organisaties Provincie Antwerpen VZW* (n 13).
[93] *Achbita* (n 46).
[94] *Bougnaoui* (n 46).
[95] *Achbita* (n 46).
[96] *Bougnaoui* (n 46).
[97] ibid.
[98] *Achbita* (n 46) *Bougnaoui* (n 46).

her headscarf constitutes direct discrimination. She held that 'Ms Bougnaoui was treated less favourably on the ground of her religion since a design engineer who had not chosen to manifest his or her religious belief would not have been dismissed'.[99] Reasoning that the freedom to conduct business is also subject to limitations that include the protection of the rights of others, AG Sharpston argued that direct discrimination could not be justified by appealing to the potential financial loss incurred by the employer.[100] Her approach provides for a robust protection of the rights of employees and religious believers.

On the other hand, AG Juliane Kokott submitted a more restrictive (from the employee's perspective) and business-friendly interpretation. She argued that wearing the headscarf was a subjective decision and, therefore, was not an immutable characteristic:[101]

> … G4S does not prohibit its employees from belonging to a particular religion or from practising that religion, but requires only that they refrain from wearing certain items of clothing, such as the headscarf, which may be associated with a religion.[102]

However, this view rests on an arbitrary distinction between religious beliefs and the manifestation of such beliefs. AG Kokott justified her position on the separation of 'belonging or practicing a particular religion' from 'the wearing or practicing of religious symbols'. However, for some religious adherents, the wearing of a religious symbol is part of belonging to and practicing a religion. In effect, the belief/manifestation dichotomy that AG Kokott relied on tends to favour some religions over others, usually putting minority religions into a position of stark disadvantage vis-à-vis the religion of the majority. The CJEU's endorsement of neutrality policies at the workplace require that such policies apply equally to all beliefs. This is problematic, as will be further elaborated in chapter three.

According to Ronan McCrea, the CJEU rulings on Islamic headscarves upheld the compatibility of rules that prohibit religious symbols at work with the Employment Equality Directive while ensuring that 'such rules do not target adherents to minority or unpopular faiths'.[103] However, empirical evidence has shown that Muslim women face greater barriers in the European labour market.[104] The CJEU's rulings were overly deferential towards employers.[105]

---

[99] *Bougnaoui* (n 46), Opinion of AG Sharpston EU:C:2016:553.

[100] ibid.

[101] *Achbita* (n 46), Opinion of AG Kokott EU:C:2016:382, paras 44–45.

[102] ibid.

[103] R McCrea, 'Faith at Work: The European Court's Headscarf Ruling' (28 March 2017), www.ucl.ac.uk/european-institute/analysis/2016-17/cjeu-headscarf-ruling.

[104] See K Alexandra, 'Muslim Women at "disadvantage" in Workplace' *BBC News* (11 August 2016) at www.bbc.co.uk/news/uk-37042942; N Akthar, 'Muslim Women Face Triple Discrimination at Work – and Taking Off the Hijab Won't Help' *New Statesman* (11 August 2016), www.newstatesman.com/politics/staggers/2016/08/muslim-women-face-triple-discrimination-work-and-taking-hijab-wont-help; and L Kaas and C Manger, 'Ethnic Discrimination in Germany's Labour Market – A Field Experiment' (2012) 13 *German Economic Review* 1.

[105] F Raza, 'The Continuity of the Headscarf Controversy: From Politics to Fashion' (OxHRH Blog, 17 December 2017), available at https://ohrh.law.ox.ac.uk/the-continuity-of-the-headscarf-controversy-from-politics-to-fashion.

In 2021, the CJEU heard two conjoined cases that had arisen in Germany.[106] One case centred on a special-needs caregiver at WABE eV whilst the other involved a sales assistant at Müller Handels GmbH. Both companies had required women to stop wearing their headscarves at the workplace. The cases were heard in the Labour Court in Germany which then made a request for a preliminary ruling in accordance with Article 267 of the Treaty on the Functioning of the European Union. The CJEU held that there was no direct discrimination and argued that there had been a consistent application of the rules given that another employee had been asked to remove a religious cross. The Court then analysed the case under the prohibition of indirect discrimination. It held that an employer's desire to display, in relation to its customers, a policy of political, philosophical or religious neutrality constitutes a legitimate aim. However, a 'genuine need' on part of the employer must exist whilst account of the rights and legitimate wishes of customers or users could also be taken into consideration.[107] In the case of WABE eV this included the wishes of the parents 'to have their children supervised by persons who do not manifest their religion or belief when they are in contact with the children'.[108] The business, it was argued, would suffer adverse outcomes in the absence of a neutrality policy. The Court did emphasise that such a policy must be applied consistently and systematically[109] so as to avoid 'difference of treatment'. However, the need for the 'consistent and systematic' application of rules does not eliminate the reality of systematic bias and discrimination that tends to be entrenched by a neutrality policy.

This section identified the key weaknesses in the decisions on the right to FORB that have been handed down by the European supra-national courts in recent years. In light of the current polarised political climate, courts have missed an opportunity to adopt a robust and bold approach to the question of religious symbols and to religious accommodation in general. Such a bold approach would have constituted an important symbolic milestone. Rather, the CJEU rulings signal a disappointing turn for protection of religious freedom at the European supranational level.

v. *The National Constitutional and Human Rights Framework*

Liberal states across the globe protect religion and the right to FORB in a variety of ways. Most states enshrine religious freedom and/or freedom of conscience in their constitutions as a qualified fundamental right. Religion is protected at least in the formal sense. This section will briefly set out the legal sources that protect religion in the US, Canada, France, Germany, and the UK as this book draws on the case law from these jurisdictions. Religion and what constitute protected religious

---

[106] Joined cases C-804/18 and C-341/19 *IX and MJ v Germany* EU:C:2021:594.
[107] ibid para 65.
[108] ibid para 65.
[109] ibid para 70.

beliefs and practices continue to be contested public issues in each of these jurisdictions. Although each state is considered to be a secular, liberal state, the respective constitutional arrangements are very different. The US Constitution enshrines the non-establishment principle and freedom of speech, press and assembly as stipulated in the First Amendment:

> Congress shall make no law respecting an establishment of religion, or prohibiting the free exercise thereof; or abridging the freedom of speech, or of the press; or the right of the people peaceably to assemble, and to petition the government for a redress of grievances.[110]

The interpretation of the First Amendment has been controversial, and the jurisprudence has continued to evolve in the face of political contestation.[111]

Similarly, section 2 of the Canadian Charter of Fundamental Rights stipulates:

Fundamental freedoms

2. Everyone has the following fundamental freedoms:

a.   freedom of conscience and religion;
b.   freedom of thought, belief, opinion and expression, including freedom of the press and other media of communication;
c.   freedom of peaceful assembly; and
d.   freedom of association.[112]

The Canadian Supreme Court has developed a duty to accommodate unless undue hardship would result.[113] However, there are criticisms that the current Canadian approach is still too narrow.[114] The German Constitution, known as the Basic Law (*Grundgesetz*), does not permit formal Church establishment. However, religion remains influential in Germany because the Basic Law protects religious individuals and groups in a number of important ways. In particular in light of events during the Nazi period, religious freedom is considered a fundamental right that is explicitly protected in the 1949 Constitution and is a priority right as highlighted by its respective position in the Basic Law (Article 4 of the Basic Law).

---

[110] US Constitution, First Amendment.

[111] Z Robinson, 'The First Amendment Religion Clauses in the United States Supreme Court' in M Breidenbach and O Anderson (eds), *The Cambridge Companion to the First Amendment and Religious Liberty* (Cambridge, Cambridge University Press, 2019); N Tebbe et al, 'How Much May Religious Accommodations Burden Others?' in F Lynch et al (eds), *Law, Religion, and Health in the United States* (Cambridge, Cambridge University Press, 2017).

[112] Section 3 of the Quebec Charter also protects conscience and religion.

[113] See L Vickers, 'Conscientious Objections in Employment: Is a Duty of Reasonable Accommodation the Answer?' in J Adenitire, *Religious Beliefs and Conscientious Exemptions in a Liberal State* (Oxford, Hart Publishing, 2019) 185–204.

[114] J Adenitire argues that the Canadian jurisprudence privileges religious beliefs over non-religious beliefs: see J Adenitire, *A General Right to Conscientious Objection: Beyond Religious Privilege* (Cambridge, Cambridge University Press, 2020) 130. See also MA Waldron, *Free to Believe: Rethinking Freedom of Conscience and Religion in Canada,* 3rd edition (Toronto, University of Toronto Press, 2013).

In addition, Article 1 of the Basic Law codifies human dignity as a foundational principle.[115] The Basic Law also permits religions to apply for the status of Public Law Corporation,[116] which constitutes a significant form of state accommodation of religion as it enables the mainstream Churches to levy taxes.[117] The two main Catholic and Protestant churches benefit from church tax and profit from the general positive economic conditions in the country.[118] Germany, unlike France, is based on a federal system and is composed of 16 federal states (*Länder*). Each federal state has its own Constitution, allowing for local variation of law. There are a number of specific legal sources in Germany that protect religious freedom: German anti-discrimination law protects individuals from discrimination on the grounds of religion. The Employment Equality Directive, which established a framework for equal treatment in employment and occupation, was implemented in Germany through the General Equal Treatment Act (*Allgemeines Gleichbehandlungsgesetz*), which came into force in August 2006.[119] This Act is the first comprehensive anti-discrimination legislation in Germany.

In France, religion, in particular Islam, has been very controversial. The French Constitution emphasises the need for the separation between church and state and its theoretical foundations are based on *laïcité*, which includes the principles of *liberté, égalité and fraternité*. The challenge lies in the practical application of secularism as discussed in chapter four. Article 1 of the 1958 French Constitution of the Fifth Republic codifies the principles of secularism and equality and accordingly adopts the vision of the 1905 Law. Article 1 of the 1905 Law of Separation between Church and State guarantees individuals the right to freedom of conscience and religious freedom whilst Article 2 prohibits the state from officially recognising or subsidising any religion.[120] However, *laïcité* can be interpreted in a number of ways and is a complex requirement that entails the balancing of competing goods.[121] As Charles Taylor argues, 'the struggle against the Catholic Church in French constitutional history meant that the state had to be founded on a *new morality* – and that new morality was liberty'.[122] This 'new founded morality' based on liberty does not necessarily tell us *how* to accommodate religion in specific cases.

In the UK, religious freedom is protected by a mixture of statute and common law principles. In particular, religion is enshrined as a human right and as a protected characteristic in discrimination law. The UK has an uncodified

---

[115] Basic Law for the Federal Republic of Germany (8 May 1949).

[116] ibid Article 140.

[117] See the case of *Klein v Germany* [2017] ECHR 327 where the applicants complained of paying the Church fee of their spouses when they themselves were not members. They also complained that Church tax was very high. The ECtHR ultimately found no violation of Article 9.

[118] O Müller et al, 'The Religious Landscape in Germany' in O Müller et al, *The Social Significance of Religion in the Enlarged Europe* (Farnham, Ashgate Routledge, 2012) 99.

[119] Allgemeines Gleichbehandlungsgesetz of 14 August 2006 (BGBl I S 1897).

[120] Loi du 9 décembre 1905 relative à la séparation des Églises et de l'État.

[121] See C Taylor, 'The Meaning of Secularism' (2010) *The Hedgehog Review* 23.

[122] ibid 27.

constitution, which means that the totality of sources that make up the UK constitution are not identifiable in an exhaustive list or in one superior source of law
as in France and Germany. The lack of a codified constitution offers the advantage of flexibility. However, there is a greater risk of weak protection of human
rights, which are safeguarded in the UK through a complex mix of common law,
public law and private law remedies. Under the 'modern' constitution, the church
has a limited role in the Constitution. There are 26 Lords Spiritual who sit in the
House of Lords, and calls for reform have generally supported retaining church
representation.[123] There have been calls for increasing religious representation in
the House of Lords to reflect the multi-faith nature of the UK, although there is no
current political appetite for changing the established church-state relations in the
foreseeable future.[124]

In the absence of a codified constitution, the two key statutory sources for the
protection of religion are the Human Rights Act 1998 (HRA 1998), which directly
incorporates the ECHR, as well as the Equality Act 2010, which implements the
Employment Equality Directive. The HRA 1998 only applies to public bodies or
bodies performing a 'public function' (HRA 1998, s 6). The scope of the HRA 1998
is problematic where services are privatised and contracted out[125] because human
rights claims in such cases can be more difficult to make. The HRA 1998 and the
Equality Act 2010 are not necessarily a permanent source of law because Acts of
Parliament can be repealed. There are two recent key developments in this regard:
first, the UK's vote in the 2016 referendum on membership of the European Union
and the its subsequent withdrawal from the Union has created the prospect that
the Equality Act 2010 may eventually be repealed or amended, thus reducing
current legal protections.[126] Second, the stability of the HRA 1998 is not immune
from the larger political context since members of the Conservative party have
advocated to repeal the HRA 1998[127] due to concerns that parliamentary sovereignty is undermined by the European supranational courts.[128] Such claims,
however, can be countered by pointing to the architecture of the HRA 1998

[123] The Wakeham Report on the Reform of the House of Lords concluded that the Church of England
should continue to be explicitly represented in the Second Chamber. See *A House for the future; reform
of the House of Lords*, available at www.gov.uk/government/publications/a-house-for-the-future-royal-
commission-on-the-reform-of-the-house-of-lords.
[124] T Baldry, 'Parliament and the Church' (2015) *Ecclesiastical Law Journal* 202.
[125] See CM Amhlaigh et al, *After Public Law* (Oxford, Oxford University Press, 2013).
[126] See House of Commons, 'Report: Ensuring Strong Equalities Legislation after the EU Exit –
Women and Equalities' Seventh Report of Session 2016–17, HC 799 (24 February 2017), available at
publications.parliament.uk/pa/cm201617/cmselect/cmwomeq/799/799.pdf.
[127] See M Zander, 'Theresa May up a Gum Tree' (2016) 166 *New Law Journal* 13.
[128] The status of the HRA 1998 came under pressure when the Conservative government indicated
that the Act should be repealed. See J Stone, 'Scrapping the Human Rights Act will help Protect Human
Rights, Attorney General says' *The Independent* (25 February 2016), available at www.independent.
co.uk/news/uk/politics/scrapping-the-human-rights-act-will-help-protect-human-rights-attorney-
general-says-a6894966.html. A Bill of Rights was put before Parliament before being shelved by then
Prime Minister Liz Truss, but at the time of writing (November 2022) it seems likely that it will be
brought back again under Prime Minister Rishi Sunak.

which strikes an appropriate institutional balance between Parliament and the Courts in that the latter does not have the power to invalidate primary Acts of Parliament.[129]

Taken together, there is a consensus that the right to FORB is worthy of protection in law. States cannot simply ignore religion. Given the varieties of church–state models across jurisdictions – ranging from religious establishment, strict secularism to partial separation[130] – the right to FORB operates within a variety of constitutional frameworks. Whilst church–state models can be evaluated by their adherence to upholding democracy and the rule of law,[131] an additional challenge lies in fashioning consistent standards for the protection of the right to FORB. Moreover, the recognition of the importance of the right to religion or conscience in national constitutions is no guarantee that religion is adequately protected. Formal legal recognition does not necessarily translate into practical and effective safeguards of the right to exercise religious freedom.

B. A Narrow or Wide Interpretation of the Right to Freedom of Religion or Belief?

There remains considerable disagreement about how exactly religion should be treated in law. Proponents in favour of a wide interpretation of the right to FORB support policies such as a duty of reasonable accommodation to achieve substantive equality.[132] Pro-accommodationists argue that the state *as well as* private-sector employers should be subject to a range of positive obligations that protect religious freedom and religious minorities.[133] However, critics argue that a generous approach to religious freedom is unnecessary and unfair to non-religious individuals.[134] Proponents of the limited protection of religion point out that both

---

[129] See the HRA 1998, ss 3 and 4 and S Fredman et al, *Oxford Human Rights Hub Submission to the Independent Review of the Human Rights Act* (2021).

[130] C Laborde, 'Political Liberalism and Religion: On Separation and Establishment' (2013) 21 *Journal of Political Philosophy* 67.

[131] AJ Nieuwenhuis, 'State and Religion, a Multidimensional Relationship: Some Comparative Law Remarks' (2012) 10 *International Journal of Constitutional Law* 153.

[132] See Fredman's four-dimensional approach to equality as articulated in S Fredman, 'Substantive Equality Revisited' (2016) 14 *International Journal of Constitutional Law* 712.

[133] Katayoun Alidadi argues that reasonable accommodation is important for protecting minorities in K Alidadi, 'Reasonable Accommodations for Religion and Belief: Adding Value to Article 9 ECHR and the European Union's Anti-Discrimination Approach to Employment?' (2012) 37 *European Law Review* 693. Kristin Henrard argues that reasonable accommodation upholds substantive equality and argues that ECtHR has not taken enough steps to develop a duty of reasonable accommodation in K Henrard, 'Duties of Reasonable Accommodation on Grounds of Religion in the Jurisprudence of the European Court of Human Rights: A Tale of (Baby) Steps Forward and Missed Opportunities' (2016) 14 *International Journal of Constitutional Law* 961.

[134] Select works include: C Eisgruber and L Sager, *Religious Freedom and the Constitution* (Cambridge: Harvard University Press 2007); B Leiter, *Why Tolerate Religion* (Princeton: Princeton University Press, 2013); R Dworkin, *Religion Without God* (Cambridge, Harvard University Press, 2013); Yossi Nehushtan, 'Secular and Religious Conscientious Exemptions: Between Tolerance and Equality'

the principles of neutrality and equality mean that religion should not benefit from special protection in law. For example, religious believers should not be afforded tailored exemptions from general laws applying to everyone.[135]

In addition to these diverging interpretations of religious freedom, an emerging alternative option entails either subsuming or 'disaggregating' the right to FORB. For instance, James Nickel maintains that religious freedom can be subsumed under other basic goods and fundamental rights. In particular, he identifies nine liberties, including the rights to freedom of expression or association, which could provide full protection of religion.[136] Nickel claims that this strategy allows for a broader scope of religious freedom in a range of areas such as association, movement, politics and business without exaggerating the importance of religion.[137] Accordingly, a claim to wear a religious symbol could be considered under the right to freedom of expression. However, subsuming religion under (other) general liberties will lead to weakening the protection of religious freedom. A related but distinct and nuanced account of what is referred to as the 'disaggregation theory' has been developed by Cécile Laborde. Her theory disaggregates religion by identifying the values that are being protected in a given case.[138] She argues that since religion captures a diverse expression of different aspects of life, 'different parts of the law should capture different dimensions of religion for the protection of different normative values'.[139] Thus, the disaggregation strategy aims to interpret the notion of religion in law irrespective of whether the explicit category of freedom of religion is upheld or not. The disaggregation strategy suggests that different parts of the law should capture different dimensions of religion in order to protect the different normative values that religion itself seeks to safeguard which include, amongst others, a conception of the good life; a conscientious moral obligation; a feature of identity; a totalising institution; and a inaccessible doctrine.[140] Laborde's theory protects religion without singling it out for special treatment.[141] However, each of the options (wide, narrow or disaggregation) outlined above must address the need for a delicate balancing of competing interests. The scrutiny of limitations is necessary to protect the core aspect of religious freedom, whether religious freedom is interpreted widely, narrowly, or is subsumed or disaggregated under other categories. Moreover,

---

in P Cane, C Evans and Z Robinson (eds), *Law and Religion in Theoretical and Historical Context* (Cambridge, Cambridge University Press, 2008).

[135] BM Barry, *Culture and Equality: An Egalitarian Critique of Multiculturalism* (Cambridge, Polity Press, 2001).

[136] J Nickel, 'Who Needs Freedom of Religion?' (2005) 76 *University of Colorado Law Review* 941.

[137] ibid.

[138] C Laborde, 'Religion in the Law: The Disaggregation Approach' (2015) 34 *Law and Philosophy* 581.

[139] ibid 594.

[140] ibid 595–96.

[141] Laborde's theory focuses on the ethically salient aspects of religion and culture so as to protect 'integrity-protecting commitments' (IPCs), which include obligation-IPCs and identity-IPCs, where fair exemptions in law are afforded when there is a disproportionate burden or majority bias in Laborde, *Liberalism's Religion* (n 88).

there is a strong case for providing robust protections of religious freedom given the fragility of the right to FORB across jurisdictions.

C. The Need for Guidelines on Limitations

With religious persecution and discrimination continuing to persist, religious freedom should be considered a *fundamental* human right. The right to FORB is empowering for individuals who consider religion as a way of life and a fundamental aspect of their identity.[142] Religious freedom is also intimately related to individual autonomy because it concerns choices about lifestyle, including everything from clothing[143] to diet[144] and employment.[145] Since the right to FORB is potentially very broad, there is also wide scope for different interests to conflict. Therefore, a principled approach to managing religious claims is an urgent desideratum. Stacie Strong proposes a new theoretical framework in which religious disputes can be resolved. Her proposed model is entitled 'the religiously orientated original position' and includes an eight-pronged analytical framework that classifies and resolves religious conflicts and is based on adaption of John Rawls' original position.[146] Strong's thesis focusses on the different effects of religion on society[147] but these are in need of further elaboration: hence the need for further criteria regarding their interpretation. Limitations must be grounded in consistent normative standards that recognise the importance of religious belief without at the same time elevating religion to a category for exclusive constitutional protection. Religious claims can adversely limit the fundamental rights of others and often entail normative disagreements that are not readily resolved by the proportionality test.[148] Jeremy Gunn notes that 'The language of the limitations clauses does not explain, for example: (1) how deferential courts should be to state authorities; (2) how important the right to manifest religion should be in comparison to state interests; (3) what evidence should be considered in resolving competing claims; (4) which party has the responsibility for providing what evidence; and (5) which party bears the "burden of proof"'.[149] Given the importance of balancing

---

[142] Gunn (n 49) 208.

[143] *SAS* (n 21).

[144] *Jewish Liturgical Association Chaàre Shalom Ve Tsedek v France* App no 27417/95 (ECtHR GC, 27 June 2000).

[145] *Francesco Sessa v Italy* App no 28790/08 (ECtHR, 3 April 2012); *Eweida and others* (n 27).

[146] S Strong, *Transforming Religious Liberties: A New Theory of Religious Rights for National and International Legal Systems* (Cambridge, Cambridge University Press, 2017) 119–20.

[147] ibid 122.

[148] Leigh argues that proportional balancing is not always appropriate in I Leigh, 'The Courts and Conscience Claims' in J Adenitire (ed), *Religious Beliefs and Conscientious Exemptions in a Liberal State* (Oxford, Hart Publishing, 2019) 109. Arguably, proportionality might obscure the real moral considerations at the heart of human rights issues in S Tsakyrakis, 'Proportionality: An Assault on Human Rights?' (2009) 7 *International Journal of Constitutional Law* 468, 493.

[149] Gunn (n 49) 262–63.

competing interests in cases concerning religious freedom, more attention needs to be paid to scrutinising the reasons offered for limiting religious freedom in liberal states. The diversity and inconsistencies of current approaches to limitations throw into relief the need to develop fair and consistent standards. The legitimacy of the right to FORB depends, therefore, on its limitations.

D. Five Arguments in Favour of Religious Accommodation

Religious accommodation is a politically sensitive policy option. However, I argue that it does not necessarily have to be controversial or unachievable. Religious accommodation is often misunderstood as favouring religion over other interests, or mistakenly, as necessarily requiring decision-makers to be more deferential.[150] There are a number of ways in which religious accommodation can be conceptualised or realised. For Brett Scharffs, accommodation can be understood from a number of perspectives: (i) state accommodation of religious exemptions; (ii) individuals adapting their practices to fit within the frameworks of the state; or (iii) accommodation as a place of safety wherein the state's and individual's perspectives are woven closer together.[151] John Bowers identifies some of the benefits of reasonable accommodation which include the following: it can lead to better outcomes such as a more individualised approach that better takes into account the individual's needs; it addresses more barriers to participation of particular groups in an objective manner; it may lead to a more structured yet clearer approach so that the employee would ask for a specific accommodation on religious or beliefs grounds and the employer would either decide 'that is not reasonable in my circumstances' or accepts that it is reasonable.[152] My approach favours religious accommodation and an expansive interpretation of the right to FORB while at the same time being especially attuned to the reasons that make limitations necessary. My model offers a nuanced and balanced approach to religious freedom. Once religious accommodation is embedded within a model that identifies the reasons for limitations, it is practically possible to implement it as a duty or favoured policy approach.

---

[150] According to Myriam Hunter-Henin, the 'accommodationist view' is a 'hands-off approach' that 'leads to deferring to religious requests and therefore to accommodating religious claims extremely generously. In this view, courts are to refrain from assessing the legitimacy of religious claims ...': M Hunter-Henin, *Why Religious Freedom Matters for Democracy: Comparative Reflections from Britain and France for a Democratic 'Vivre Ensemble'* (Oxford, Hart Publishing 2020) 10. However, 'accommodationist' views do not *necessarily* lead to an 'extremely' generous approach towards religious claim, nor are they immune from an assessment of legitimacy as I demonstrate in this book. A more nuanced account of religious accommodation is possible both conceptually and in practice.

[151] BG Scharffs, 'Conceptualising reasonable accommodation' in PT Babie et al (eds), *Freedom of Religion or Belief: Creating the Constitutional Space for Fundamental Freedoms* (Cheltenham, Edward Elgar, 2020) 59.

[152] J Bowers, 'Accommodating difference; how is religious freedom protected when it clashes with other rights; is reasonable accommodation the key to levelling the field?' (2021) 10 *Oxford Journal of Law and Religion* 275–97.

Religious accommodation is usually referred to as 'reasonable accommodation', a term which corresponds with duties of reasonable accommodation in disability law.[153] Whilst a duty to accommodate disability is widely accepted as a legal tool for assisting people who face burdens, the 'reasonable' accommodation of religion is more controversial. Whereas disability is (rightly) deemed to be an important characteristic in anti-discrimination and equality law since it can have the effect of limiting the physical and personal autonomy of individuals, religious accommodation is not as widely accepted partly because it is still a controversial proposition that religious belief constitutes an 'immutable characteristic' (see also chapter two).

There are at least five core arguments in favour of religious accommodation. First, religious accommodation is about protecting identity-forming commitments. The right to FORB should be interpreted expansively because it constitutes a fundamental right for many individuals. A legal duty or policy approach in favour of religious accommodation upholds the religious identity of religious believers, which is important in enabling minorities and others to be 'recognised' within the political domain.[154] Second, religious accommodation helps to combat inter-sectional discrimination and upholds substantive equality. Sandra Fredman argues that the aim of substantive equality should be to respect and accommodate difference in order to remove the *detriment*, but not the difference itself.[155] Her conception of substantive equality addresses Peter Westen's famous critique of equality as an 'empty idea'[156] because she demonstrates why equality matters and how it can be achieved in practice through a multi-dimensional and dynamic conception of substantive equality.[157] Religious accommodation can achieve substantive equality by ensuring that religious adherents receive recognition and are afforded equal employment opportunities. Accordingly, they would not be forced to make a difficult choice between employment or religious observance as employers would be open to accommodation and negotiating interests. Moreover, religious accommodation would also help to achieve equality of opportunity[158] which is a corollary of substantive equality, by widening access and removing barriers in employment. Thirdly, religious accommodation upholds the dignity of the individual by respecting the identity and equal worth of those who wish to

---

[153] UN Convention on the Rights of Persons with Disabilities 2006 and Directive 2000/78/EC, Art 5.
[154] C Taylor, 'The Politics of Recognition' in G Baumann and S Vertovec (eds), *Multiculturalism* (London, Routledge, 2011) 93.
[155] S Fredman, *Discrimination Law*, Clarendon Law Series (Oxford, Oxford University Press, 2010) 25–33.
[156] P Westen, 'The Empty Idea of Equality' (1982) 95 *Harvard Law Review* 537.
[157] Fredman (n 155) 25–33. Her conception of substantive equality is multi-dimensional with four aims. It includes (i) breaking the cycle of disadvantage to include a redistributive dimension; (ii) promoting dignity and respect which aims at recognition; (iii) the accommodation of difference and structural change to include the transformative dimension and (iv) full participation in society.
[158] M Gibson, 'The God "Dilution"? Religion, Discrimination and the Case for Reasonable Accommodation' (2013) 72 *The Cambridge Law Journal* 578, 592.

practise their religion in public or at the workplace.[159] Fourthly, religious accommodation helps to realise personal autonomy by enabling individuals to pursue their conception of the good life, as Martha Nussbaum has argued.[160] Finally, religious accommodation is a flexible policy tool that can be achieved through a range of measures such as workplace human resource (HR) policies in addition to granting legal exemptions from generally applicable laws. In this way, religious accommodation can include a wider range of cases. In sum, there are at least five compelling reasons that support a legal duty or policy approach in favour of religious accommodation.

E. Is Religious Accommodation Necessary?

The necessity or 'added-value' of a legal duty or policy approach in favour of religious accommodation is doubted by scholars and practitioners. A legal duty codified in statute would make it a formal obligation for institutions such as employers to implement a duty to accommodate religious beliefs. A policy approach might be a 'softer' way of encouraging accommodation but falls short of imposing legal duties.

For some, religious accommodation is unnecessary because the current legal frameworks provide adequate legal protection and thus remove the need to 'go any further'. The argument is that current equality legislation prohibits indirect discrimination – that is, rules and practices that disadvantage an individual based on a protected characteristic – and is considered an effective means of protection.[161] However, Matthew Gibson argues that reasonable accommodation should be a free-standing duty rather than considered as an aspect of indirect discrimination.[162] This is because indirect discrimination often offers weak protection because it can be justified albeit subject to certain conditions being met. For example, a rule at work forbidding head-coverings will put Muslim women at a disadvantage but it is possible that this could be justified for various reasons. The removal of the need of a comparator to prove disadvantage or unfavourable treatment could enhance protection too. Indirect discrimination has made the introduction of limitations to the right to FORB too easy, as has been demonstrated by the CJEU rulings on Islamic headscarves at the workplace in the *Achbita* and *Bougnaoui* cases. In *Achbita*, the CJEU did not consider that prohibiting the wearing of political, philosophical and religious signs constituted direct discrimination. The Court considered the possibility of indirect discrimination, which it deemed justifiable provided employers apply generally neutral policies equally to all. The consequences of the CJEU rulings are that a blanket 'neutrality policy'

---

[159] P Bou-Habib, 'A Theory of Religious Accommodation' (2006) 231 *Journal of Applied Philosophy* 109.
[160] MC Nussbaum, *The New Religious Intolerance* (Cambridge, Harvard University Press, 2012).
[161] Vickers (n 113) 185–204.
[162] Gibson (n 158) 614.

puts employers in a position in which they do not need to consider the reasonable accommodation of religious practices provided that the equality policy is consistently applied to other beliefs. Accordingly, the standard of protection for religious believers is potentially lower if certain conditions are met.

In the European context, both Katayoun Alidadi and Kristin Henrard have argued in favour of reasonable accommodation. Alidadi, a leading proponent of a duty of reasonable accommodation, points out that its implementation in the workplace would mark a progressive shift to the de-commodification of employees.[163] She emphasises the importance of allowing employees to exercise their religion at the workplace since this is intimately linked with the need to integrate into the workplace, and ultimately, society at large.[164] According to Alidadi, both the ECHR and EU discrimination law have gaps that limit protection of religious freedom. For example, the discretion afforded to Contracting States as demonstrated by the jurisprudence of ECHR can prevent religious claims from being considered as indirect discrimination in EU law.[165] Moreover, Alidadi points out that employment contractual obligations ignore power asymmetries when the former override human rights.[166] As noted by the European Network of Legal Experts in the Non-discrimination Field, 'the very concept of indirect discrimination is overlooked in many Member States'.[167] Kristin Henrard therefore urges that the ECtHR should recognise reasonable accommodation duties in order to allow equal opportunities for everyone.[168] Moreover, the inter-sectional nature of discrimination[169] means that reasonable accommodation can provide better, consistent and fairer protection.

Some scholars make a case against religious accommodation because they do not think that religious beliefs are to be prioritised when they conflict with other fundamental rights. Moreover, the accommodation of religious organisations is a complex task. As Samia Bano has emphasised, a cautious and nuanced approach is needed towards the accommodation of religious bodies such as sharia councils.[170] This is a point also made by Aileen McColgan, who argues against exempting religious organisations from equality laws because such exemptions would inevitably result in strengthening 'the conservative elements of the organisations rather than protecting internal minorities'.[171] The 2016 UK Casey Review

---

[163] K Alidadi, *Religion, Equality and Employment in Europe* (Oxford, Hart Publishing, 2017) 18–19.
[164] ibid 2.
[165] Alidadi (n 133) 695.
[166] ibid 705.
[167] E Bribosia and I Rorive, 'Reasonable Accommodation beyond Disability in Europe?' (2013) *European Commission, European Network of Legal Experts in the Non-discrimination Field* 7.
[168] Henrard (n 133).
[169] S Atrey, *Intersectional Discrimination* (Oxford, Oxford University Press, 2019).
[170] S Bano, 'Muslim Family Justice and Human Rights: The Experience of British Muslim Women' (2007) 2 *Journal of Comparative Law* 38.
[171] A McColgan, 'Religion and (in)equality in the European Framework' in L Zucca and C Ungureanu (eds), *Law, State and Religion in the New Europe* (Cambridge, Cambridge University Press, 2012) 233.

found that several ethnic and faith minority women's groups were treated as 'second class citizens' within their communities, and that this attitude was often reinforced by religious councils or courts.[172] The Report highlighted the sensitive issue of the need to protect minorities within minorities. Moreover, a more recent government report in the UK has foregrounded the nexus between intersectionality and religious freedom.[173] There are legitimate concerns about the consequences that flow from a generous policy of religious accommodation for women, religious minorities and other groups such as LGBTQ+ persons. A duty or policy approach in favour of religious accommodation should not, however, be rejected on the ground that it tends to reinforce the conservative elements of religion as that is precisely why some legal exemptions are granted: so that certain groups can maintain the integrity of their traditional belief systems (even if they are unpopular or conservative). That is not to say that all such beliefs trump other fundamental rights. Rather, the challenge lies in finding a basis on which an accommodative approach towards religion can be maintained whilst recognising the limits of such accommodations.

Religious accommodation has the potential to encompass a wide range of valuable beliefs, practices and rituals that are important to safeguard the personal autonomy of religious individuals in a liberal society. For example, religious accommodation of beliefs implies a highly pluralist vision of religious freedom that might require employers or institutions to take *positive* measures to accommodate religion by, for example, providing prayer facilities, allowing prayer breaks or days off, and changing work schedules. The implementation of reasonable accommodation depends on the version of secularism that a liberal state adopts,[174] but there is also a need for an over-arching framework and set of guidelines.

F. How to Implement a Duty of Religious Accommodation

The implementation of religious accommodation requires a set of flexible guidelines. There are several ways in which religious accommodation can be attained in practice. Religious accommodation could be achieved in varying degrees, beginning with its codification in statute as a legal duty, as a general policy approach, or as an optional and discretionary institution-specific approach. There are

---

[172] Dame Louise Casey, *The Casey Review: A Review into Opportunity and Integration* (5 December 2016) 106, available at www.assets.publishing.service.gov.uk/government/uploads/system/uploads/attachment_data/file/575973/The_Casey_Review_Report.pdf.

[173] Commission on Race and Ethnic Disparities, *Commission on Race and Ethnic Disparities: The Report* (March 2021), available at https://assets.publishing.service.gov.uk/government/uploads/system/uploads/attachment_data/file/974507/20210331_-_CRED_Report_-_FINAL_-_Web_Accessible.pdf.

[174] G Alida du Plessis, 'Is reasonable accommodation sufficient protection for the right to religious freedom in secular societies?' in JWC Durham et al (eds), *Law, Religion, and Freedom: Conceptualizing a Common Right* (London, Routledge, 2021).

a number of pragmatic benefits of implementing a duty or policy approach of religious accommodation, including better compliance with the law, empowerment of employees, and an improvement of the public image of employers, to name but a few.

It is worth listing the relevant kinds of religious questions that come up time and again across jurisdictions:

• Should religious symbols be allowed at the workplace?

• Does it make any difference if religious symbols are permitted when they are displayed in the context of state institutions, that is, either by state employees or at a state school?

• Should religious individuals and businesses be allowed to refuse to serve others on conscientious grounds?

• Should religious exemptions (for religious symbols, ritual slaughter, ritual circumcision, etc) be permitted?

• Should dietary requests be accommodated?

• Should time off for religious holidays and prayers be permitted at the workplace?

• What should be the scope of religious education?

There are at least two stages in providing answers to the question of limitations. The first is to apply a particular standard for 'measuring' and evaluating religious claims to decide whether or not they are to be accommodated. The second stage is to contextualise the issues further. This means that once the standard or criteria are identified, their application is context-specific. The purpose of the book is to offer a model of religious accommodation that lays down the general principles and criteria for what reasons are justifiable for limiting a religious claim. My model sets out a systematic approach to the right to FORB by developing a model based on a categorisation of harms to the autonomy of others. This strategy does not solve all of the complexities raised by religion, and its status, in liberal states. However, it does provide a specific principled and pragmatic approach to limitations to the right to FORB.

III. Conclusion

This chapter has identified the multiple complexities that the right to FORB gives rise to whilst highlighting the need for the development of clear guidelines on how to implement it in practice. The chapter has set out five inter-related arguments in favour of religious accommodation by emphasising how the latter plays a crucial role in protecting identity-forming commitments; achieving substantive equality; safeguarding the dignity of the individual; realising personal autonomy; and implementing a flexible policy to manage religious diversity. Religious accommodation is both necessary *and* achievable. The book makes an original contribution to the field of law and religion by mapping out and evaluating different approaches to limitations to the right to FORB before proposing a novel model of religious accommodation. This model is underpinned by a perfectionist version of the harm principle that can be applied in practice. To that end, the proposed model of religious accommodation respects and fulfils more than the 'minimum core' of the right to FORB.

2

Exemptions and Religion's 'Special Cage'

The right to FORB in liberal states is often fraught with tensions that require the resolution of conflicting interests. The expanding literature on the relationship between law and religion often frames the accommodation of religion in a way that predominantly focuses on the permissibility of religious exemptions from generally applicable laws.[1] Exemptions are a specific legal technique that allows individuals or groups not to comply with a specific law or rule, or disapplies it for those individuals/groups. Exemptions can be codified in statute or granted on a case-by-case basis. There are persuasive arguments on both sides of the so-called 'exemptions debate'. This is a normative debate that concerns the nature of the distinction between religious and non-religious/secular beliefs. The 'exemptions debate' raises important questions for my proposed model of religious accommodation, as detailed in Part II of this book. This chapter has two aims: first, to critically engage with the arguments made by proponents on either side of the debate; and second, to highlight the limits of the 'exemptions debate' by showing that legal exemptions are only *one* form of religious claims made in liberal societies. In particular, I argue that the workability of exemptions is more appropriately understood within a general framework of religious accommodation. Finally, this chapter establishes that religion has a proper place in liberal states and that religious claims can be accommodated, subject to certain limitations. The chapter concludes by arguing that a legal duty or policy approach in favour of religious accommodation is defensible in light of a model that defines the limits of the right

---

[1] The 'exemptions debate' continues to rage on ever since Brian Barry's provocative book *Culture & Equality* made the case for limiting religious and cultural exemptions against the backdrop of anti-multiculturalist policies (B Barry, *Culture and Equality: An Egalitarian Critique of Multiculturalism* (Cambridge, Polity Press, 2001). There has been an ongoing debate about both the legitimacy and scope of exemptions. A powerful critique of religious exemptions has been made by C Eisgruber and L Sager in their work *Religious Freedom and the Constitution* (Cambridge, MA, Harvard University Press, 2007). More accommodative accounts were subsequently developed by MC Nussbaum, *The New Religious Intolerance* (Cambridge, MA, Harvard University Press, 2012); J Maclure and C Taylor, *Secularism and Freedom of Conscience* (Cambridge, MA, Harvard University Press, 2011); and K Greenawalt, *Exemptions* (Cambridge, MA, Harvard University Press, 2016). More recent titles on exemptions include John Adenitire's book *A General Right to Conscientious Objection: Beyond Religious Privilege* (Cambridge, Cambridge University Press, 2020) in which he comprehensively argues that a general right to conscientious objection is defensible and should apply to both religious and non-religious conscientious beliefs.

to FORB, as set out in Part II. Religion in liberal states belongs in a 'special cage'. It is the boundary of that cage that needs to be properly defined.

I. Introducing the 'Exemptions Debate'

Much of the 'exemptions debate' has been premised on the underlying assumption that it is necessary to establish that religion is 'special' in order to justify its accommodation. More specifically, the questions at stake are the following: is it justified to set apart religion as a distinct category for protection *in law*? What types of religious exemptions are there? Should *only* religious exemptions be permissible or should exemptions be extended to include other categories of secular and comparable beliefs? These questions touch on a set of complex issues for liberal states and the right to FORB. In the absence of a fixed, universal and satisfactory answer or approach to the question of 'whether religion is special', this chapter ultimately argues that the analysis should shift to focusing on the manifestations of harmful religious practices.

The expansion of laws, case law and public discourse on religious exemptions and conscience claims across jurisdictions are evidence of the importance of this debate. Since the US Supreme Court's decision in *Burwell v Hobby Lobby Stores* in 2014,[2] the 'exemptions debate' has been violently re-ignited in the context of increasing pluralism and the escalating 'culture wars'.[3] Whilst religious exemptions are not a recent phenomenon, Susanna Mancini and Michel Rosenfeld argue that the new generation of conscience claims are 'interventionist, intrusive, and represent attempts to withdraw from mainstream collective undertakings'.[4] This concern was voiced by Justice Ginsburg in *Hobby Lobby*: 'The Court, I fear, has ventured into a minefield.'[5] She added: 'I would confine religious exemptions [under that Act] to organizations formed "for a religious purpose," "engage[d] primarily in carrying out that religious purpose," and not "engaged … substantially in the exchange of goods or services for money beyond nominal amounts."'[6] In other words, Justice Ginsburg adopted a narrow approach to exemptions, limiting the field in which they ought to apply. Key controversial examples of religious exemptions include permission for Jews and Muslims to conduct religious slaughter of animals in the European context[7] and the controversial case

---

[2] *Burwell v Hobby Lobby Stores, Inc*, 134 S Ct 2751 (2014).
[3] See S Mancini and M Rosenfeld, 'Introduction: The New Generation of Conscience Objections in Legal, Political, and Cultural Context' in S Mancini and M Rosenfeld (eds), *The Conscience Wars: Rethinking the Balance between Religion, Identity, and Equality*, Reprint ed (Cambridge, Cambridge University Press, 2019).
[4] ibid 1.
[5] *Burwell v Hobby Lobby Stores, Inc* (n 2) 2781–82.
[6] ibid.
[7] A key case heard in the ECtHR concerning ritual slaughter is *Jewish Liturgical Association Cha'are Shalom Ve Tsedek v France* App no 27417/95 (ECtHR GC, 27 June 2000).

of religious male circumcision in Germany,[8] as well as exemptions from wearing a motorcycle helmet for Sikh men.[9] In addition, exemptions for non-religious beliefs include, among others, exemption from military service on conscientious grounds[10] and exemptions for doctors and healthcare professionals to allow them to refuse to perform an abortion.[11] The central importance of one's conscience was recognised by Lady Hale in the UK case of *Doogan v NHS Greater Glasgow & Clyde Health Board*: 'The exercise of conscience is an internal matter which each person must work out for herself. It is bound to be subjective'.[12] It is no surprise then that the scope of these conscience-based exemptions is subject to complex litigation.

Given the deeply contested nature of religious and non-religious claims for accommodation, a range of views on the question of exemptions, and the 'special treatment' they allegedly afford to religion, have emerged in recent years. The importance of religious beliefs has been placed into doubt. The broad contours of the debate can be mapped in the following way: there is a clear division between positions that hold that religious beliefs should be treated with *less* deference and those that urge that religious beliefs should be afforded *more* deference. There is another position that occupies some sort of middle ground insofar as it makes a case for religious reasons to be treated with the *same* deference as secular reasons.[13] Ultimately, these divergent positions on the question of religious exemptions create irreconcilable conflicts and disagreements.

The combination of a number of complex and inter-related arguments against religious exemptions amount to a significant challenge to the legitimacy of granting such exemptions and, by extension, to religious accommodation more generally. These arguments encompass claims that religious exemptions are unnecessary, unfair, and unmanageable. They are considered unnecessary where religious individuals voluntarily *choose* to manifest their religious beliefs or where there are alternative options available to them. Religious exemptions are unfair to non-believers or those with similarly 'intensely held' beliefs because they unduly privilege religious believers.[14] Some commentators argue that

---

[8] *Landgericht Köln*, 151 Ns 169/11, 7 May 2012.

[9] See the UK Deregulation Act 2015, s 6 – Requirements to wear safety helmets: exemption for Sikhs.

[10] See *Thlimmenos v Greece* (App no 34369/97) (2001) 31 EHRR 15 which concerned a member of the Jehovah's Witness community who refused to serve in the army and was subsequently charged with a criminal offence which then affected his employment opportunities.

[11] Several jurisdictions have granted exemptions to doctors from performing abortions: see the UK Abortion Act 1967, s 4.

[12] *Doogan and Another v NHS Greater Glasgow & Clyde Health Board* [2013] ScotCS CSIH 36, para 31.

[13] J Corvino, 'Is Religion Special? Exemptions, Conscience and the Culture Wars' in J Adenitire (ed), *Religious Beliefs and Conscientious Exemptions in a Liberal State* (Oxford, Hart Publishing, 2019) 14.

[14] Calls for expanding the category of religious exemptions to include other comparable beliefs have been made by numerous scholars. Jocelyn Maclure and Charles Taylor argue that 'convictions of conscience, which include religious beliefs, form a particular type of subjective preference that calls for special legal protection' in Maclure and Taylor (n 1) 73. Whereas, John Adenitire argues that there is a moral case for a more 'General Right to Conscientious Exemption' in Adenitire (n 1).

religious beliefs could be characterised as mere habits or preferences.[15] Therefore, treating religious beliefs as unique or special results in unequal outcomes for religious and non-religious individuals. Accordingly, religious exemptions are deemed to breach the rule of law. Finally, religious exemptions are difficult to manage in practice due to institutional and resource constraints. This argument has found favour in some of the case law. In the ECHR case *Francesco Sessa v Italy*, the government argued that non-accommodation of a request made by to reschedule court hearings in order to avoid a conflict with a religious holiday was justified. It was argued that, by refusing accommodation, the authorities 'had simply sought to ensure that the applicant did not hamper the smooth operation of essential State services in exercising his right to request that the hearing be adjourned' and that 'The administration of justice was an essential State service which had to take priority'.[16] In other words, institutions and employers are not bound to accommodate religious practices at any costs and not where legitimate concerns about the effective administration of justice are undermined. In short, the objections against religious exemptions are collectively weighty and worthy of consideration.

This chapter will arrange the various key claims about whether religious beliefs 'deserve special treatment' into the following three broad categories of arguments: (i) 'the preference-choice' argument; (ii) the 'intensity-cost' argument; and (iii) the 'equality/rule of law' argument. This grouping best captures the very rich range of arguments found in the literature on exemptions. Before critically engaging in detail with these three arguments, the chapter will first address an important preliminary challenge to religious exemptions which revolves around the definition of religion.

II. The Problem of Defining Religion

The problem of defining religion is relevant to the 'exemptions debate' and religious accommodation more generally, as it raises questions about how liberal states treat religion as a category in law and thus determines and delineates the scope of the right to FORB. This is important for claimants who want to fall within the scope of FORB and potentially benefit from legal recognition and the range of attendant privileges. This section deals with a range of complex arguments that are here subsumed under the umbrella heading of 'the definitional problem'. This is basically a problem of determining what counts as religion or belief in the context of increasing pluralism. Religion, as a concept, can be defined too narrowly so as to be exclusionary, or too widely so as to be very expansive. For some scholars

---

[15] See G Cornelissen, 'Belief-Based Exemptions: Are Religious Beliefs Special?' (2012) 25 *Ratio Juris* 85.

[16] *Francesco Sessa v Italy* App no 28790/08 (ECtHR, 3 April 2012) paras 31–32.

within critical religious studies, religion has no distinct core or essence and is not necessarily a universal feature of human life, and, accordingly, any belief or practice can subjectively be considered as 'religious'.[17] The implications of this can be potentially wide-ranging. This section will first critically set out how the case law has dealt with the problem of definitions and, as a second step, engage with the 'semantic critique', that is, the claim that there is 'no stable, universally valid empirical referent for the category of religion'.[18]

A. The Case Law on Definitions of Religion

There are two predominant ways in which religion has been defined in court: one 'functional' and the other 'content-based'. 'Functional' approaches focus on the role that beliefs play in the individual's life or in society or both[19] whilst 'content-based' approaches focus on the characteristics of religion and rely on a 'definition by analogy'.[20] Definitions of religion can contain 'objective' or 'subjective' elements. Objective definitions seek to evaluate a belief system in accordance with a set of external criteria. Subjective definitions, by contrast, highlight the individual's beliefs and the sincerity of these beliefs.[21] In this sense, subjective definitions focus on how individuals make sense of their religious beliefs.

Despite the different ways in which religion can be defined, the centrality of religious belief to the religious person has been captured by the Preamble to the 1981 UN Declaration on the Elimination of All Forms of Intolerance and of Discrimination Based on Religion or Belief which states that 'religion or belief, for anyone who professes either, is one of the fundamental elements of his conception of life'.[22]

Increasingly, the law must address the reality of an ever-expanding range of religious, ethical, and secular beliefs.[23] Defining what constitutes religion is a

---

[17] M McIvor, 'The Impossibility of Religious Freedom: "Legal religion" and its discontents' in R Sandberg (ed), *Leading Works in Law and Religion* (London and New York, Routledge, 2019) 100.

[18] C Laborde, 'Rescuing Liberalism from Critical Religion' (2020) 88 *Journal of the American Academy of Religion* 58.

[19] PL Berger, 'Some Second Thoughts on Substantive versus Functional Definitions of Religion' (1974) 13 *Journal for the Scientific Study of Religion* 125, 126: 'Religion has been substantively defined, in terms of the meaning contents of the phenomenon. And it has been functionally defined, in terms of its place in the social and/or psychological system'.

[20] A Deagon, 'Towards a Constitutional Definition of Religion: Challenges and Prospects' in PT Babie et al (eds), *Freedom of Religion or Belief: Creating the Constitutional Space for Fundamental Freedoms* (Cheltenham, Edward Elgar, 2020) 59. See also LA Mercadante, *Belief Without Borders: Inside the Minds of the Spiritual but not Religious* (Oxford, Oxford University Press, 2014) 96.

[21] Berger (n 19).

[22] Declaration on the Elimination of All Forms of Intolerance and of Discrimination Based on Religion or Belief, adopted by General Assembly Resolution 36/55 of 25 November 1981 (UN Doc A/RES/2312(XXII)).

[23] As outlined in C Taylor, *A Secular Age* (Cambridge, MA, Harvard University Press, 2007). Increasingly pluralism brings with it new possibilities and ways of thinking about religious and ethical beliefs. The definitional problem, although not new, does face novel challenges in light of increasing pluralism and 'cross-fertilisation' of beliefs.

difficult, or even impossible, task: as Winnifred Sullivan puts it, 'who is to say what is the authentic way to be a Christian or Jewish or Muslim or Inuit or Daoist ...'.[24] Whilst most major world religions are accepted as 'valid' religions, many other comparable belief systems do not always meet the definitional threshold of what generally counts as religion. Increasingly, individuals consider themselves to be 'spiritual but not religious' (SBNRs). However, the category of 'spiritual' is also difficult to define as many SBNRs do not match the criteria associated with the more familiar claims made by religious freedom claimants[25] which means that there is a real fluidity and diversity in the field. Moreover, defining the category of 'nonreligion' has also become a topic of interest given that protection under the right to FORB extends to the *areligious and nonreligious* and covers a wide range of spiritual and philosophical beliefs. Nonreligion is usually conceptualised in relation to religion. Some nonreligious people ignore religion, while others engage in 'traditional' religious practices such as prayer or devotions although outside of the framework of the historically established religions.[26] Certainly, there is a shift towards adopting a broader understanding of religion in both the scholarly literature[27] and the case law.

A number of beliefs have been litigated under the right to FORB across jurisdictions such as veganism,[28] environmentalism,[29] Scientology[30] and a belief in the existence of some form of extra-terrestrial beings.[31] Movements such as Jediism,[32] Matrixism, and The Church of the Flying Spaghetti Monster are what some scholars refer to as new religious movements based on fiction or 'fandom'.[33] These movements are evidence of the different ways in which spirituality and belief systems are being conceptualised in a post-modern context.[34] How the law should

---

[24] WF Sullivan, *The Impossibility of Religious Freedom* (Princeton, Princeton University Press, 2005) 1–2.

[25] J Patrick, 'A La Carte' Spirituality and the Future of Freedom of Religion' in PT Babie, et al (eds), *Freedom of Religion or Belief: Creating the Constitutional Space for Fundamental Freedoms* (Cheltenham, Edward Elgar, 2020) 59. See also Mercadante (n 20).

[26] L Strumos, 'Ethical Veganism as Nonreligion in Mr J Casamitjana Costa v the League Against Cruel Sports' (2020) 51 *Studies in Religion / Sciences Religieuses* 295, 3.

[27] See most recently R Dworkin, *Religion without God* (Cambridge, MA, Harvard University Press, 2013).

[28] See the UK case of *J Casamitjana Costa v The League Against Cruel Sports* [2020] UKET 3331129/2018 (21 January 2020) which held that ethical veganism is a valid protected belief within the meaning of the Equality Act 2010, s 10 and in accordance with the principles set out in *Grainger plc and Others v Nicholson* [2010] ICR 360, EAT.

[29] *Grainger plc v Nicholson* (n 28).

[30] See *Hodkin v Registrar of General of Births, Deaths and Marriages* [2013] UKSC 77.

[31] See *Mouvement Raëlian Suisse v Switzerland* App no 16354/06 (2013) 56 EHRR 14.

[32] Charity Commission for England and Wales, The Temple of the Jedi Order – Application for Registration Decision of the Commission (Charity Commission for England and Wales 2016) para 35. See T Cheung, 'Jediism: Religion at Law?' (2019) 8 *Oxford Journal of Law and Religion* 350.

[33] CM Cusack, *Invented Religions: Imagination, Fiction and Faith* (Farnham, Ashgate, 2010).

[34] An interesting account of the distinction between 'fiction-based' religion and conventional 'history-based' religion is offered by MA Davidsen, 'Fiction-Based Religion: Conceptualising a New Category Against History-Based Religion and Fandom' (2014) 14 *Culture and Religion* 378.

be applied to find solutions for the conflicts created by such increasing pluralism is a question difficult to answer because the distinction between religious, philosophical and political beliefs is far from clear-cut.

Accordingly, courts across jurisdictions have defined religion in different ways. The Supreme Court of Canada in *Syndicat Northcrest v Amselem* defined religion in subjective terms:

> Freely and deeply held personal convictions or beliefs connected to an individual's spiritual faith and integrally linked to one's self-definition and spiritual fulfilment, the practices of which allow individuals to foster a connection with the divine or with the subject or object of that spiritual faith.[35]

In the US case of *Seeger*, conscientious objectors to military service argued that their beliefs should fall within the scope of the relevant legal exemption. The Court expanded the definition of religion by adopting the following test:

> We believe that, under this construction, the test of belief 'in a relation to a Supreme Being' is whether a given belief that is sincere and meaningful occupies a place in the life of its possessor parallel to that filled by the orthodox belief in God of one who clearly qualifies for the exemption.[36]

In the UK case *Hodkin v Registrar of General of Births, Deaths and Marriages* the Supreme Court adopted a broad view of religion. Lord Toulson set out relevant criteria for identifying what constitutes religion:

> For the purposes of the PWRA, I would describe religion in summary as a spiritual or non-secular belief system, held by a group of adherents, which claims to explain mankind's place in the universe and relationship with the infinite, and to teach its adherents how they are to live their lives in conformity with the spiritual understanding associated with the belief system. By spiritual or non-secular I mean a belief system which goes beyond that which can be perceived by the senses or ascertained by the application of science. I prefer not to use the word 'supernatural' to express this element, because it is a loaded word which can carry a variety of connotations. Such a belief system may or may not involve belief in a supreme being, but it does involve a belief that there is more to be understood about mankind's nature and relationship to the universe than can be gained from the senses or from science. I emphasise that this is intended to be a description and not a definitive formula.[37]

In the UK Employment Appeal Tribunal case of *Grainger plc v Nicholson* the Tribunal, drawing on the jurisprudence of the ECtHR, identified criteria to limit the number of beliefs that count as a 'philosophical belief' within the scope of the Equality Act 2010:

(i) the belief must be genuinely held;
(ii) it must be a belief and not an opinion or viewpoint based on the present state of information available;

---

[35] *Syndicat Northcrest v Amselem* [2004] 2 SCR 551, para 39.
[36] *United States v Seeger*, 380 US 163 (1965), at 166.
[37] *Hodkin v Registrar of General of Births, Deaths and Marriages* (n 30) para 57.

(iii) it must be a belief as to a weighty and substantial aspect of human life and behaviour;

(iv) it must attain a certain level of cogency, seriousness, cohesion and importance; and

(v) it must be worthy of respect in a democratic society, not be incompatible with human dignity and not conflict with the fundamental rights of others.[38]

These tests were applied to subsequent case law in order to extend protection to a range of additional ethical beliefs. In the UK case *Forstater v CGD Europe*, an employment tribunal held that the gender critical belief that 'sex was immutable' failed to meet the fifth limb of the *Grainger* test. Employment Judge Tayler stated that:

> I consider that the Claimant's view, in its absolutist nature, is incompatible with human dignity and fundamental rights of others. She goes so far as to deny the right of a person with a Gender Recognition Certificate to be the sex to which they have transitioned. I do not accept the Claimant's contention that the Gender Recognition Act produces a mere legal fiction. It provides a right, based on the assessment of the various interrelated convention rights, for a person to transition, in certain circumstances.[39]

The Employment Appeal Tribunal allowed the claimant's appeal and held that:

> The Claimant's belief does not get anywhere near to approaching the kind of belief akin to Nazism or totalitarianism ... It is a belief that might in some circumstances cause offence to trans persons, but the potential for offence cannot be a reason to exclude a belief from protection altogether.[40]

Meanwhile, the ECtHR has adopted an expansive approach in the absence of a definition of religion provided in Article 9 of the ECHR. As emphasised in the leading case of *Kokkinakis v Greece* the Court held that Article 9 covers religious *as well as* other beliefs:

> Article 9 is one of the foundations of a plural democratic society that protects the identity of religious believers and others such as atheists and agnostics.[41]

In *Eweida and others v UK*, the ECtHR further elaborated that Article 9 extends beyond religion:

> The Court recalls that, as enshrined in Article 9, freedom of thought, conscience and religion is one of the foundations of a 'democratic society' within the meaning of the Convention. In its religious dimension it is one of the most vital elements that go to make up the identity of believers and their conception of life, but it is also a precious asset for atheists, agnostics, sceptics and the unconcerned.[42]

---

[38] *Grainger plc v Nicholson* (n 28) para 24.

[39] *Forstater v CGD Europe* Case no 2200909/2019 (ET, 18 December 2019) para 84.

[40] *Forstater v CGD Europe* Appeal no UKEAT/0105/20/JOJ (EAT, 10 June 2021) para 111.

[41] *Kokkinakis v Greece* App no 14307/88 (1994) 17 EHRR 397, para 31.

[42] *Eweida and others v UK* App nos 48420/10, 59842/10, 51671/10 and 36516/10 [2013] ECHR 37 (ECtHR, 15 January 2013), para 79.

The ECtHR has, however, laid down a number of criteria that place limits on what counts as a relevant religion or belief for the purposes of Article 9. Accordingly, beliefs must attain a 'certain level of cogency, seriousness, cohesion and importance'.[43] Whilst the ECtHR has generally adopted a wide approach to religion, 'convictions must be worthy of respect in a democratic society and should not be incompatible with human dignity'.[44] In *Pretty v UK*, the ECtHR held that 'Article 9 § 1 does not cover each act which is motivated or influenced by a religion or belief'.[45] Ms Pretty, who suffered from a degenerative disease, and wished to end her life but could not without assistance, sought a declaration from the UK Director of Public Prosecutions (DPP) to not prosecute her husband for homicide for assisting her to end her life. The DPP refused to make an undertaking to that effect.[46] Ms Pretty argued that the DPP's refusal infringed her fundamental rights. However, the ECtHR held that 'although it did not doubt the "firmness" of the applicant's views concerning assisted suicide, it nevertheless could not accept that all opinions or convictions could constitute beliefs in the sense protected by Article 9 § 1 of the Convention'.[47] Therefore, even if a belief meets the test of 'attaining a level of cogency', it does not follow that a belief will necessarily fall within the scope of the Convention. *Pretty v UK* raises the question of whether individuals can claim protection when a dominant view is codified in law, in this case, the dominant moral view against euthanasia.[48]

The case law highlights the complexity of the intersectionality of religion with other fundamental rights. Any definition of religion, nonreligion or philosophical belief is inherently limited and problematic. Thus, the definition of religion poses a number of challenges. These include questions about just how a belief can be assessed and tested for its sincerity; the extent to which extending the category of religion is desirable; and which methodological approach ought to be adopted in order to determine what should count as religion.

B. Criticisms of Definitions of Religion

Rex Ahdar and Ian Leigh argue that a too narrow definition of religion risks excluding deserving religious groups, whereas, a too broad definition could render the concept useless for legal purposes.[49] Ahdar and Leigh's argument requires a normative judgement as to which beliefs *should* count. Thus, there is

---

[43] *Campbell and Cosans v UK* App no 7511/76 (1982) 4 EHRR 293, para 36.
[44] ibid.
[45] *Pretty v UK* App no 2346/02 (2002) 35 EHRR 1.
[46] ibid para 80.
[47] ibid para 82.
[48] P Dijk et al, *Theory and Practice of the European Convention on Human Rights* (Antwerpen, Intersentia, 2006) 759.
[49] R Ahdar and I Leigh, *Religious Freedom in the Liberal State* (Oxford, Oxford University Press, 2005) 141–142.

no easy answer to the question of how to define religion as any definition raises difficulties. In particular, there is always the risk that definitions are either 'under-inclusive' or 'over-inclusive', depending on whether religion is conceptualised narrowly or broadly. The semantic critique holds that attempts to define religion are either futile or problematic because of the lack of a method from which a clear and universally accepted definition of religion could be derived.[50] Accordingly, the law is inherently inadequate and unable to include all forms of religion and comparable beliefs.[51] Moreover, since religion has been the product of historical contingencies, no *single* conceptualisation of religion can fully account for the sheer diversity of religious pluralism in practice. The semantic critique points to a problem that cannot be resolved partly because the category of religion and belief evolves over time. It is also true that the liberal state cannot be neutral towards religion, especially where religion challenges the authority or foundational legitimacy of the liberal state.

A stinging critique of liberalism and its conception, or treatment, of religion has been advanced by a number of scholars, particularly by a number of academics in the fields of political philosophy, anthropology and religious studies who are sometimes grouped together under the label 'critical religious scholars'.[52] Cécile Laborde discusses the key arguments of what she refers to as the 'critical religion challenge'.[53] Laborde identifies three types of critique of the liberal treatment of religion: the semantic critique (that there is no stable universally valid empirical referent for the category of religion); the Protestant critique (that liberal law is biased toward individualistic, belief-based religions); and the realist critique (that liberal regulation of religion is arbitrary). The 'critical religion challenge' raises several inter-related challenges for religious exemptions and casts doubt on the claim that religion can be subject to stable regulation in law. Religion, as a category, is allegedly too vague, unstable, inadequate and conceptually indeterminate.[54] These are important criticisms that point to the difficulties that accompany any attempt to use the law as a means to regulate a complex and ever-changing phenomenon such as religion.

---

[50] C Laborde (Cambridge, MA, Harvard University Press, 2017) 18.

[51] See Laborde (n 50) 20; T Asad, *Formations of the Secular: Christianity, Islam, Modernity* (Redwood City, CA, Stanford University Press, 2003); and S Mahmood, *Religious Difference in A Secular Age* (Princeton, Princeton University Press, 2015). See also T Fitzgerald, 'Encompassing Religion, Privatized Religions and the Invention of Modern Politics in Timothy Fitzgerald' in T Fitzgerald (ed), *Religion and the Secular: Historical and Colonial Formations* (London, Equinox Press 2008) 211–40. Fitzgerald argues that non-European and non-Christian religions were analogised in accordance with a Christian understanding of religion. Fitzgerald argues 'a notion of the secular as the non-religious, the natural, the rational, was generated as the superior ground from which to observe and order the world' (at 235). The argument here is that our understanding of religion is itself constructed by certain assumptions that have exclusionary implications.

[52] Critical religion scholars include works by Talal Asad, Saba Mahmood, Winnifred F Sullivan, Timothy Fitzgerald and others.

[53] In Laborde (n 50) 18.

[54] ibid 18–21.

In his genealogical critique of secularism, Talal Asad has taken aim at one of the core tenets that underpins liberalism and the secular state, namely the notion of neutrality. Asad argues that secularism is far from neutral. Secular constitutional arrangements in fact often favour some forms of religion over others.[55] The category of religion itself, Asad demonstrates, bears the indelible imprint of its Western and particularly (Protestant) Christian origins. As a consequence, a normative bias is inscribed in the modern concept of religion and the debate about the status and role of religious beliefs in liberal societies. The ideals of neutrality and equality, as codified in the liberal constitution, are thus revealed to be context-specific and do not enjoy universal validity.[56] Specifically, legal categories of religion are a product of a complex, historical genealogy, which often favours some forms or manifestations of religious beliefs over others.[57]

Although his arguments are distinct from Asad's critique, Jürgen Habermas, too, acknowledges the limitations of secular public reason:

> ... the secular character of the state is a necessary though not a sufficient condition for guaranteeing equal religious freedom for everybody. It is not enough to rely on the condescending benevolence of a secularized authority that comes to tolerate minorities hitherto discriminated against. The parties themselves must reach agreement on the always contested delimitations between a positive liberty to practice a religion of one's own and the negative liberty to remain spared from the religious practices of the others.[58]

Habermas recognises that the secular constitution and public reason might place unfair burdens on religious believers.[59] He therefore emphasises the 'need for secular reason to be reflexive and open to religious dialogue'.[60] However, the distinction between the secular and religious is not necessarily binary in that distinguishing between what constitutes secular and religious reasons is sometimes difficult and not readily evident.[61] Thus, defining religion is further complicated by the plurality of secularism, which makes it difficult to simply juxtapose religion against secularism.

The criticisms outlined above have several implications for the law. Firstly, current legal definitions cannot be taken for granted since they are constructed with reference to a theoretical framework that excludes, or favours, some religions and beliefs over others.[62] Secondly, with the expansion of the range of worldviews, defining religion or belief becomes more complex and inevitably political. In sum, the 'critical scholars challenge' highlights the problems that follow from all too

---

[55] Asad (n 51).
[56] ibid.
[57] Laborde (n 50).
[58] J Habermas, 'Religion in the Public Sphere' (2006) 14 European Journal of Philosophy 1, 4.
[59] ibid 13.
[60] ibid 9–10.
[61] Asad (n 51).
[62] See Fitzgerald (n 51) 211–40.

readily using religion as a catch-all category. There are consequences that follow from these complexities in practice as demonstrated in the case law. For example, Article 9 of the ECHR distinguishes between the 'internal' and 'external' aspects of belief which has the consequence of prioritising some religious beliefs over others. In *Eweida and others v UK* the Court reiterated that:

> *Religious freedom is primarily a matter of individual thought and conscience.* This aspect of the right set out in the first paragraph of Article 9, to hold any religious belief and to change religion or belief, is absolute and unqualified.[63] (my emphasis)

The Court prioritises thought and conscience over actions and manifestation of religious beliefs, which has in some cases led to adverse outcomes for those who hold that a belief must be accompanied by its manifestation. For example, in *Dahlab v Switzerland* the appellant was a school teacher who wanted to wear her Islamic headscarf at school. The ECtHR emphasised that:

> … even if it is particularly important to the appellant and does not merely represent an expression of a particular religious belief but complies with an imperative require-ment of that belief, the wearing of a headscarf and loose-fitting clothes remains an outward manifestation which, as such, is not part of the inviolable core of freedom of religion.[64]

Yet, for many religious believers the external manifestation of their belief is funda-mental. Whilst acknowledging the validity of the criticisms made by the critical religion scholars, Laborde defends her version of liberal egalitarianism. She argues that liberal egalitarianism can be defended on the grounds that it does not single out religion as an area of uniquely special concern, thus preventing it from becom-ing 'embroiled in controversial definitions of what religion is'.[65] According to Laborde, liberal egalitarianism respects all citizens; it is therefore able to bypass the semantic critique.[66] Arguing that 'it is *not* for liberal egalitarianism to ask whether the law accurately captures what religion *is*',[67] Laborde notes that the law cannot avoid the need to engage in some *interpretative* task and must define religion on a case-by-case basis. The law does not seek to provide an ultimate definition of reli-gion; rather, the definitions used will depend on the specific issues that are being litigated.[68] Likewise, the proposed model of religious accommodation developed in this book offers a categorisation of harms that limit religious accommodation so that the focus shifts to the consequences and outcomes of a claim instead of conducting an evaluation of the beliefs in question. The strength of the 'critical religion challenge', however, is limited because the reality is that there remains a

---

[63] *Eweida and others* (n 42) para 80.
[64] *Dahlab v Switzerland* App no 42393/98 (ECtHR, 15 February 2001) 3.
[65] ibid 31.
[66] ibid 30–32.
[67] ibid 31.
[68] Laborde (n 50).

need for a workable solution to managing religious claims. Religion is not special per se, but it deserves to be placed within a 'special cage' within the liberal framework. In other words, there is a need for a workable normative framework that respects, and places appropriate limits to, the right to FORB.

The following sections of this chapter critically engage in more detail with a set of arguments made by liberal egalitarians. The 'egalitarian critique' has been developed in a number of ways by Brian Barry, Christopher Eisgruber, Lawrence Sager, Ronald Dworkin and, more recently, by Cécile Laborde. These scholars envision different outcomes for relegous exemptions, ranging from Barry's strict and narrow approach to Laborde's nuanced approach. The chapter does not address all of the arguments presented under the 'egalitarian critique' and focuses instead on a specific set of sub-arguments that are developed in terms of a general 'egalitarian critique.' What will emerge from this discussion is a clearer understanding of the ultimate limits of the 'exemptions debate' as it has been carried out by political philosophers and legal scholars and practitioners.

III. The 'Preference-Choice' Argument

Characterising religious beliefs as merely another kind of personal preference or choice has been a powerful argumentative strategy against religious exemptions. According to this view, religious beliefs do *not* constitute a distinctive set of preferences that would justify specific accommodation in law. The core of the preference-choice argument rests on the claim that religious believers have the ability or the option to choose their beliefs. Alternatively, it is maintained that even if religious beliefs or conscience claims are the kinds of beliefs that some individuals consider themselves to be morally bound by, acting upon these beliefs in practice is ultimately a choice. It follows that the manifestation of a particular belief in a particular context constitutes a choice. Accordingly, actions that are motivated by religious reasons are not *in and of themselves* unique. This is because individuals typically have different sets of preferences based on various important motivations and reasons. They might or might not be motivated by religion. Religious reasons are only one set of reasons. For example, an individual might wear particular headgear because of a religious belief, whilst another individual might wear headgear because they are simply a 'hat lover'.[69] In both cases, the individuals *choose* to wear a particular type of headgear even if their motivations are different. Religious rules, like other norms, leave room for religious believers to make choices about how and when they should adhere to religious obligations.

'Voluntarist' accounts of religious freedom argue that religious practice is a choice, thus demoting religious choices and preferences by claiming that they

---

[69] Barry (n 1) 46–50.

are neither distinct nor special as compared to other preferences.[70] In the leading US case of *Employment Division v Smith* the respondents were fired by a private drug rehabilitation organisation because they consumed peyote, a hallucinogenic drug, for sacramental purposes at a ceremony of their Native American Church.[71] They then applied for employment benefits. However, the relevant law of the State of Oregon disqualified employees who had been discharged for work-related 'misconduct'. The consumption of the drug in question had been, however, for religious reasons. The issue that the Supreme Court had to consider was whether the Free Exercise Clause of the First Amendment permitted the State of Oregon to include religiously inspired peyote use within the scope of its general criminal prohibition on use of drugs, and whether it permitted the State to refuse unemployment benefits to persons dismissed from their jobs *because* of such religiously inspired use. The Supreme Court held that it was lawful for the State to prohibit sacramental peyote use and thus to deny unemployment benefits to employees who had consumed it.[72] The First Amendment did not require an exemption to be granted. Justice Scalia delivered the majority verdict of the Court. The reasoning of the Court ran as follows: 'we have never held that an individual's religious beliefs excuse him from compliance with an otherwise valid law prohibiting conduct that the State is free to regulate';[73] 'the only decisions in which we have held that the First Amendment bars application of a neutral, generally applicable law to religiously motivated action have involved not the Free Exercise Clause alone, but the Free Exercise Clause in conjunction with other constitutional protections'; and 'It may fairly be said that leaving accommodation to the political process will place at a relative disadvantage those religious practices that are not widely engaged in; but that unavoidable consequence of democratic government must be preferred to a system in which each conscience is a law unto itself or in which judges weigh the social importance of all laws against the centrality of all religious beliefs'.[74] The Court held that the respondents sought 'to carry the meaning of "prohibiting the free exercise [of religion]" one large step further'.[75] The retreat of the Supreme Court from an earlier more generous reading of the First Amendment to narrowing the scope of religious exemptions was both significant and marked, as it meant that a religious adherent might not benefit from wide protection.

Brian Barry draws on a sophisticated account of choice in order to develop his thesis against religious exemptions.[76] He uses the specific example of ritual

---

[70] Voluntarist accounts of religious freedom include a range of arguments advanced by Barry (n 1); Eisgruber and Sager (n 1); and Cornelissen (n 15).

[71] *Employment Division v Smith*, 494 US 872 (1990), at 890.

[72] ibid.

[73] ibid.

[74] ibid.

[75] ibid.

[76] I have discussed Barry's argument about choice in a working paper (F Raza, 'Working Paper: Accommodating Religious Slaughter in the UK and Germany: Competing Interests in Carving Out

slaughter to illustrate his argument against religious and cultural exemptions. The practice of ritual slaughter is relevant to a sizeable number of Jews and Muslims who follow dietary laws that require animals to be slaughtered in accordance with specified religious rites.[77] Ritual slaughter is, however, in conflict with the general laws on animal slaughter in most European states. Barry argues that Jews and Muslims are not *required* to eat meat, and therefore, eating meat is a preference like any other.[78] He concludes that religious preferences are 'expensive tastes'[79] since most laws, inevitably, have the effect of burdening some groups more than others. Barry develops his argument along the following lines:

> If we consider virtually any law, we shall find that it is much more burdensome to some people than to others. Speed limits inhibit only those who like to drive fast ... Only smokers are stopped by prohibitions on smoking in public spaces ... this is not, of course, to deny that the unequal impact of a law may in some cases be an indication of its unfairness. It is simply to say that the charge will have to be substantiated in each case by showing exactly how the law is unfair. It is never enough to show no more than that it has a different impact on different people.[80]

There need to be additional reasons, then, for supporting religious exemptions. Thus, since religious adherents choose to practise their religion, it follows that they choose to place themselves in situations of conflict, and therefore, any burden of the religious practice should be borne by the individual rather than the general public. In other words, the public should not bear the cost of another's religious beliefs and preferences. Barry's argument against religious exemptions is powerful and is part and parcel of a more general critique of multiculturalist policies.[81]

Legal Exemptions' (2018) Max Planck Institute for Social Anthropology 1, 22–25), however, there was not enough space to do justice to Barry's very sophisticated general account against multi-culturalism, identity politics, and religious exemptions. In this book, I defend my argument in the narrow sense. Specifically, I do not offer a general account of political theory or religious accommodation. Rather, I seek to develop a model of religious accommodation.

[77] See Raza (n 76).
[78] Barry (n 1) 34–38.
[79] ibid 40.
[80] ibid 34.
[81] ibid. Barry's thesis is impressive as it is comprehensive. This chapter only focuses on Barry's arguments on religious exemptions and cannot engage in a more detailed discussion of his critique of multicultural policies. Barry opposes policies of the kind that he refers to as 'the politics of difference'. He makes a distinction between two kinds of such policies: negative and positive. He states that 'negative policies are those that provide individual exemptions from generally applicable laws on the basis of cultural practices or (very often) religious beliefs' (at 17). Moreover, 'the strategy of privatisation entails a rather robust attitude towards cultural diversity. It says, in effect, "Here are the rules which tell people what they are allowed to do. What they choose to do within those rules is up to them. But it has nothing to do with public policy." A simple model of rational decision-making, but one adequate for the present purpose, would present the position as follows: the rules define a choice set, which is the same for everybody; within that choice set people pick a particular course of action by deciding what is best calculated to satisfy their underlying preferences for outcomes, given their beliefs about the way in which actions are connected to outcomes' (at 32). Barry rejects what he calls the 'rule-and-exemption' approach as required by egalitarian liberal justice, although he concedes that it might sometimes be defensible as a matter of political prudence (at 33).

However, the choice to eat *ritually* slaughtered meat is not all-or-nothing. First and foremost, there are various methods of animal slaughter; moreover, the methods of stunning animals prior to slaughter also differ. For example, common methods of stunning either involve the use of captive bolt, electrical shock, water-bathing or the administration of certain gases.[82] Though there is reasonable disagreement about the best method of stunning animals prior to slaughter, some religious communities do in fact permit some forms of stunning.[83] Since there are a range of methods used to stun and slaughter animals, ritual slaughter also includes a range of methods. This means that the different methods of religious slaughter are not necessarily an 'expensive taste' as compared to other methods of animal slaughter. There exists a spectrum of views on the ethics of various methods of animal slaughter, which makes ritual slaughter a complex issue and not 'an all or nothing' choice. Therefore, the choice is not between choosing to eat meat or not, the choice concerns a more complex debate about the correct balancing of ethical considerations including animal welfare, hygiene standards within the meat industry, and the right to FORB. As I have argued elsewhere:

> While it might be the case that, at one level, Jews and Muslims do make the choice to (a) eat meat and (b) eat religiously slaughtered meat, for many religious adherents meat is a necessary part of their diet. Once the choice/need to eat meat is established, many Jews and Muslims consider themselves *bound* by their legal religious obligations. In this way, choices pertaining to food are not merely part of a particular lifestyle but form a central aspect of a thicker conception of the good in the Rawlsian sense.[84]

The preference-choice argument is limited in the following ways: first, even if religious believers are free to choose to practise their beliefs and therefore are *fully* autonomous, the case for religious accommodation is not necessarily undermined. For example, if a religious believer is free to choose whether or not to eat ritually slaughtered meat or wear an Islamic headscarf, the choice to follow that practice might still be worthy of protection, just as a range of other preferences and choices are protected as part of individual autonomy and/or the right to FORB.

Secondly, the importance of the embodiment of religious beliefs highlights the complexity of the right to FORB, as Laborde and others have argued, who point out that religion relates to a range of human goods and values that are necessary to lead a fulfilling life. Laborde suggests moving beyond the reference to 'the good' or 'religion' and instead refers to the various *dimensions* of religion.[85] To put it another way, precisely because religion refers to a range of goods and has a number of dimensions, its complexity is not fully understood by asking

---

[82] C Needham, 'Religious Slaughter of Animals in the EU', Briefing Paper of the Library of the European Parliament (2012) 3.
[83] Raza (n 76) 16.
[84] ibid 23.
[85] Laborde (n 50).

'whether religion is special' or a 'choice'. For example, religion can relate to a set of beliefs, rituals or ceremonies that can cover everything from birth and marriage to diet and death. Religion clearly encompasses a range of human goods relevant in different contexts. More specifically, the preference-choice argument does not provide an adequate account of the role of choice in the context of religious freedom – a strict 'outsiders'' or external viewpoint does not appreciate that the role of choice in religious life is multi-faceted and can depend on the 'internal' viewpoint of the religious adherent or community.

Yet, it is also arguable that even if religious belief is a choice, religious practice falls within an 'exceptional category of behavioural choice'.[86] In other words, religious practice constitutes a special choice/set of preferences. In sum, 'choice' in the context of the right to FORB turns out to be complex, contested, and not an appropriate method for deciding limitations, as will be argued in chapter three.

IV. The 'Intensity-Cost' Argument

The 'Intensity-Cost' argument includes a challenge to two interrelated claims that are made in favour of religious beliefs. The first is the 'intensity claim' which rests on the assumption that religious beliefs *are* special since they are more intensely held when compared to other beliefs. The second claim is that of 'greater cost', which holds that a breach of a religious belief involves a greater *cost* or entails more serious consequences for religious believers. The twin claims of 'intensity' and 'cost' are inter-related in that they both seek to distinguish religious beliefs from other sets of beliefs. One claim focuses on the subjective understanding or feelings of the religious believer whilst the other claim zeroes in on the 'moral' consequences of a breach.

Both claims are disputed. Gemma Cornelissen, for instance, argues that the 'intensity' argument is weak and fails to demonstrate *why* religious beliefs are more intensely held than other beliefs. She points out: 'Not every intensely felt belief is religious and not every religious belief is intensely felt by all believers'.[87] It is uncontroversial to claim that other nonreligious beliefs and preferences can also be intensely held. Thus, the argument of intensity inevitably involves a subjective assessment. A focus on the 'intensity' of belief does not fully capture the ways in which religious beliefs relate to the important aspects of one's conception of a good life. Assessing intensity of belief, therefore, leaves open the question of whether different sets of beliefs, preferences or hobbies can be legitimately ranked in a hierarchy in order to establish the kinds of beliefs or preferences that ought to be considered to be more than trivial daily habits or pursuits.

---

[86] N Ofrath, 'R v NS: The Niqab in Court and Lessons in Religious Exemptions' in K Vallier and M Weber (eds), *Religious Exemptions* (New York, Oxford University Press, 2018).
[87] Cornelissen (n 15) 90.

A number of persuasive accounts about the nature of religious belief and conscience claims have been developed by scholars. Paul Tillich's philosophical account of the nature of religious belief is particularly illuminating as it persuasively explains why religion is central to many people's lives. Tillich submitted that religious beliefs are those beliefs that pertain to one's 'ultimate concern'.[88] Ultimate concern does not cover trivial concerns or hobbies. His account of how religious beliefs can be distinguished from other sets of beliefs and preferences is useful in highlighting why religion matters. Of course, Tillich's conception of religion can also be subject to the 'semantic objection'; however, his account goes some way to explain the nature and importance of the right to FORB. Tillich provides an overarching understanding, rather than a specific definition, of religion. Although his conception of religion is abstract and the notion of 'ultimate concern' can be criticised for its ambiguity, his concept of 'ultimate concern' captures the idea that religious beliefs are not a mere habit or preference. Religious practices might appear to be similar to preferences and habits at first sight, but they also relate to something *more*. It is for these 'meta' reasons that there might be a 'cost' attached to breaching a religious belief where they relate to one's ultimate concern. This is why nonreligious exemptions such as a conscientious objection to military services also exist in some jurisdictions[89] as such exemptions recognise the importance of deeply-held convictions that relate to a certain set of 'higher' beliefs – religious or otherwise. These might be more appropriately categorised as 'higher-order' preferences. As such, Martha Nussbaum argues 'the faculty with which people search for life's ultimate meaning – frequently called 'conscience' – is a very important part of people, closely related to their dignity, or an aspect of it.'[90]

In a similar vein, Jocelyn Maclure argues that a distinction can be made between 'meaning-giving beliefs and commitments' and 'mundane preferences', and acknowledges that the former can be *either* secular or religious.[91] Religious beliefs fall within a category of 'special' beliefs and commitments. Maclure argues that there is something special about religion that merits reasonable accommodation provided that certain conditions are met:[92]

> My argument is that there is a special category of interests that humans have that has more normative weight and that deserve special legal treatment. These interests have to do with the capacity to act in accordance with one's deepest and meaning-giving convictions. *'Meaning-giving beliefs and commitments'* should be seen as special and be singled out, at least for normative purposes. Such beliefs and commitments should not

---

[88] P Tillich, *The Dynamics of Faith* (first published Harper & Row 1957, Harper Collins, 2001).
[89] See *Papavasilakis v Greece* (App no 66899/14) (ECtHR, 15 September 2016).
[90] Nussbaum (n 1) 65.
[91] J Maclure, 'Conscience, Religion, and Exemptions: An Egalitarian View' in K Vallier and M Weber (eds), *Religious Exemptions* (Oxford, Oxford University Press, 2018) 12–13.
[92] ibid.

be treated on a par with the kind of beliefs, values, attachments, and preferences that agents have but that are not related in strong and significant way to their sense of self or to their conception of what is a life worth living.[93] [my emphasis]

It is true that non-religious beliefs might also be intensely held, and therefore, both religious beliefs and similar kinds of secular or ethical conscience-related beliefs that pertain to 'ultimate concern' are both worthy of legal protection. In order for an individual to fulfil their conception of the good, in practical terms, there is a need to protect intensely held beliefs that relate to 'ultimate concern' or 'meaning-giving beliefs and commitments'.[94] These kinds of beliefs are not only intensely held, but also entail a 'cost' to the religious believer. The cost might be calculated in terms of immediate (loss of a job etc) or immanent costs (disobeying religious rules). But religious exemptions are not concerned with intense feelings or cost *per se*, and seek to protect a certain category of beliefs that are comparably as important as religious convictions.

Whilst religious beliefs might be intensely held, this alone does not justify religious exemptions. Rather, the 'intensity-cost' argument seeks to demonstrate that certain categories of beliefs are worthy of respect. The 'intensity-cost' argument bolsters protections for *both* religious and non-religious believers. However, the 'intensity-cost' argument is not a standalone justification for religious accommodation. It is made relevant to religious accommodation once the relationship of the intensity-argument is related to the goods, such as religious freedom and conscience, that liberal states (should) protect.

V. The Rule of Law and Equality Argument

The preference-choice and the intensity-cost arguments can be situated within the broader and, arguably, more challenging liberal egalitarian critique of religious exemptions as chipping away at the rule of law. As set out earlier, a key objection to religious exemptions is that they treat non-religious beliefs unfairly and unequally. Unfair and unequal treatment, in turn, breaches the rule of law. Religious exemptions unfairly prioritise the beliefs and practices of religious individuals by distinguishing between religious beliefs and non-religious beliefs. Not only do religious exemptions constitute an *unfair privilege* afforded to a certain category of individuals, but they also result in unequal treatment of non-religious citizens.

Christopher Eisgruber and Lawrence Sager offer a leading account of why religious exemptions result in unequal treatment of different citizens. They argue that all citizens must accept the imposition of a myraid of rules and carry the

---

[93] ibid 11–12.
[94] Nussbaum (n 1).

burdens of generally applicable laws.[95] As Eisgruber and Sager put it, 'since laws are (usually) not arbitrary as they address legislative concerns, people must generally honour those laws *despite* their personal convictions'.[96] Someone might find a number of laws and rules disagreeable or in conflict with their personal convictions, but that does not permit them to break the law or request an automatic exemption. Where individuals do not agree with a specific law or rule in their jurisdiction, they can exercise their political power at the ballot box in elections. Similarly, Brian Barry asserts that 'usually either the case for the law is strong enough to rule out exemptions or the case for exemptions is strong enough that there should be no law anyway'.[97] Barry suggests that exemptions should be narrowly interpreted whilst current categories of exemptions should not be further expanded.[98]

The 'rule of law' argument against religious exemptions relies on a formal conception of equality. Yossi Nehushtan and Stella Coyle maintain that the principle of equality should be used to decide the limits to religious exemptions and the right to FORB. They distinguish between two types of conscientious objections: the first type is directly fuelled by 'repugnant, unjustly intolerant, anti-liberal and ultimately illegitimate views'.[99] The second type of views 'may be irrational or morally misguided but are not necessarily unjustly intolerant or morally illegitimate'.[100] The first type of claims, in Nehushtan and Coyle's scheme of categorisation, would include refusals to serve homosexuals, whereas the second type would include practices such as the wearing of religious symbols. Nehushtan and Coyle argue that 'where the content of some conscience claims is grossly repugnant then neutral considerations on part of the state need not apply especially as anti-discrimination and equality laws adopt a certain moral standpoint which necessarily conflict with other views'.[101]

However, the distinction between the two types of claims is problematic since type-one exemptions, which are considered to be 'illegitimate' and 'irrational', rest on thick moral theories. Nehushtan and Coyle's classification invites the courts and decision-makers to enter into thick evaluations about what constitutes morality; in other words, the courts would need to make substantive judgements about a range of religious beliefs. Since religious claims are made in an increasing number of areas of law as well as in other contexts such as education, goods and services, and private business, it is difficult to determine when a claim is 'irrational' since the scope and rationale for an exemption varies considerably.

---

[95] Eisgruber and Sager (n 1) 86.
[96] ibid 82.
[97] Barry (n 1) 39, also known as Barry's 'pincer argument'.
[98] ibid 51.
[99] Y Nehushtan and S Coyle, 'The Difference between Illegitimate Conscience and Misguided Conscience: Equality Laws, Abortion Laws and Religious Symbols' in J Adenitire (ed), *Religious Beliefs and Conscientious Exemptions in a Liberal State* (Oxford, Hart Publishing, 2019) 114.
[100] ibid.
[101] ibid 114–15.

Certainly, equality is an important principle when determining the limits of the right to FORB; it does, however, not assist with how to strike the balance between competing interests in the absence of further criteria. Ian Leigh correctly argues that 'it is a misunderstanding of the rule of law to equate it with identical treatment of all persons'.[102] Rather, what the rule of law requires is that everyone is subject to one system of (administrative) law, but this is not the same as requiring a *uniform* application of the law.[103] The reality is that law, in an increasingly regulated state, relies on various forms of *discretion*. For example, discretion is indispensable for modern administrative law[104] where general rules need to be modified or implemented at various levels of decision-making. Discretion is a necessary part of the application of human rights law and central to the adjudication of claims of religious accommodation that are made outside of the traditional human rights framework.[105]

The reasons or motivation for requesting a religious exemption are usually not due to a desire to intentionally disobey a law that is considered disagreeable or burdensome. Jeremy Waldron points out that the case for an exemption is not based on the intensity of the objection to the law, but because of a more complex social reality that exists for those religious or cultural groups that already have a system of rules that govern the area that the states wishes to rule.[106] The conflicts of norms that often arise when the right to FORB is at stake are not to be understood as a disregard for general laws. As Waldron asserts, 'the case for exemption should not be regarded as though it were in any sense proportionate to the extent or intensity of one's opposition to the law'.[107] Requests for religious exemptions typically arise because of opposition or inability to comply with a rule that is perceived or believed to go against the grain of one's comprehensive worldview or conscience.[108]

For example, in the ECtHR case of *Jakóbski v Poland*, a prisoner requested a vegetarian diet in accordance with his religious beliefs. His request was refused and he was obliged to accept the general meat-based diet which was offered to all prisoners.[109] The claimant's request was based on his religious beliefs and therefore related to his conception of the good. The request can be distinguished from other kinds of requests. The nature of certain kinds of rules differ: a rule to ensure that people stop at a traffic light is different from a religious rule that

---

[102] I Leigh, 'The Courts and Conscience Claims' in J Adenitire (ed), *Religious Beliefs and Conscientious Exemptions in a Liberal State* (Oxford, Hart Publishing, 2019) 10, 90–91.
[103] ibid.
[104] See C Harlow and R Rawlings, *Law and Administration* (Cambridge, Cambridge University Press, 2009).
[105] In the context of the UK there are exemptions under discrimination law, see Equality Act 2010, Sch 11.
[106] J Waldron, 'The Logic of Accommodation' (2002) 59 *Washington & Lee Law Review* 3, 23–24.
[107] ibid 23–24.
[108] Chapter six will address the issue of religious organisation and group-based claims.
[109] *Jakóbski v Poland* App no 18429/06 (2012) 55 EHRR 8.

requires individuals to pray or fast. The rules are different in nature and in consequences. Dietary rules are often an integral aspect of a religious or ethical worldview for members of religious communities such as Jews, Muslims and Hindus and the sizeable number of individuals who keep to a strictly vegetarian or vegan diet only.

Jeremy Waldron emphasises that the question of granting religious exemptions is not one of regulation versus anarchy; rather, the issue is better framed as a choice between different *types* of regulation.[110] This view makes sense once we consider the range of rules imposed on individuals and the different consequences that flow from breaching them. Religious exemptions, following Waldron's line of argument, do not automatically undermine the rule of law and could even have the positive effect of enhancing the legitimacy of the rule of law. Waldron's point ties in with the argument made by Anthony Ellis who maintains that it is in the interest of the rule of law not to place citizens in a dilemma where they must choose between disobeying religious laws or state laws.[111] The need to reduce potential conflicts within a legal system is evidently a sensible policy approach. The expectation that all groups within a polity will be able to fulfil the demands of all laws and rules is both unreasonable and unattainable. Moreover, religious exemptions advance substantive equality, as outlined in chapter one.

VI. Is Religion Special?

The arguments assessed in the sections above culminate in the wider question of whether religion is special as a distinct category (in law). Several liberal egalitarian theorists have developed accounts of legal exemptions that address concerns about inequality and unfairness. There have been various argumentative strategies employed by liberal egalitarians that range from demoting religion or constructing proxies for the category of religion or equivalent and comparable beliefs to religion in order to expand protection in law.

Limiting religious exemptions to theistic faiths is manifestly unfair, whilst a more expansive approach to exemptions is potentially unworkable. Ronald Dworkin's response to the practical and definitional challenge of religion is to demote the category of religious freedom and replace it with a more general right to 'ethical independence'.[112] Dworkin argues in favour of a wider definition of religion:

> Religion is a deep, distinct, and comprehensive worldview: it holds that inherent, objective value permeates everything, that the universe and its creatures are awe-inspiring,

---

[110] Waldron (n 106) 16.
[111] A Ellis, 'What is Special about Religion?' (2006) 25 *Law & Philosophy* 219, 240.
[112] R Dworkin, *Religion without God* (Cambridge, MA, Harvard University Press, 2013) 129–30.

that human life has purpose and the universe order. A belief in a god is only one possible manifestation or consequence of that deeper worldview.[113]

However, Dworkin maintains that the general right to 'ethical independence' should not be considered a 'special right' such as the right to freedom of speech and thereby making it easier to justify limitations. He states 'we should abandon the idea of a special right to religious freedom with its high hurdle of protection'.[114] Thus Dworkin's right to 'ethical independence' does not prevent the government from limiting religious freedom without providing a 'compelling' justification.[115] The consequences of his thesis are that religion is neither special nor does it warrant any specific protection in law.

There are three key problems with Dworkin's proposed solution: first, Dworkin's demotion of religion reduces the legal protection for religious believers, which can have particularly disadvantageous effects for minority groups. If a very high threshold is to be met before a government action limiting religious freedom can be challenged successfully, some groups are bound to face higher burdens.[116] Second, Dworkin's concept of 'ethical independence' is too narrow. Whilst an interpretation of religious freedom that exclusively focuses on theistic religions is inadequate as well, 'ethical independence' does not sufficiently account for the role of rituals in religious life. Dworkin's conception of 'ethical independence' potentially includes a wide range of moral and ethical beliefs; however, one key question remains unaddressed: what is the relationship between 'ethical independence' and the *manifestation* of beliefs?[117] For example, some religious practices such as male circumcision, ritual slaughter and religious clothing often have ritual or cultural dimensions that are not fully captured by the category of 'ethical independence'. The result is that Dworkin's 'ethical independence' potentially excludes a significant number of religious practices from its scope. There is the risk that state institutions and employers could place religious believers at a particular disadvantage. The extent to which his theory supports neutrality is questionable since even if his theory seeks to uphold a version of an agnostic state – one that does not explicitly acknowledge religion X or belief Y as correct – his concept of ethical independence favours certain kinds of beliefs over others. Accordingly, Dworkin's translation of religious freedom as 'ethical independence' favours less ritualist beliefs. This criticism explicitly spelled out by Laborde beliefs and this criticism is explicitly.[118]

---

[113] ibid 1.
[114] ibid 132.
[115] ibid 131.
[116] ibid 132–33.
[117] Here the critique of the critical religion scholars such as Talal Asad and Saba Mahmood is relevant because they argue that the category of religion itself can reveal biases towards some belief systems.
[118] Laborde (n 50).

Moreover, the category of 'ethical independence' carries a number of problematic assumptions. Paul Horwitz argues that the argument against casting religious freedom as a special right is a product of Dworkin's definitions that are themselves not properly defended or universally accepted.[119] Horwitz argues that 'the gloss of abstraction in his argument overstates the problems and gives an undue air of inevitability to his demotion proposal'.[120] Dworkin's ethical independence focuses too heavily on individual conscience because it does not take into account the practical and communal elements of religion such as rituals. Laborde similarly argues that Dworkin's theory is itself not neutral as he takes a substantive position on what he considers to be 'religious matters'.[121] Finally, by replacing religious freedom with 'ethical independence', it is unclear what the added-value is in practice, since the problem about the limits of religious accommodation persists. In sum, some religious beliefs do potentially fall within a broader category of 'ethical independence', but in many cases the categories do not neatly overlap. The answer depends on how religious, ethical or cultural practices and beliefs are classified. For example, the case of *Papavasilakis v Greece* concerned a conscientious objection to military service[122] which could fall within the scope of the right to ethical independence. However, a case such as *Cha'are Shalom ve Tsedek v France*, which concerned a specific point about the regulation of ritual slaughter,[123] might only fit very awkwardly, if at all, within the scope of this category.

Charles Taylor and Jocelyn Maclure have developed another sophisticated theory of exemptions which is compatible with the liberal egalitarian framework and yields more equitable outcomes for religious minorities. Taylor and Maclure argue that both religious and secular beliefs should be granted exemptions since both potentially fall under the category of conscience (or beliefs comparable to religious beliefs).[124] However, Laborde argues that Taylor and Maclure's thesis is also too narrow because religious beliefs are collapsed into the category of conscience. Taking issue with Taylor and Maclure's assumption that conscience is a broad, all-encompassing category that captures a wide range of beliefs, Laborde maintains that religion cannot entirely be subsumed under it.[125] 'The unexpected consequence of the reduction of religion to conscience', she notes, 'is that it seems to deny protection to the cultural, habitual, embodied, and collective dimensions of religion'.[126]

---

[119] P Horwitz, 'A Troublesome Right: The Law in Dworkin's Treatment of Law and Religion' (2014) 94 *Boston University Law Review* 1225, 1229.
[120] ibid 1237.
[121] Laborde (n 50) 82.
[122] *Papavasilakis v Greece* (n 89).
[123] *Jewish Liturgical Association Cha'are Shalom ve Tsedek v France* App no 27417/95 (ECtHR GC, 27 June 2000).
[124] Maclure and Taylor (n 1).
[125] Laborde (n 50) 66–68.
[126] ibid.

According to Laborde, standard liberal egalitarian objections to exemptions are flawed for two key reasons. Firstly, she argues that the need to uphold a version of liberal neutrality (on which the liberal egalitarian objection to exemptions is based) does not prohibit the ethical evaluation of the salience of different conceptions, beliefs and commitments.[127] That is to say, liberalism for all its claim to neutrality, nevertheless, ends up making judgements about different beliefs. Secondly, although religion is not ethically salient in and of itself, religion does fall within a broader set of commitments that are ethically salient.[128] Thus, Laborde argues that liberals must clarify what exactly it means to treat religious and nonreligious commitments equally. Laborde's thesis demonstrates that liberal neutrality does not preclude the state from making *certain kinds of* assessments about the value of religious beliefs. In fact, there is a need to make finer distinctions about how liberalism *should* treat religion, and these distinctions reveal that religion is indeed relevant and can be protected under a range of goods. Nevertheless, Laborde maintains that religion per se is not special and worthy of unique protection. Her 'disaggregation strategy' is particularly advantageous in that it addresses the gap in the literature on the 'exemptions debate', whilst offering a consistent method for deciding when to grant religious exemptions within the liberal egalitarian framework. Hers is a novel and impressive strategy. Although Laborde concludes that religion is not special she stresses that several of its disaggregated features are worthy of special protection.[129]

My proposed model of religious accommodation differs from Laborde's project. First, the solution I propose is a model that is not formally rooted in the liberal egalitarian framework. Certainly, equality has to be taken seriously by any approach to religion within the liberal state. However, the starting premises of liberal egalitarianism and my approach differ. My model is based on the premise that religious accommodation is justifiable and beneficial for a number of inter-related reasons. Secondly, my model interprets the limitations to FORB through the categorisation of harms to autonomy and focuses on the practical outcomes of a particular claim. My model evaluates, or more specifically, weighs up harms to autonomy caused by a religious claim. Accordingly, for the purposes of this book – and given the range of potential cases arising from the right to FORB – it is impossible and unnecessary to demonstrate that religion is special. Any attempt to do so is also undesirable: the category of religion is in constant flux. It remains important and central whether it is disaggregated or taken to be a special category of unique beliefs. The simple fact that some individuals treat religion and conscience as a distinct human good, together with the need to uphold substantive equality, provides a strong justification in favour of exemptions.

---

[127] ibid 198–202.
[128] ibid.
[129] Laborde (n 18).

VII. Conclusion

Religion in the liberal state deserves to be placed into its own 'special cage'. Religion is not *necessarily* special. Yet, religion does and ought to have a special place in the liberal constitution. What counts as a genuine 'religion or belief' for the purposes of the law is important for claimants who seek to fall within the scope of the relevant legislation in order to make a successful claim. The 'all or nothing' approach to religious accommodation, as famously articulated in *Employment Division v Smith*, is not the only option available to the liberal state. Exemptions are one key way in which the liberal state can recognise the value of plural societies and accommodate different conceptions of justice and the good. The model of religious accommodation proposed in this book offers a more nuanced account of religious accommodation by taking into account the various interests of parties involved. More specifically, a legal duty or policy approach in favour of religious accommodation can be realistically implemented without compromising the legitimacy of the liberal constitution. This chapter has argued that religious exemptions are only one form of accommodation and that the 'exemptions debate' has its limitations. Religious beliefs as well as secular (analogous and comparable) sincerely held beliefs are worthy of legal protection. A nuanced account of the rule of law, which is based on substantive equality, is capable of accommodating a range of exemptions without compromising the integrity of the legal system. I offer a solution by proposing a model of religious accommodation as set out in Part II of this book.

3

Approaches to Limitations*

Courts and decision makers across jurisdictions decide on the limitations to the right to FORB by interpreting the legal sources that protect religion and by applying different legal tests. The central questions at stake in this process are the following: how exactly is the right to FORB to be limited? And what approach is the most appropriate? This chapter identifies the shortcomings of the four dominant approaches to limitations, which include the following categories: (i) practices deemed to breach or undermine the key tenets of the liberal democratic order; (ii) practices that breach the duty of neutrality; (iii) practices that do not constitute a core religious belief; and (iv) the choice of alternatives. The focus of the discussion rests on democratic liberal states that uphold a minimal commitment to secular constitutionalism, although the utility of the analysis is not limited to these jurisdictions. The approaches are not necessarily mutually exclusive or applied as distinct categories to limitations in the jurisprudence. Yet, there are two key advantages to categorising key approaches to limitations in this way. First, by systematising different approaches, it is possible to make sense of how courts approach the increasing complexity raised by religious freedom. Second, enhanced scrutiny of the different reasons given under each approach can lead to better protection of religious freedom by ensuring fair and overall consistent standards. Part II of this book then goes on to propose an alternative model of religious accommodation.

I. Practices Deemed to be against the Liberal Order

International human rights law does not prescribe a specific church–state model that a state should adopt, but it does require that both the rights to FORB and non-discrimination are adequately protected.[1] The ECtHR, by contrast, in its

---

* This chapter reproduces large sections in Farrah Raza, 'Limitations to the Right to Religious Freedom: Rethinking Key Approaches' (2020) 9 *Oxford Journal of Law and Religion* 435–62. Reprinted with permission of Oxford University Press. To consult and cite the original article: Raza F, Limitations to the Right to Religious Freedom: Rethinking Key Approaches, *Oxford Journal of Law and Religion* 2020; 9 (3): 435–462, https://doi.org/10.1093/ojlr/rwaa025, © The Author(s) 2020. All rights reserved. For permissions, please email: journals.permissions@oup.com.

[1] D Moeckli et al, *International Human Rights Law*, 3rd edition (Oxford, Oxford University Press, 2018) 213.

jurisprudence on religious freedom additionally requires states to uphold the principles of pluralism[2] and neutrality.[3] Whilst the constitutional establishment of religion per se does not necessarily breach the ECHR, a theocratic system that upholds religious laws would breach it. Therefore, any role that religion plays in a liberal state must be subordinate to the secular constitution. Raymond Plant, in his discussion of religion and the liberal state, raises the pertinent question of 'whether a religion seeking a role in a liberal society can do so only if it is a liberalised form of that religion.[4] In other words, can the tension experienced by some religious believers, who are confronted with a clash between their religious commitment and the liberal framework, only be resolved in favour of the secular constitution? This question can partly be answered by reference to the jurisprudence.

In liberal democratic states, the right to FORB can justifiably be limited where a particular belief or practice is contrary to the foundational principles of the secular order. There are 'thin' and 'thick' versions of liberalism. For example, Jahid Bhuiyan and Darryn Jensen distinguish between 'liberalism as a truce' and 'comprehensive' liberalism where the latter promotes a set of 'enlightened' values.[5] Whilst the liberal state should not, in principle, endorse or promote a specific conception of the good,[6] this does not mean that *every* conception of the good, religious organisation or religious practice will be tolerated. For example, where a religious belief or organisation seeks to overthrow or to undermine the liberal state by establishing a system of religious law or legal pluralism, then this would constitute a direct threat to the liberal order. Both liberal political theory and the ECtHR's jurisprudence on religious freedom hold that liberal democracies must meet the minimum requirements of secularism even where states have an established church.[7] Jürgen Habermas emphasises that whilst the liberal constitution can accommodate religion, the constitution itself must remain secular and grounded in non-transcendental reasons.[8] For Habermas, 'the secular character of the state is a necessary though not a sufficient condition for guaranteeing equal religious freedom for everybody.[9] Thus, religion can only be accommodated in liberal states to the extent that it does not undermine the key principles of neutrality, equality and secularism. However, this requirement is subject to litigation as set out below.

---

[2] The Court emphasised the importance of Art 9 for both religious and non-religious individuals in *Kokkinakis v Greece* App no 14307/88 (1994) 17 EHRR 397, para 31.

[3] *Lautsi v Italy* (2010) 50 EHRR 42 (App no 30814/06, ECtHR Second Section, 3 November 2009), subsequently to be referred to as *Lautsi I*.

[4] R Plant, 'Religion in a Liberal State' in G D'Costa et al (eds), *Religion in a Liberal State* (Cambridge, Cambridge University Press, 2013) 9.

[5] JH Bhuiyan and D Jensen (eds), *Law and Religion in the Liberal State* (Oxford, Hart Publishing, 2020).

[6] See J Rawls, *Political Liberalism* (New York, Columbia University Press, 1993) xxi and xxii.

[7] J Habermas, 'Religion in the Public Sphere' (2006) 14 *European Journal of Philosophy* 1.

[8] ibid.

[9] ibid 4.

Although a degree of legal and moral pluralism is a reality of modern liberal states, an important distinction is to be made between the formal *constitutional entrenchment of* legal pluralism and the everyday reality of religious believers following their religious norms in practice. In the former case, the state officially endorses and recognises legal pluralism, whereas in the latter case parallel 'minority legal orders'[10] exist that are not given explicit constitutional recognition. For example, when religious adherents choose to marry in accordance with their religious marriage laws, this does not necessarily mean that a parallel and equally valid family law system is recognised at the state level.[11] Of course, the reality of everyday moral and religious pluralism poses challenges for the liberal state, but its existence does not replace or substitute state law. In the UK, the controversy over *Sharia* councils prompted a government review that arrived at the following conclusion: 'Whilst sharia is a source of guidance for many Muslims, *Sharia* councils have no legal jurisdiction in England and Wales.'[12] The review also emphasised that *Sharia* councils could not bypass domestic laws and were bound by obligations arising from equality law.[13] It is well established in international human rights law that religious organisations must respect minimal standards of human rights, equality and non-discrimination and that states must ensure 'the actual enjoyment of rights by all and without discrimination'.[14] Thus, religious organisations must ensure that they adhere to the constitutional framework and equality laws so as to ensure that the boundaries of religious freedom are appropriately defined.

The principle of preserving the liberal order, which includes the commitment to conditions of 'minimal' secularism, is confirmed by the jurisprudence on religious freedom in many liberal states. Limitations to the right to FORB are justified where they are considered necessary to preserve the foundational normative values that uphold the legitimacy of the liberal state such as democracy, secularism, equality and the rule of law. The ECtHR has confirmed that states can legitimately justify limiting the rights of religious groups and religious practices in order to preserve the secular liberal order. In the seminal 2003 case of *Refah Partisi (Welfare Party) v Turkey*, the Court held that the dissolution of a political party

---

[10] M Malik, *Minority Legal Orders in the UK Minorities, Pluralism and the Law* (London, The British Academy, 2012).

[11] A religious marriage might be valid in accordance with state law or it might be outside of the scope of state law. For example, Muslim marriages also known as a 'nikah' that are 'unregistered' have caused a considerable amount of debate in several jurisdictions. The lack of legality of a 'nikah' marriage that fails to meet the requirements of the Marriage Act 1949 and the Matrimonial Causes Act 1973 in England and Wales or falls outside of the legal framework of a state's family law framework in other jurisdictions can mean that parties are left without remedies upon divorce. See PS Nash, 'Sharia in England: The Marriage Law Solution' (2017) 6 *Oxford Journal of Law and Religion* 523; RC Akhtar, R Probert and A Moors, 'Informal Muslim Marriages: Regulations and Contestations' (2018) 7 *Oxford Journal of Law and Religion* 367.

[12] The Independent Review into the Application of Sharia Law in England and Wales (Cm 9560, 2018) 4.

[13] ibid.

[14] H Bielefeldt, N Ghanea and M Wiener, *Freedom of Religion or Belief: An International Law Commentary* (Oxford, Oxford University Press, 2016) 340.

that promoted the implementation of Islamic law did not breach Article 11 of the ECHR (freedom of assembly and association).[15] According to the Constitutional Court of Turkey, the party had become 'a centre of activities contrary to the principle of secularism'.[16] The applicant party (Refah) claimed that the dissolution of the party and the prohibition barring its leaders from holding similar office in any other political party amounted to a breach of Article 11 of the ECHR. However, the government contended that Refah's dissolution was pursuant to a number of legitimate aims listed in Article 11(2) of the ECHR and that the interests of public safety and the freedom of others were informed by the principle of secularism as enshrined by the Turkish Constitution.[17] In other words, the legitimate aims had to be interpreted in light of secularism. The ECtHR emphasised that a plural legal system which rests on a distinction based on religion is incompatible with the Convention. The Court pointed out that the entrenchment of a religious-based legal system would '… introduce into all legal relationships a distinction between individuals grounded on religion …'.[18] The ECtHR further stated:

> It is difficult to declare one's respect for democracy and human rights while at the same time supporting a regime based on sharia, which clearly diverges from Convention values, particularly with regard to its criminal law and criminal procedure, its rules on the legal status of women and the way it intervenes in all spheres of private and public life in accordance with religious precepts …[19]

The Court held that the constitutional entrenchment of religious laws is incompatible with the values of the Convention. However, David Schilling argues that the Court departed from its jurisprudence on Article 11 in *Refah* because of European concern about the growing influence of Islam in Turkish politics.[20] Although Turkey has a secular constitution, it is generally not considered to be a *liberal* state in the sense that many Western liberal democracies are.[21] Despite the political dimensions of *Refah*, the Court clarified that the Convention is incompatible with a system of religious law because it would breach state neutrality, equality and human rights.

More recently, in *Molla Sali v Greece*,[22] the ECtHR addressed the legality of applying religious inheritance laws in a case that concerned a dispute about the

---

[15] *Refah Partisi and others v Turkey* App nos 41340/98, 41342/98, 41343/98, 41344/98 (2003) 37 EHRR 1.
[16] ibid para 25.
[17] ibid para 42.
[18] ibid para 70.
[19] ibid para 72.
[20] D Schilling, 'European Islamaphobia and Turkey – Refah Partisi (The Welfare Party) v. Turkey' (2004) 26 *Loyola of Los Angeles International and Comparative Law Review* 501.
[21] The current Turkish secular order is distinct from liberal states and the question of the appropriate church–state model in Turkey is beyond the scope of this discussion.
[22] *Molla Sali v Greece* App 20452/14 (ECtHR, 9 December 2018).

validity of a public will made by a Muslim man (Mr Sali). In light of the special status of the Muslim community in the region of Thrace in Greece, *Sharia* law ordinarily applied to cases concerning family and inheritance matters. However, the wife of the deceased argued that *Sharia* could not be applied against her late husband's will because of his intention to not follow *Sharia*. His intention to not apply *Sharia* had been evidenced by the fact that he had taken the necessary steps to notarise his will. His will left all of his property to his wife, rather than apportioning it amongst relatives in accordance with the principles of *Sharia* (according to dominant interpretations). However, the sisters of the deceased argued that *Sharia* did apply and that they had a legitimate interest in his estate. The sisters contended that the Civil Code did not apply to the case. The Court of Cassation held that Mr Sali's will was subject to *Sharia* law[23] whilst the deceased's wife argued that this finding amounted to religious discrimination. The ECtHR held that there had been a breach of Article 14 of the ECHR (Prohibition of discrimination) read in conjunction with Article 1 of Protocol No 1 (Protection of property). The Court reiterated the principles governing church–state relations:

> … freedom of religion does not require the Contracting States to create a particular legal framework in order to grant religious communities a special status entailing specific privileges. Nevertheless, a State which has created such a status must ensure that the criteria established for a group's entitlement to it are applied in a non-discriminatory manner.[24]

Moreover, the Court emphasised the right to 'opt-out' of a religious system and stated that:

> Refusing members of a religious minority the right to voluntarily opt for and benefit from ordinary law amounts not only to discriminatory treatment but also to a breach of a right of cardinal importance in the field of protection of minorities, that is to say the right to free self-identification.[25]

The Court drew on the principles of self-determination and non-discrimination to justify its decision. An approach to limitations that deems a practice to be illiberal is informed by the principles of neutrality, self-determination, equality and non-discrimination, as the case law demonstrates. But these are complex principles that need to be interpreted and given content in specific cases which means that approaches to limitations based on the need to protect the liberal order encompass a range of internal normative conflicts. This approach does not in and of itself resolve conflicts and inconsistencies. When exactly is a practice 'illiberal' or against the liberal order? Courts have often relied on additional principles such as neutrality to justify their decisions.

---

[23] ibid, para 18.
[24] ibid, para 155.
[25] ibid para 157.

II. The Duty of Neutrality

The duty of neutrality is commonly invoked as a justification for limitations to religious freedom, but neutrality is also multi-faceted. The duty of neutrality is underpinned by the commitment of liberal states to moral pluralism and minimal secularism, as outlined above. Although limitations based on neutrality and the need to preserve the liberal order are related, important differences remain between the two approaches. Some manifestations of religious belief that are considered to be 'illiberal' are not necessarily deemed to undermine the liberal state as such. For example, segregated prayer spaces, religious marriages that tend to entrench gender inequality, and religious clothing for women are illiberal practices that could nevertheless be accommodated. However, some permissible illiberal practices might breach the duty of neutrality. In particular, the duty of neutrality is a specific duty of certain sectors in some jurisdictions such as state schoolteachers[26] and the judiciary.[27] Neutrality, as a ground for limitations, deserves specific attention because of its variations and complexity as highlighted by the conflicts raised by the application of neutrality in the case law. However, different versions of secularism[28] and church–state models generate different normative accounts of the duty of neutrality. Thomas Jefferson's famous description of 'a wall of separation' is commonly used to describe the church–state model in the US and its separation of state and religion as codified in the Constitution.[29] The First Amendment of the American Constitution states:

> Congress shall make no law respecting an establishment of religion, or prohibiting the free exercise thereof.

However, separation does not necessarily entail hostility or strict separation as confirmed by the jurisprudence and as articulated by Chief Justice Warren E Burger in *Lynch v Donnelly*:

> the 'wall' of separation between church and state is a useful metaphor, but is not an accurate description of the practical aspects of the relationship that in fact exists. The

---

[26] See *Dahlab v Switzerland* App no 42393/98 (ECtHR, 15 February 2001).

[27] See the recent controversy in Germany over the wearing of Islamic headscarves in courts: 'Bavarian court upholds headscarf ban for judges, prosecutors' *Deutsche Welle* (18 March 2019) at www.dw.com/en/germany-bavarian-court-upholds-headscarf-ban-for-judges-prosecutors/a47960676.

[28] Veit Bader identifies no less than 12 versions of secularism which include versions of secularism that are: 'inclusive, passive, moderate, weak, strong and aggressive' in V Bader, 'Beyond Secularisms of All Sorts' (SSRN, The Immanent Frame, 11 October 2011).

[29] Thomas Jefferson's reference to 'the wall of separation' is widely quoted including in case law such as in the seminal decision of *Everson v Board of Education* (1947) 330 US 1 although Kerry notes the divergence between multiple understandings of the relationship between church and state in the USA: see PE Kerry, 'Religious and Secular Presuppositions in First Amendment Interpretations' in MD Breidenbach and O Anderson (eds), *The Cambridge Companion to the First Amendment and Religious Liberty* (Cambridge, Cambridge University Press, 2019).

Constitution does not require complete separation of church and state; it affirmatively mandates accommodation, not merely tolerance, of all religions, and forbids hostility toward any.[30]

The French Constitution entrenches secularism through the constitutional principle of *laïcité*,[31] which generates a strict(er) duty of neutrality. German Basic Law (*Grundgesetz*) codifies the separation between state and church but enables religious organisations to obtain special constitutional status.[32] However, the duty of neutrality has generated litigation in both France[33] and Germany.[34] Conflicts about the relationship between church–state can raise deep normative disagreements about precisely when the principles of secularism and/or neutrality are breached in practice. Cécile Laborde argues that secularism is a normative precondition of the liberal state but clarifies that 'secularism and neutrality should not be reduced to one value, but explicated in relation to a constellation of liberal values'.[35] This means that neutrality is an important value but is subject to variation. The case law illuminates that the application of the duty of neutrality varies in different jurisdictions.

The duty to uphold neutrality is emphasised in the case law of several national courts as well as in case law on Article 9 of the ECHR either directly or indirectly. In *Kokkinakis v Greece*, the ECtHR emphasised the duty of state neutrality in the context of the right to proselytise.[36] In *Konrad v Germany*, the Court emphasised the need to uphold state neutrality in the context of education.[37] The duty of neutrality has also been invoked to justify limitations in a number of the Islamic headscarf cases as outlined below. The duty of neutrality is multi-faceted and, accordingly, has resulted in different outcomes in similar cases. Most notably, in *Lautsi v Italy*, which concerned the display of a crucifix in a school classroom in Italy, the contentious issue was whether the display of a crucifix in a state school breached the duty of neutrality in the context of education where state neutrality is a duty. In *Lautsi I* the applicant submitted that 'The concept of secularism required the state to be neutral and keep an equal distance from all religions, as it should not be perceived as being closer to some citizens than to others'.[38]

---

[30] *Lynch v Donnelly* (1984) 465 US 668.
[31] See art 1 of the 1958 French Constitution of the Fifth Republic and Taylor's discussion of the values of 'liberty, equality and fraternity' in C Taylor, 'The Meaning of Secularism' (2010) 12 *The Hedgehog Review* 23.
[32] See Art 140 of the Basic Law for the Federal Republic of Germany 1949.
[33] *Dogru v France* App no 27058/05 (ECtHR, 4 December 2008); *Kervanci v France* App no 31645/04 (ECtHR, 4 December 2008); see E Daly, 'Public Funding of Religions in French Law: The Role of the Council of State in the Politics of Constitutional Secularism' (2014) 3 *Oxford Journal of Law and Religion* 103 for a nuanced account of litigation of religious organisations and the duty of neutrality.
[34] BVerfGE 93, 1 1 BvR 1087/91 Krucifix-decision 'Crucifix Case (Classroom Crucifix Case)' 12 May 1987 and n 59.
[35] C Laborde, *Liberalism's Religion* (Cambridge, MA, Harvard University Press, 2017) 115.
[36] *Kokkinakis v Greece* (n 2) para 15.
[37] *Konrad v Germany* App no 35504/03 (2007) 44 EHRR SE8, 3.
[38] *Lautsi I* (n 3) para 32.

The applicant argued that the display of the crucifix breached the principle of secularism and that '… the crucifix, over and above all else, had a religious connotation …'.[39] The government, on the other hand, argued that 'While the sign of the cross was certainly a religious symbol, it had other connotations'.[40] The government emphasised that:

> The message of the cross was therefore a humanist message which could be read independently of its religious dimension and was composed of a set of principles and values forming the foundations of our democracies.[41]

According to the government, the crucifix had acquired a neutral secular meaning, which complimented the constitutional values of the state.[42] The ECtHR, however, held that the crucifix carried a number of meanings of which the religious meaning was the predominant one[43] and argued that the display of the crucifix did breach the applicant's right to education in accordance with Article 2 of Protocol No 1 (Right to education).[44] The outcome of the case attracted considerable controversy and public attention.[45] However, the Italian government successfully appealed the decision of the Chamber. On appeal, in *Lautsi II* the Grand Chamber of the Court held that there was no violation of Article 2 of Protocol No 1 (and that no separate issue arose under Article 9 of the ECHR). The Grand Chamber emphasised the wide margin of appreciation afforded to contracting states in the sphere of cultural and historical development.[46] The Court held that the crucifix was essentially 'a passive symbol'.[47] Judge Power reasoned that 'A preference for secularism over alternative world views – whether religious, philosophical or otherwise – is not a neutral option'.[48]

Neutrality, then, was a vehicle for submissions about what secularism *should* entail. Joseph Weiler argues that there was no neutrality as such because both a wall with a crucifix, and without, are not neutral.[49] On the other hand, Lorenzo Zucca argues that Judge Power confuses *secularist* ideology with secularism as a legal/constitutional concept – and the latter, Zucca claims, is not necessarily ideological.[50] *Lautsi II* highlights the malleability of neutrality as an approach to limitations and stands in contrast to the Court's earlier case law on religious symbols.

---

[39] ibid para 31.
[40] ibid para 35.
[41] ibid para 35.
[42] ibid para 31.
[43] ibid, para 51.
[44] ibid.
[45] See *Lautsi v Italy* App no 30814/06 (18 March 2011) Grand Chamber (*Lautsi II*) para 47 for submissions of the third-party interveners.
[46] ibid para 61.
[47] ibid para 72.
[48] J Weiler, '*Lautsi*: A Reply' (2013) 11 *International Journal of Constitutional Law* 230.
[49] ibid.
[50] L Zucca, '*Lautsi*: A Commentary on a Decision by the ECtHR Grand Chamber' (2013) 11 *International Journal of Constitutional Law* 218, 225.

The duty of neutrality has been disputed in a range of cases concerning religious symbols. The case law on religious symbols can be divided into two broad categories: (i) religious symbols displayed by the state and (ii) religious symbols worn by individuals. The Grand Chamber's reasoning in *Lautsi v Italy* appears to depart from the Court's earlier case law on religious symbols. In *Dahlab v Switerzland,* a state school teacher was barred from wearing an Islamic headscarf to work.[51] The Commission held that the Islamic headscarf constitutes a 'powerful external symbol' and that 'the wearing of a headscarf might have some kind of proselytising effect'.[52] In *Şahin v Turkey,* a medical student was denied entry to her university examinations because she was wearing the Islamic headscarf.[53] The ECtHR found that the interference with the applicant's Article 9 rights was justified and proportionate as they pursued the legitimate aim of upholding secularism. Therefore, the ECtHR held that visibility of the Islamic headscarf could breach the principle of secular neutrality, whereas the Grand Chamber in *Lautsi II* held that the crucifix did not do so.

The Court's jurisprudence reveals an inconsistent application of the principle of neutrality. Should neutrality entail an 'inclusive' secularism as Zucca argues or do the dimensions of neutrality require, as Laborde emphasises, different solutions depending on the specific context? Or alternatively, does the Court's interpretation of secularism promote 'a discriminatory and hegemonic' understanding of neutrality?[54] In the context of Article 9, critics have accused the Court of bias or not going far enough to protect minority rights.[55] Satvinder Juss points out that the Court has too readily decided in favour of the interests of the state over individual rights,[56] whilst Samuel Moyn highlights the Court's fragile institutional legitimacy.[57] The ECtHR's jurisprudence on religious symbols and neutrality is left in an unsatisfactory state. Notwithstanding the debates about how exactly the principles of secularism and neutrality should be applied in a given case, neutrality persists as a justification for limitations. However, neutrality has failed to generate a consistent approach to limiting religious practices, in particular with regards to the display of religious symbols. The *Lautsi* cases demonstrate that state neutrality can be interpreted in radically different ways that result in different outcomes. The *Lautsi* cases were unable to satisfy all parties precisely because there were competing versions of neutrality and secularism at stake. Such variation and inconsistency are problematic for developing standards that can be applied across jurisdictions with fairer outcomes.

---

[51] *Dahlab v Switzerland* (n 26).

[52] ibid 13.

[53] *Leyla Şahin v Turkey* App no 44774/98 (ECtHR GC, 10 November 2005).

[54] B Gökarkiksel and K Mitchell, 'Veiling, Secularism, and the Neoliberal Subject: National Narratives and Supranational Desires in Turkey and France' (2005) 5 *Global Networks* 147.

[55] C Joppke, 'Pluralism vs. Pluralism: Islam and Christianity in the European Court of Human Rights' in JL Cohen and C Laborde (eds), *Religion, Secularism, and Constitutional Democracy* (New York, Colombia University Press, 2015).

[56] S Juss, 'Burqa-bashing and the Charlie Hebdo Cartoons' (2016) 26 *King's Law Journal* 27.

[57] S Moyn, 'Christian Human Rights: An Introduction' (2017) 28 *King's Law Journal* 1, 33.

More recently, the CJEU's application of it as a blanket principle to address religious diversity at the workplace further reveals why neutrality is problematic. At stake in both *Samira Achbita and Centrum voor Gelijkheid van Kansen en voor Racismebestrijding v G4S Secure Solutions NV*[58] and *Asma Bougnaoui, Association de Defense des Droits de l'Homme (ADDH) v Micropole Univers SA*[59] was the application of policies of neutrality at the workplace. In *Achbita* the applicant worked for the security company G4S, which had an unwritten rule of prohibiting visible signs of their employees' 'political, philosophical and religious' beliefs.[60] *Achbita* refused to remove her headscarf, which led to her dismissal. The CJEU did not classify this as an instance of direct discrimination. Rather, the Court considered that a policy of banning religious symbols could constitute indirect discrimination. However, indirect discrimination could be objectively justified if applied equally to other beliefs. In the case of *Bougnaoui*, the applicant had been told by her employer that her headscarf might upset customers. The question for the CJEU was whether the wishes of customers to not see the headscarf could constitute 'a genuine and determining occupational requirement'.[61] The Court ruled that such a requirement is only permissible in very narrow circumstances and must be based on a justification that is grounded in an objective assessment. As Ronan McCrea argues, 'in *Achbita*, the Court appears to say that the need of the employer to present a neutral image to clients makes it more justifiable to impose a neutrality requirement on employees with customer-facing roles. On the other hand, in *Bougnaoui*, the Court found that compliance with a client's request for "no veil next time" could not be seen as a "genuine and determining occupational requirement"'.[62]

In *IX v WABE eV* the Court in Germany requested a preliminary ruling from the CJEU for cases concerning the wearing of the Islamic headscarf at the workplace.[63] One of the claimants 'IX' was employed at a childcare centre, and after a period of parental leave, she returned to work wearing her headscarf. She was requested to remove it in line with the company's 'neutrality policy'. Specifically, the relevant rule held that employees could not 'wear any visible signs of their political, philosophical or religious beliefs'. Likewise, in *Müller Handels Gmbh v MJ* the employee was also requested to remove her headscarf in order to protect the image of neutrality. In particular, the relevant rule held that employees could 'not wear conspicuous, large-sized signs of any political, philosophical or religious

[58] Case C-157/15 *Samira Achbita and Centrum voor Gelijkheid van Kansen en voor Racismebestrijding v G4S Secure Solutions NV* EU:C:2017:203.

[59] Case C-188/15 *Asma Bougnaoui, Association de Defense des Droits de l'Homme (ADDH) v Micropole Univers SA* EU:C:2017:204.

[60] *Achbita* (n 58).

[61] Council Directive 2000/78/EC of 27 November 2000 establishing a general framework for equal treatment in employment and occupation.

[62] See www.ucl.ac.uk/european-institute/news/2017/mar/faith-work-european-courts-headscarf-ruling.

[63] C-804/18 and C-341/19 *IX v WABE eV and MH Müller Handels GmbH v MJ* EU:C:2021:594, decision handed down on 15 July 2021.

beliefs'. At issue was whether a policy that prohibits religious (and other) symbols can be lawful and whether a neutrality policy in principle is permissible. In short, was this an instance of unlawful discrimination? Or as one commentator put it: 'Can catering to the prejudiced views of customers be a legitimate aim within the scope of the Equal Treatment Framework Directive 2000/78?'[64] The CJEU held that a prohibition on wearing any visible form of expression of political, philosophical or religious beliefs in the workplace may be justified by the employer's need to present a neutral image towards customers or to prevent social disputes.[65]

The rulings of the CJEU in these cases made it possible for employers to justify the banning of religious symbols – under the condition that such a policy of neutrality meets a genuine need and is consistently applied. The CJEU circumscribed religious freedom on weak grounds.[66] The inconsistencies of neutrality as an approach to limitations reveal that neutrality must be replaced with a stable and robust normative approach to limitations if it is to offer better guidance to decision makers.

III. Practices that do not Constitute a 'Core' Religious Belief

Most courts and decision makers adjudicating religious disputes have, either explicitly or implicitly, adopted an approach to limitations that rests on whether or not the belief or practice in question is a 'core' belief. If it is considered to be central to that faith, then there is a stronger reason to not limit it. Whereas, if the practice is not a core aspect of the faith, then limiting it is justifiable in principle. The rationale for this approach is simple: since the manifestation of the right to FORB is not absolute and not every practice can be accommodated, a distinction between 'core' and 'non-core' aspects of a faith is a helpful way of deciding the limits of religious freedom.

The ECtHR has sought to avoid making judgements about the truthfulness of particular religious claims and has repeatedly reiterated its role as a neutral arbitrator. In *Şahin v Turkey*, the ECtHR emphasised that '... the State's duty of neutrality and impartiality is incompatible with any power on the State's part to assess the legitimacy of religious beliefs or the ways in which those beliefs are expressed'.[67] The Court has generally not required a religious practice to be deemed a *mandatory*

---

[64] See www.verfassungsblog.de/preserving-prejudice-in-the-name-of-profit.
[65] Joined Cases C-804/18 and C-341/19 *IX v WABE eV and MH Müller Handels GmbH v MJ* EU:C:2021:594, decision handed down on 15 July 2021.
[66] F Raza, 'The Continuity of the Headscarf Controversy: From Politics to Fashion' (OxHRH Blog, 17 December 2017), available at https://ohrh.law.ox.ac.uk/the-continuity-of-the-headscarf-controversy-from-politics-to-fashion.
[67] *Şahin v Turkey* (2007) 44 EHRR 5, para 107.

practice before finding an interference or violation of Article 9. However, the concept of 'core' or 'essential' practice features in some of its jurisprudence and particularly in its earlier case law on Article 9. In *X v UK*, a Buddhist prisoner was prohibited from sending materials for publication in a Buddhist magazine.[68] The prisoner claimed that an exchange of ideas between Buddhists was part of his religious faith. The European Commission held that the applicant failed to show that the practice was a necessary part of his religion and his complaint was held to be manifestly ill-founded. On the other hand, in *Eweida and others v UK*, the Court emphasised that '... there is no requirement on the applicant to establish that he or she acted in fulfilment of a duty mandated by the religion in question'.[69] Yet, the 'core' beliefs approach to limitations has persisted across jurisdictions.

In the UK case of *R (on the application of Playfoot) v Governing Body of Millais School*, the High Court directly engaged with the concept of 'core' religious belief in its reasoning.[70] The case concerned a school girl who was not permitted to wear her 'purity ring' at school, which signified celibacy until marriage. The school uniform policy did not permit jewellery. The father (on behalf of his daughter) claimed that the prohibition constituted an unlawful interference of his daughter's rights under Article 9 of the ECHR. Counsel on the behalf of the school submitted that '... only those practices which are necessary or required by the belief are protected ...'.[71] The High Court noted that although there was some support for this approach in the case law on Article 9 of the ECHR, there was no consistent and settled jurisprudence that authoritatively held that *only* 'necessary' beliefs were protected.[72] Rather than using 'core' beliefs as a test, the High Court relied on the test as set out in *R (on the application of Williamson) v Secretary of State for Education and Employment*[73] and held that the purity ring was not 'intimately linked' with Ms Playfoot's belief.[74] The Court went on to argue that 'The Claimant was under no obligation, by reason of her belief, to wear the ring; nor does she suggest that she was so obliged'. Accordingly 'the Claimant was not manifesting her belief by wearing the ring and Article 9 is not engaged'.[75] Yet, the notion that a religious practice must be an 'obligation' in order for it to be considered a manifestation is arguably akin to requiring religious practices to be necessary or 'core'. In the UK case of *Ladele v Islington Borough Council*, the Employment Tribunal

---

[68] *X v UK* App no 5442/72 (1974) 1 Eur Comm'n HR Dec and Rep 41.

[69] *Eweida and others v UK* App nos 48420/10, 59842/10, 51671/10 and 36516/10 [2013] ECHR 37 (ECtHR, 15 January 2013), para 82.

[70] *R (on the application of Playfoot (a minor) v Governing Body of Millais School* [2007] EWHC 1698 (Admin).

[71] ibid para [20].

[72] ibid.

[73] *R (on the application of Williamson) v Secretary of State for Education and Employment* [2005] UKHL 15, [2005] 2 AC 246, para [32]: 'in deciding whether the claimants' conduct constitutes manifesting a belief in practice for the purposes of Article 9 one must first identify the nature and scope of the belief. If, as here, the belief takes the form of a perceived obligation to act in a specific way, then, in principle, doing that act pursuant to that belief is itself a manifestation of that belief in practice'.

[74] *Playfoot* (n 70) para [23].

[75] ibid paras [23]–[24].

held that the wearing of a visible cross did not constitute a mandatory requirement of the Christian faith, but rather was a personal choice.[76] In both *Playfoot* and *Ladele*, the courts drew on the concept of 'core' practices in some form when assessing whether there had been a manifestation of or interference with the right to FORB.

Similarly, in the South African case of *MEC for Education KwaZulu-Natal and Others v Pillay*, a schoolgirl was prohibited from wearing a nose stud at school.[77] Ms Pillay contended that wearing a nose stud was an aspect of her Hindu religion and culture and that the prohibition amounted to unfair discrimination. The Constitutional Court found that the nose stud was not a mandatory tenet of Ms Pillay's religion or culture.[78] The Court argued that:

> It follows that whether a religious or cultural practice is voluntary or mandatory is irrelevant at the threshold stage of determining whether it qualifies for protection. However, the centrality of the practice, which may be affected by its voluntary nature, is a relevant question in determining the fairness of the discrimination.[79]

The Court held that Ms Pillay suffered unfair discrimination and that there was no evidence to demonstrate that granting an exemption to her would have adversely affected school discipline or the school uniform policy in general.[80] Notably, the Court took into consideration the 'mandatory' nature of the obligation when assessing whether discrimination was fair or not – thus highlighting the relevance of the concept of 'core' beliefs to the tests that some courts adopt when balancing interests in religious claims.

Applying an approach to limitations that relies on a distinction between 'core' and 'non-core' religious beliefs is problematic for three reasons: first, an assessment of what the *obligations* of a particular religion are can lead courts to making 'thick' evaluations about religious beliefs and has the potential to draw them into irresolvable theological debates. Second, if religious beliefs are to be limited on the basis of whether they are 'core' or not, it is unclear how courts would apply the same test in cases concerning secular and other ethical beliefs. What would constitute 'core' beliefs in such categories of cases? It would be difficult, if not impossible, to determine what is not a 'requirement' and 'obligation' of a particular ethical worldview. For example, whilst it might be clear that for vegetarians not consuming animal products is a core aspect of the belief system, it is difficult to determine what constitutes a 'core' belief of other philosophical beliefs such as environmentalism.[81] Third, it is increasingly difficult to legitimately identify the key tenets of a particular faith given the increase in different interpretations of any

---

[76] As cited in *Eweida and others* (n 69) para 14 and see *Ladele v London Borough of Islington* [2009] EWCA Civ 1357.
[77] *MEC for Education KwaZulu-Natal and others v Pillay* (Case CCT 51/06) [2007] ZACC 21.
[78] ibid para 60.
[79] ibid para 67.
[80] ibid paras 99–102.
[81] See *Grainger plc and others v Nicholson* (2010) ICR 360.

religion in 'a secular age'.[82] Thus, the argument that 'non-core' or non-mandatory religious practices should attract a lower level of protection potentially limits the protection of the right to FORB.

IV. The Choice of Alternatives

The fourth key approach to limitations can be categorised as the 'choice of alternatives'. This approach justifies the non-accommodation of a religious practice in cases where viable alternatives are available to the individual or group making the claim. For example, religious adherents are free to choose a job that fits their religious needs rather than burdening employers with requests for accommodation. This line of argument rests on the assumption that religious belief and the manifestation and practice of that belief constitute a choice.

The argument of choice is related to the approach based on 'core' obligations because some religious adherents feel that they are obligated to practise the core aspects of their religion. In other words, it is possible to argue that the duty to practise the mandatory obligations of one's religion means that one does not have a free choice to act contrary to these obligations. However, approaches to limitations based on 'core' beliefs or the 'choice of alternatives' are distinguishable in certain cases because the existence of alternatives does not *necessarily* rest on a particular practice being classified as 'core' or non-core. In international human rights law, the right to FORB covers both mandatory and non-mandatory religious practices.[83] A decision-maker might consider alternative ways for the religious believer to practise their religion irrespective of whether the practice in question is considered to be mandatory. For example, in cases where a religious believer feels 'bound' to manifest a religious belief in a particular way, but alternatives to achieve the *same goal* exist, non-accommodation might be justifiable.

However, the 'choice of alternatives' approach is also both complex and contested as an assessment of the key case law reveals. In the leading UK case of *R (on the application of Begum) v Headteacher and Governors of Denbigh*, Ms Begum, a schoolgirl, was prohibited from wearing a long coat-like garment, known as a jilbab, to school.[84] Ms Begum contended that her garment was part of her Islamic faith and that she considered wearing it to be an 'absolute obligation'.[85] The headteacher, however, maintained that the school uniform policy was already flexible

---

[82] C Taylor, *A Secular Age* (Cambridge, MA, Harvard University Press, 2007).
[83] Bielefeldt, Ghanea and Wiener (n 14) 97 note 'Different believers may of course attach more importance to some aspects of religious manifestations than to others. Given the vast inter- and intrareligious diversity in this field, it cannot be the business of State agencies, domestic courts or international bodies to try to settle this issue.'
[84] *R (on the application of Begum (by her litigation friend, Rahman)) v Headteacher and Governors of Denbigh* [2006] UKHL 15.
[85] ibid para [12].

as it accommodated a range of clothing in order to meet the preferences of its student body, many of whom were of Muslim background.[86] After lengthy discussions between Ms Begum, the headteacher, and relevant parties about the matter, a committee of the school governors upheld the headteacher's refusal to permit Ms Begum to wear the *jilbab* to school. Ms Begum challenged that decision but her claim was, ultimately, unsuccessful in the House of Lords. Three of the Lords held that there had been no interference with Ms Begum's rights, whilst Lord Nicholls and Lady Hale argued that there had been an interference albeit that it was justified. The choice of alternatives was relevant to assessing whether there had been an interference with the applicant's right to religion. Lord Bingham stated:

> The Strasbourg institutions have not been at all ready to find an interference with the right to manifest religious belief in practice or observance where a person has voluntarily accepted an employment or role which does not accommodate that practice or observance and there are other means open to the person to practise or observe his or her religion without undue hardship or inconvenience.[87]

Lord Hoffmann opined that Ms Begum's right was not infringed and reasoned that:

> ... there was nothing to stop her from going to a school where her religion did not require a jilbab or where she was allowed to wear one. Article 9 does not require that one should be allowed to manifest one's religion at any time and place of one's own choosing.[88]

According to Lord Nicholls, however, the majority's finding that the school's refusal did not amount to an interference with Ms Begum's rights 'may over-estimate the ease with which Shabina could move to another, more suitable school and under-estimate the disruption this would be likely to cause to her education'.[89] Lady Hale also offered a nuanced account of the role of 'choice' in religious practice. She noted that whilst it is the parents or guardians who make the choice about which secondary school their child should attend – Ms Begum was still not yet an adult at the relevant time – nevertheless, the choices made by adolescents are potentially worthy of protection since they *can* be subject to interference.[90] Accordingly, Lady Hale found that there had been an interference with Ms Begum's right to manifest her religious beliefs, although the interference had been justified.[91]

   In the conjoined appeals in *Eweida and others v UK*, Ms Ladele argued that she could not act against her moral conscience by registering civil partnerships

---

[86] ibid para [6].
[87] ibid para [23].
[88] ibid para [50].
[89] ibid para [41].
[90] ibid paras [92]–[93].
[91] ibid para [94].

for homosexual couples as part of her job as a registrar of marriages and civil partnerships.[92] Ms Ladele's employment duties conflicted with her conscience, but from this fact alone it does not follow that her religious beliefs should automatically be accommodated. The ECtHR considered submissions about the role of choice in deciding whether there had been an interference with Article 9 of the ECHR. On the one hand, the Equality and Human Rights Commission argued that 'the question of interference must take into account not only the choices a person has made, such as the choice of particular employment, but also the actions of the employer'.[93] Accordingly, responsibility lies with both the rights-holder and the duty bearers which in *Eweida* meant both the employee and employer. On the other hand, the National Secular Society submitted that religious adherents could effectively fulfil the demands of their conscience by opting to resign from their employment.[94] Framed in this way, religious believers must make a difficult choice between their religious beliefs and their job.

In both *Begum* and *Ladele*, there is an implicit argument that the religious believer is *bound* to her religious belief. In other words, there is little or no choice. Proponents of the 'choice of alternatives' approach maintain that the religious believer *chooses* to place herself in such a dilemma especially when there are employment and educational institutions that would accommodate her beliefs. In other words, the religious believer chooses to follow her moral conscience in a particular *context*. Moreover, freedom of contract means that employees are not bound to stay in their jobs, but if they sign up to a particular job, then they must accept its terms. However, as Lord Nicholls recognises in *Begum*, the potential to make free choices can be overestimated. The choice to practise one's religion is intrinsically linked to self-determination and personal autonomy. In *Pillay*, Chief Justice Pius Langa asked, 'Are voluntary practices any less a part of a person's identity or do they affect human dignity any less seriously because they are not mandatory?'[95] Moreover, he argued 'That we choose voluntarily rather than through a feeling of obligation only enhances the significance of a practice to our autonomy, our identity and our dignity'.[96] Justifying limitations to religious freedom because there are potentially other ways for the individual to achieve her goal can undermine the principle of equal treatment because 'finding another job' is not always possible.

In a different context, in *Jewish Liturgical Association Cha'are Shalom Ve Tsedek v France*, the applicant association was refused a licence to conduct religious slaughter. The French government submitted that another organisation already provided ritually slaughtered meat for the Jewish community. However,

---

[92] *Eweida and others* (n 69).
[93] ibid para 77.
[94] ibid.
[95] *Pillay* (n 77) para 62.
[96] ibid para 64.

the association argued that they adhered to a more rigorous standard in order for their meat to be classified as *glatt* in addition to *kosher*.[97] The ECtHR held that:

> ... there would be interference with the freedom to manifest one's religion only if the illegality of performing ritual slaughter made it impossible for ultraorthodox Jews to eat meat from animals slaughtered in accordance with the religious prescriptions they considered applicable.[98]

The Court did not find an interference with the applicant's Article 9 rights. The Court noted that the applicant association could obtain meat that was classified as *glatt* from Belgium. The Court appears to have placed significant weight on the availability of alternatives in justifying its decision. However, the argument of choice can pull in different directions,[99] and as such choice is multidimensional. The key problem of an approach to limitations based on a choice of alternatives is that it assumes that all individuals are equally empowered and have a range of options to choose from. It often assumes that choice is all-or-nothing. Lady Hale's judgment in *Begum* recognises the complexity of choice as well as the barriers to free choice. The reality of discrimination and structural disadvantage means that international human rights law and the courts need to protect and interpret the right to FORB in light of this complexity and recognise that highlighting the availability of alternatives is often an unhelpful justification or unrealistic in practice. Whilst realistic alternatives could be relevant to the proportionality assessment when balancing competing rights and interests, an over-reliance on choice should be avoided and the existence of viable alternatives not be overestimated.

V. Conclusion

This chapter outlined four key approaches to limitations and identified their shortcomings. An approach based on practices deemed to be against the liberal order is too narrow because some religious practices might need to be limited or regulated even if they do not constitute a direct threat to the liberal order. The need to make a value judgement about which practices are 'illiberal' relies on a number of additional normatively complex principles. Moreover, the duty of neutrality fails to provide coherent and consistent guidance because its application can lead to wide variation so as to result in uncertain outcomes. An approach that

---

[97] *Cha'are Shalom Ve Tsedek v France* App no 27417/95 (ECtHR, 27 June 2000). 'For meat to qualify as "*glatt*", the slaughtered animal must not have any impurity, or in other words any trace of a previous illness, especially in the lungs. In particular, there must be no filamentary adhesions between the pleura and the lung. This requirement of purity mainly concerns adult sheep and cattle, which are more likely to have contracted disease at some point of their existence', para 32.

[98] ibid para 80.

[99] F Raza, 'Working Paper: Accommodating Religious Slaughter in the UK and Germany: Competing Interests in Carving Out Legal Exemptions' (2018) Max Planck Institute for Social Anthropology, 1, 22–25.

centralises 'core' beliefs is also too limiting because it excludes voluntary religious or cultural practices and, therefore, restricts personal autonomy. It also requires thick evaluations to be made about essentially theological debates. Finally, the 'choice of alternatives' approach sets the bar too low for justifying limitations. This is because many religious practices would fail to be accommodated as they could be too easily considered as voluntary. From this perspective, conflicts could be resolved by, for instance, simply 'finding another job'. Such an approach can place an undue burden on religious believers.

Whilst this chapter has highlighted how different principles underpin different approaches to limitations, the next chapter offers an interpretative framework of principles that should form the basis of an alternative model of religious accommodation.

PART II

Religious Accommodation in Practice

4

'Bridging the Gap': From Principle to Policy

Part I of this book made the case for religious accommodation by arguing that a legal duty or policy approach in favour of religious accommodation is the best way to support citizens in the pursuit of their goals and conceptions of the good life. Although the right to FORB is a complex and multi-faceted right, a wide interpretation of its scope is preferable. Religious accommodation *prima facie* offers more generous protection of religious freedom as it seeks to maximise personal autonomy to the extent that it protects choices made by individuals in both their private and public capacity. The challenge of religious accommodation lies in setting out the appropriate limits of the right to FORB. As has been demonstrated in the previous chapters, the dominant approaches to limitations suffer from a lack of normative clarity and/or consistency in application. Thus, there is an urgent need for a principled and consistent set of general guidelines that can assist decision-makers when determining and interpreting the limitations to religious freedom. Part II of this book offers a perfectionist solution to the problem of limitations by proposing a model that outlines a categorisation of harms to the autonomy of others – harms that justify limiting religious freedom.

The area of law and religion is fraught with tensions arising from how exactly to balance the various principles and interests raised by the case law. It is necessary to clarify, and sketch out, how the key principles should work in practice. The role of secularism in constitutional theory and constitutional rights has been somewhat neglected by legal scholars. Secularism is considered supremely important, but its status in constitutional theory remains awkward. There exists confusion about what secularism as a constitutional norm entails in the context of limitations to the right to FORB. That is to say, the liberal state is necessarily committed to moral pluralism, but this is evidently a complex requirement which stands in need of being fleshed out by further normative criteria. Likewise, limitations to the right to FORB in liberal states can only be justified by a number of additional normative principles that I will set out in what follows as part of my proposed model.

This chapter lays down the theoretical foundations for my model of religious accommodation. The overall argument is organised around *three* central claims: the *first* is the normative claim that secularism is a fundamental constitutional norm in liberal states. Since the content and scope of secularism as a constitutional norm are subject to dispute, it is necessary to draw on additional principles in order to develop a coherent model framework of religious accommodation. Whilst the secular legitimacy of the liberal constitution is a necessary condition, it is not a sufficient one. Secularism, and its relationship with the constitutional principles of state neutrality and equality, has generated much debate and confusion. I argue that clarification of different conceptions of secularism is necessary for determining the scope of the right to FORB. There are two broad categories of secularism: thin and thick. Thin versions of secularism leave room for a wide(r) interpretation of neutrality and equality, whereas thicker versions of secularism are (more) prescriptive and substantive in content. Accordingly, the *second* claim is that secularism as a constitutional norm *should* aim to maximise personal autonomy by protecting moral pluralism. A substantive version of secularism that upholds, and is consistent with, the principle of autonomy is best suited to addressing the problem of how to place limitations on religious freedom. More than that, secularism as a constitutional norm must also be interpreted within a framework of liberalism. Drawing on Joseph Raz's perfectionist version of liberalism, which focuses on an autonomy-based doctrine of freedom,[1] provides a solid framework for the implementation of a model of religious accommodation.

The long-standing debate about different versions of liberalism in its various perfectionist and anti-perfectionist strands is beyond the scope of this book. However, my model is underpinned by Joseph Raz's conception of the harm principle as autonomy, and therefore, it is worth setting out a few key points for clarification in the following order: a working definition of perfectionist liberalism, its core claims outlined by Raz, and its relationship with religion in the liberal state. Martha Nussbaum defines perfectionist liberalism as 'a species of a genus of liberal views that might be called "comprehensive liberalisms," liberalisms that base political principles on some comprehensive doctrine about human life that covers not only the political domain but also the domain of human conduct generally'.[2] Most forms of comprehensive liberalism are perfectionist as they involve doctrine about the good life and the nature of value(s).[3] In contrast, the political liberalism of Charles Larmore and John Rawls focus on reasonable disagreement over comprehensive doctrines and the merits of pluralism. Political liberalism is based on 'thin' core morality that embeds political principles so that political autonomy is favoured and requires citizens to agree to principles that are not based on

---

[1] According to Raz, three main features characterise the autonomy-based doctrine of freedom. 'First, its primary concern is the promotion and protection of positive freedom which is understood as the capacity for autonomy, consisting of the availability of an adequate range of options, and of the mental abilities necessary for an autonomous life. Second, the state has the duty not merely to prevent denial of freedom, but also to promote it by creating the conditions of autonomy. Third, one may not pursue any goal by means which infringe people's autonomy unless such action is justified by the need to protect or promote the autonomy of those people or of others.' J Raz, *The Morality of Freedom* (Oxford, Oxford University Press, 1986), 425.

[2] M Nussbaum, 'Perfectionist Liberalism and Political Liberalism' (2011) *Philosophy & Public Affairs* 39.

[3] ibid.

comprehensive metaphysical, religious and ethical doctrines.[4] For Raz, however, the central value is autonomy, but this, controversially, requires an acceptance of the doctrine of pluralism. The doctrine of pluralism entails the co-existence of different comprehensive worldviews which results in the existence of conflicting, but equally, legitimate worldviews. Accordingly, the government ought to endorse pluralism as morally worthy by protecting the doctrine of pluralism.[5]

The status of religion in a liberal state is complex and multi-layered. Religion is never entirely absent and there are plenty of conflicts between law and religion as already established in the previous chapter. Raz's perfectionist liberalism is well suited to regulating religion because of the importance it places on individual autonomy, moral pluralism and comprehensive neutrality. Raz's perfectionist liberalism generates certain obligations for the state with regard to the limits of religious freedom. The state should protect religious freedom as part of individual autonomy, but not in cases where it conflicts with and infringes upon the autonomy of others. It follows that secularism as a constitutional norm cannot be value-neutral or merely restricted to institutional requirements. Hostile versions of secularism that view religion as *a priori* a threat or problematic undermine the goal of protecting personal autonomy of a section of society (that is, religious believers). Therefore, it is necessary that different versions of secularism are evaluated in light of their respective capacities to uphold key liberal values. From this perspective, Raz's perfectionist liberalism offers the most appropriate framework within which the constitutional principles of secularism, neutrality, equality and autonomy can be negotiated. The problem with neutrality is that it does not offer adequate guidance or protection of the right to FORB. In particular, a thicker version of secularism that supports personal autonomy is preferable to alternative (thin) conceptions of secularism since personal autonomy is central to both perfectionist liberalism and the right to FORB.

The *third* claim is that a version of secularism that upholds autonomy best suits my model of religious accommodation which provides a framework in which the core principles – that is, secular neutrality, equality and autonomy – and conflicting interests can be appropriately balanced. Accordingly, my model identifies four key categories of harm to the autonomy of others. The advantages of my model are that it offers a principled and consistent approach that seeks to achieve the maximum autonomy of all parties involved, and its practical application can assist decision-makers when interpreting the right to FORB. Thus, the particular interests of the relevant parties in each individual case can be negotiated and balanced against the liberal touchstone of maximising autonomy. This seemingly straightforward approach to limitations can best be summarised as follows: religious claims should not be accommodated where they harm the autonomy of others. Whilst the importance of autonomy in religious freedom cases is generally acknowledged,

---

[4] Rawls argues that citizens will be motivated to do this because they will treat fellow citizens as equals in the democratic process.
[5] Nussbaum (n 2).

what is often neglected in the literature is the relationship between a perfectionist version of liberalism and thicker versions of secularism, as elaborated on later in this chapter.

As this chapter will establish, there is a gap that needs to be bridged between the key constitutional principles governing the relationship between liberal states and religion which includes secularism and the determination of limitations to the right to FORB in practice.

I. Secularism as a Constitutional Norm

A. Secular Neutrality and the Liberal Constitution

This section makes the normative claim that secularism is a core constitutional principle. Secularism has a fundamental place in the liberal constitution. It is now fairly uncontroversial to claim that secularism is a pre-requisite for the liberal state's democratic legitimacy, although the 'legitimacy' of the liberal constitution is subject to debate. Political philosophers have asked whether substantive sources of legitimacy have largely been dislodged and displaced. 'With the erosion of religion and natural law as substantive sources of legitimacy in the contemporary secular state', Vincent Depaigne has argued, 'the issue is whether the dominant form of legitimacy in contemporary constitutional law can be purely procedural or whether substantive elements are required to ensure its coherence'.[6] What exactly 'fills the gap' as the legitimating source of the modern liberal constitution is unclear. The status of secularism in the liberal constitution is well established in the literature on law and religion, as well as in practice, either through the codification of secularism in constitutions themselves or through institutional design or as confirmed by case law. Secularism as a *constitutional norm* is necessary to the regulation of the right to FORB in law as it helps to determine the precise scope of religious freedom. Yet, the normative consequences of secularism for the liberal constitution are not readily clear. Like all constitutional norms, it, too, is subject to various interpretations. Secularism can lead to radically different outcomes for religious accommodation across different liberal states, especially since neutrality and secularism are often treated as synonymous. Chapter three outlined key approaches to limitations to the right to FORB, two of which included practices that are 'deemed to be against the liberal democratic order' and breaches of the 'duty of neutrality'. The principle of secularism underpins both of these approaches to limitations; however, its precise interpretation in specific cases is far from self-evident.

---

[6] V Depaigne, *Legitimacy Gap: Secularism, Religion, and Culture in Comparative Constitutional Law* (Oxford, Oxford University Press, 2017) 52.

The source of secularism as a constitutional norm has a textual basis in some liberal states or is found in the case law. In particular, since the content of secularism as a constitutional norm is disputed, it generates a need for further clarity about its role in interpreting the constitutional right of FORB. Essentially, secularism can be a source of legitimation of the liberal state, an organising principle, and a goal *all at once*. Part of this might appear to be a 'legal fiction' so that secularism is considered a core constitutional norm although the historical developments point to a more complex picture regarding the acceptance of secularism. That aside, for the purpose of interpreting the limitations to the right to FORB, secularism clearly has a complex multi-layered role in the liberal constitution.

Why should secularism be considered to be a fundamental constitutional norm? Both Jürgen Habermas and Cécile Laborde have maintained that the liberal state has to be grounded in some form of secularism. According to Habermas, 'The principle of separation of state and church obliges politicians and officials within political institutions to formulate and justify laws, court rulings, decrees and measures only in a language which is equally accessible to all citizens'.[7] He argues that religious communities in liberal states must accept the separation of church and state in addition to the restrictions that follow from public reason.[8] However, religious reasons have the potential to enrich public discourse and should not be barred altogether – so long as religious reasons are translatable. Habermas recognises that this 'translation proviso' creates an asymmetrical burden between (some) secular reasons and religious reasons. He therefore cautions against the enforcement of the institutional separation of religion and politics/law as an 'undue mental and psychological burden for those of its citizens who follow a faith'.[9] Rather, a 'reflexive open attitude' from both believers and non-believers is necessary. 'Whilst deep conflicts and disagreements will exist between believers, believers of others denominations, and non-believers', Habermas notes that 'the constitutional right to religious freedom is the appropriate political answer to challenges to religious pluralism'.[10] It follows that for Habermas the liberal state's legitimacy depends on a commitment to secularism that is to be institutionalised to provide protection to both believers and non-believers; at the same time, however, there exists an obligation on the part of believers and non-believers to accept the epistemic superiority of the secular liberal state. Whether this can truly be achieved (normatively and empirically) is questionable. Laborde develops a sophisticated account of liberalism that includes the need for minimal secularism. Her version of secularism is not hostile to religion, but neither is it *overly* deferential to religious claims. Drawing on a Rawlsian conception of justice, she argues that freedom of religion

---

[7] J Habermas, 'Religion in the Public Sphere' (2006) 14 *European Journal of Philosophy* 1, 4.
[8] ibid, 6.
[9] ibid, 10.
[10] ibid.

and non-establishment of religion can be interpreted through the ideals of equal liberty and state neutrality.[11] Laborde argues that:

'... the category of religion is less than adequate *as a politico-legal category.* We can explicate the values implicit in freedom of religion, equality between religions, and neutrality of the state toward religion – to mention just a few of the relevant liberal ideals – without direct recourse to the semantic category of religion at all.'[12]

Laborde defends a version of liberal egalitarianism which holds that the secular democratic state must decide on the contested questions of the boundary and scope of the freedom of religion.[13] This, in turn, means that the state cannot be entirely neutral towards religion. The relationship between secularism and the principle of neutrality then requires elaboration. In particular, two inter-related conceptions of neutrality are relevant to the constitutional regulation of religion: (i) neutrality towards different conceptions of the good; and (ii) justificatory neutrality.[14] Neutrality towards conceptions of the good means that the liberal state should not favour one religion over the other, nor favour nonreligion over religion. Justificatory neutrality requires the liberal state and its institutions to ground the justification of laws in non-comprehensive 'neutral' reasons. A range of conceptions of neutrality have been developed by liberal political theorists. For John Rawls, political liberalism aims to be impartial between different conceptions of good.[15] According to Gerald Gaus, political neutrality is not concerned with protecting conceptions of the good *per se*, but is concerned with neutrality between *persons* since conceptions of the good cannot be protected themselves as they are always attached to persons.[16] For Ronald Dworkin neutrality is derived from the principle of equality. Neutrality is fundamental because individuals are entitled to equal concern and respect, and therefore, government should be neutral towards conceptions of the good.[17] Will Kymlica, finally, argues that liberalism should provide a neutral framework that makes it possible to negotiate between conflicting conceptions of the good.[18] These leading theorists have laid the philosophical groundwork for neutrality's role in managing religious claims as they have sketched out broad conceptions of and justifications for neutrality. As their respective theories demonstrate, neutrality can encompass a range of liberal goals and values.

---

[11] C Laborde, *Liberalism's Religion* (Cambridge, MA, Harvard University Press, 2017) 5.
[12] ibid 2.
[13] ibid 9. Laborde calls this the 'jurisdictional boundary problem'.
[14] See W Kymlica, Liberal Individualism and Liberal Neutrality (1989) 99 *Ethics* 883, E Sarajilic, 'Are Liberal Perfectionism and Neutrality Mutually Exclusive?' (2015) 4 *Canadian Journal of Philosophy* 515 and RE Goodin and A Reeve (eds), *Liberal Neutrality* (London, Routledge 1989).
[15] J Rawls, *Political Liberalism* (New York, Columbia University Press, 1993, 1996) xxi–xxii.
[16] G Gaus, 'State Neutrality and Controversial Values in *On Liberty*' (2009) at www.gaus.biz/Gaus-MillNeutralistLiberalism.pdf at 5.
[17] In D Paris, 'Theoretical Mystique: Neutrality, Plurality, and the Defense of Liberalism' (1987) 31 *American Journal of Political Science* 909, 911.
[18] Kymlica (n 14) 883.

The ideal of neutrality is not, however, without its critics. Even scholars within the liberal tradition acknowledge that neutrality is problematic: not only is it difficult to achieve in practice, but neutrality itself requires justification. For example, Thomas Nagel argues that 'the Rawlsian requirement of fairness in the original position (a position that does not permit the selection of the principles of justice to be based on any thick conception of the good)[19] is impossible because neutrality between conceptions of the good *itself* requires justification'.[20] Gerald Gaus, moreover, maintains that liberal neutrality is a radical principle and one that challenges many state policies.[21] These criticisms highlight the need to give further content to the principle of neutrality.

Neutrality is not only a complex requirement of political liberalism; its normative content is variable as emerges clearly from legal cases in which the right to religious freedom is at stake. This variation exposes a weakness inherent in neutrality, especially as it has been interpreted in a way that has resulted in lower levels of protection for minority religions in the European supranational courts. Neutrality does not tell us how to treat religious and non-religious citizens equally or how to deal with laws that burden the majority and minority dissimilarly.[22] Thus far, appeals to neutrality have often concealed the normative choices that need to be made with regard to the scope of the right to FORB. Furthermore, such appeals sometimes have had the effect of undermining personal autonomy and other liberal values. Neutrality has often been employed as a technique for managing religion that has, in turn, led to indeterminacy, confusion and inconsistent outcomes.

Leading liberal scholars do, however, propose complex versions of liberal neutrality that uphold key liberal values whilst overcoming some of the criticisms outlined above. Laborde has recently expanded on what neutrality entails for liberal states in the context of religious freedom. She notes that different theorists have actually been referring to different *subsets of neutrality*.[23] According to Laborde, 'secularism and neutrality should not be reduced to one value, but explicated in relation to a constellation of liberal values'.[24] Her nuanced analysis of neutrality is helpful because she clarifies two central points in relation to neutrality and religion in the liberal state. On the one hand, she highlights that the liberal, secular state should not *always* be neutral towards conceptions of the good including religion; rather, the liberal state has to be neutral to certain *dimensions of the good*. The liberal state should uphold a commitment to minimal secularism and one that is neutral towards the good at specific levels such as by not favouring one religion over others when implementing the rule of law.

---

[19] T Nagel, 'Rawls on Justice' (1973) 82 *The Philosophical Review* 220, 227.
[20] ibid 227.
[21] GF Gaus, 'Liberal Neutrality: A Compelling and Radical Principle' in S Wall and G Klosko (eds), *Perfectionism and Neutrality* (Lanham, Rowman & Littlefield Publishers Ltd, 2003) 149.
[22] Laborde, *Liberalism's Religion* (n 11) 134.
[23] ibid.
[24] ibid 115.

On the other hand, Laborde emphasises that neutrality relates to a variety of *values*. She maintains that neutrality is not 'an all or nothing' requirement for the liberal state, and it is possible to identify which set of values should be subject to neutrality. In particular, the liberal state should not be neutral toward religion or the good in general, for example, when they are inaccessible, divisive and comprehensive.[25]

Neutrality offers no guidance on the 'meta-jurisdictional' question of competence ['who gets to decide on issue x'] and sovereignty.[26] That is to say, the liberal state must make sovereign decisions on what exactly state neutrality is about. This includes determining and defining where the boundaries of religion/nonreligion and public/private are to be drawn in the first place.[27] However, the debate about neutrality is likely to remain unsettled, with some scholars continuing to defend both a broad conception of neutrality (as opposed to Laborde's restricted version) and a stance of general liberal scepticism towards religion.[28]

From the discussion above, it is possible to distil the following requirements a state has to meet in order to be considered liberal:

- The liberal state must commit itself to minimal secularism for its legitimacy.
- The liberal state must be neutral towards conceptions of the good (both religious and nonreligious).
- The liberal state must uphold justificatory neutrality vis-à-vis the requirement of public reason.
- The liberal state must treat all religions equally.
- Secularism is a core constitutional norm and relevant to interpreting human rights.
- Secularism is a necessary but not a sufficient condition of the liberal state.

B. Translating Secular Neutrality in Practice

At the abstract level, the role of secularism in the liberal constitution is indispensable. However, we are left with several open-ended questions and options

---

[25] Laborde (ibid) argues: 'Instead of drawing on vague notions of neutrality or secularism, I identify three central liberal values and map them onto three specific dimensions of religion or the good. The *justifiable* state appeals to the idea that laws should be justified only by reasons that are accessible to citizens. The *inclusive* state is a state that honors the equal status and citizenship of all. The *limited* state respects individual self-determination in private matters. Each picks out a different feature of disaggregated religion: religion as *nonaccessible*; religion as *divisive*; and religion as *comprehensive*. Disaggregating religion allows me to specify that religion is not uniquely special: nonreligious ideologies and practices can be inaccessible, divisive, and comprehensive too. This also means that the state need not be separate from religion when religion is not divisive, inaccessible, or comprehensive', at 8.

[26] ibid 70.

[27] ibid 70.

[28] JW Howard, 'Defending Broad Neutrality' (2020) 23 *Critical Review of International Social and Political Philosophy* 36.

such as the following: What kind of secularism should be upheld? Does neutrality entail 'strict' neutrality that imposes specific requirements that religion ought to meet or 'open' neutrality which is more dynamic and receptive to religious accommodation? What does it mean to treat religious beliefs equally? At the level of practice, courts across liberal states have emphasised the importance of the principle of secularism but have offered competing visions of its 'true meaning', that is, of its normative content.

Whilst there is a need for the liberal state to protect its secular normativity, the complex requirements of 'public reason'[29] do not readily resolve the question of the scope of the right to the FORB. Both Rawls and Habermas revised their theories of public reason to include a 'translation proviso' so as to allow religious reasons to be translated into 'accessible public reasons'. However, the translation of religious reasons is a complex and discursive process. Since religion, as lived experience, is subject to incessant change, its status in society and, therefore, in the constitution is fluid. It may or may not be possible to translate religious reasons into accessible 'public reason'. The threshold at which religious, or comprehensive, reasons violate the institutional or 'jurisdictional boundary' will vary. Moreover, the *translation* of religious reasons (the category itself) rests on a conception of secularism which itself is based on procedural or substantive versions. This means that although the concept of 'public reason' provides the liberal state an overarching framework in which religion and religious reasons can be negotiated, public reason itself is subject to contestation about the extent to which it can accommodate religious reasons.[30]

A brief overview of a few select cases serves to highlight these variations. In the US case of *Lynch v Donnelly*, which concerned the public display of a crèche in a park owned by a non-profit organization and located in the heart of the city's shopping district, the Supreme Court stated the following:

> Rather than taking an absolutist approach in applying the Establishment Clause and mechanically invalidating all governmental conduct or statutes that confer benefits or give special recognition to religion in general or to one faith, this Court has scrutinized

---

[29] Public reason essentially seeks to limit or define the boundaries of the role of religion in a liberal state. It rests on the ideal of justificatory neutrality – that laws and policies should not be justified by appealing to substantive conceptions of the good. Public reason seeks to achieves both (i) neutrality towards the good; and (ii) equality between individuals. According to Rawls' famous account of public reason, a number of conflicting reasonable comprehensive doctrines exist in democratic states, and, therefore, laws should be justified by reasons acceptable to all so that all citizens can be treated fairly. See J Rawls, *The Law of the People* (Cambridge, MA, Harvard University Press, 2001). Rawls stipulates that public reason is public in three ways: 'it is the reason of free and equal citizens; it is the reason of the public; its subject is the public good concerning questions of fundamental political justice that concern constitutional essentials and matters of basic justice': J Rawls, 'Idea of Public Reason Revisited' (1997) 64 *University of Chicago Law Review* 765, 767.

[30] V Bader, 'Secularism, Public Reason or Moderately Agnostic Democracy?' in GB Levey and T Modood (eds), *Secularism, Religion and Multicultural Citizenship* (Cambridge, Cambridge University Press, 2009).

challenged conduct or legislation to determine whether, in reality, it establishes a religion or religious faith or tends to do so.[31]

The Supreme Court rejected an 'absolutist' strict approach to the question of the separation of state and religion. Non-establishment is not to be equated with a comprehensive secularist view that seeks to remove all signs, or government support, of religion in the public sphere. In *Leyla Sahin v Turkey*, the applicant wore a headscarf to a university examination and was refused entry because the university did not permit the wearing of Islamic clothing. The applicant argued that the policy infringed her rights under Article 9 of the ECHR. The ECtHR found no violation of Articles 9 or 14 of the ECHR. The majority held that the government was entitled to preserve secularism:

> … the principle of secularism … is the paramount consideration underlying the ban on the wearing of religious symbols in universities … where the values of pluralism, respect for the rights of others and, in particular, equality before the law of men and women are being taught … it is understandable that the relevant authorities should wish to preserve the secular nature of the institution.[32]

Yet, in *Lautsi v Italy* (*Lautsi I*) the government submitted that the principle of secularism precluded any substantive content:

> Furthermore, there was no European consensus on the way to interpret the concept of secularism in practice, so that states had a wider margin of appreciation in the matter. More precisely, although there was a European consensus concerning the principle of the secular nature of the state, there was no such consensus about its practical implications or the way to bring it about. The Government asked the Court to show caution and reserve and consequently to refrain from giving a precise definition going so far as to prohibit the mere display of symbols. Otherwise, it would be giving a predetermined substantive content to the principle of secularism, and that would run counter to the legitimate diversity of national approaches and lead to unforeseeable consequences.[33]

In *Lautsi v Italy* (*Lautsi II*), Judge Power emphasised that secularism itself was not neutral:

> A preference for secularism over alternative world views – whether religious, philosophical or otherwise – is not a neutral option. The Convention requires that respect be given to the first applicant's convictions … It does not require a preferential option for and endorsement of *those* convictions over and above all others.[34]

Evidently, different judges subscribe to different versions of secularism and neutrality. Thus, the principles or ideals of secularism and neutrality can either complement or be in conflict with each other. In particular, secularism as a

---

[31] *Lynch v Donnelly* 465 US 668 (1984), at 669.
[32] ibid para 116.
[33] *Lautsi v Italy* (2010) 50 EHRR 42 (App No 30814/06, ECtHR Second Section, 3 November 2009) para 41.
[34] *Lautsi v Italy* App no 30814/06 (ECtHR, 18 March 2011) Grand Chamber at p 44.

constitutional norm allows for a wide range of approaches to determining the scope of the right to FORB. The relationship between state, law and religion is very diverse in liberal states. Church–state models, for example, can be organised into three broad categories: the first is the constitutional and/or institutional establishment of a church as in England;[35] the second is the formal separation of church and state as in France;[36] and the third is a kind of 'mixed state' whereby religion benefits from some privileges and recognition in the constitution, as is the case in Germany.[37] Thus, secularism plays a complex and multi-layered role in the liberal constitution and is a necessary, but not a sufficient, condition for the liberal state.

There is a need to balance the various conflicting interests through institutional mechanisms. Secularism as a constitutional norm, and its interpretation in the jurisprudence on the right to FORB, is fiercely contested. Whilst a range of theories on religious exemptions and accommodation have been developed as outlined in the previous chapters, a number of questions remain in terms of bridging the gap between principle and policy, making it necessary to identify the different conceptions of secularism at work in the constitution.

II. Thin and Thick Versions of Secularism

The previous section established that secularism is a fundamental constitutional norm that has a complex relationship to other constitutional principles such as neutrality and equality. This section builds on that analysis by subsuming the different conceptions of secularism under two broad categories: thin and thick. This broad categorisation is helpful because, by distinguishing between different kinds of secularism, it sheds light on how exactly secularism as a constitutional norm is applied in practice and the question of whether religion should play a strong or weak role in the public sphere.

An increasing body of literature on secularism across disciplines and jurisdictions highlights the complexity of defining secularism. Terms such as 'post-secular' and 'multiple secularities' are often employed both descriptively and normatively to explain the role of secularism in modern states.[38] The increase of pluralism, coupled with the persistence of pockets of religious fundamentalism, means that the interpretation of constitutional principles such as secularism and neutrality

---

[35] See www.churchofengland.org see also T Baldry, 'Parliament and the Church' (2015) 17 *Ecclesiastical Law Journal* 202.

[36] Loi du 9 décembre 1905 relative à la séparation des Églises et de l'État.

[37] Article 137 (Weimar Constitution) of the Basic Law states that 'there shall be no state church'. See Basic Law for the Federal Republic of Germany, 1949, translated version (www.btg-bestellservice. de/pdf/80201000.pdf, accessed 6 March 2022). The translation from German to English is provided by Professor Christian Tomuschat et al, in cooperation with the Language Service of the German Bundestag and Art 137(6) (Weimar Constitution) of the Basic Law.

[38] See T Modood and T Sealy, *Secularism and the Governance of Religious Diversity* (2019) GREASE Concept paper 1.

are not straightforward: 'thick' value judgements about the limits of religion are necessary in order to police its boundaries. The retreat of religion from public spaces is only one reason why the display of religious symbols has been a hotly litigated area across jurisdictions and is considered by some to breach secular neutrality. The increase in pluralism entails that religion is no longer considered 'special'; hence there has been widespread support for the demotion of religion as a distinct category for constitutional protection. However, some scholars have offered a more nuanced account of secularism by discrediting the claim that there has been a 'resurgence of religion' – a claim that is not empirically sound since it assumes that religion has declined globally. Rather, as Veit Bader has argued, there is no general decline of religious beliefs and practices, but there are country and institution specific changes.[39]

Whilst sociological claims about its history and function in modern societies are widely disputed, secularism has been a central reference point for discussing religious freedom. However, secularism and religion are far from being 'two sides of the same coin', as secularism is multi-dimensional. Charles Taylor's discussion of secularism, as outlined in his seminal book *A Secular Age*, is an appropriate starting point as it sheds light on the different ways in which the concept of the 'secular', or the process of secularisation, manifests in reality. Taylor identifies three modes of 'secularity'. The first relates to the retreat of religion from various public spaces whereby political organisation today comprises a separation of church and state, so much so that 'in our "secular" societies, you can engage fully in politics without ever encountering God'.[40] In various public spaces and activities we no longer need to encounter God or reference to ultimate reality. The second mode relates to 'the conditions of belief' which concerns 'a move from society where belief in God is unchallenged and indeed, unproblematic, to one in which it is understood to be one option amongst others, and frequently not the easiest to embrace'.[41] The third mode relates to 'the whole context of understanding in which our moral, spiritual or religious experience and search takes place'.[42] This is harder to define or 'pin point' but relates to 'different kinds of lived experience' of belief and unbelief.[43] *A Secular Age* is not merely about religion in the public sphere; it charts out the conditions that have made religious, ethical and moral pluralism possible. Of course, this has implications for the legal definition of religion itself. As has been discussed in chapter two, the definition of religion is under permanent strain. Taylor highlights that secularism is a complex requirement for the liberal state since there is more than one good being sought. The goals of liberty, equality and fraternity (the trinity of the French Revolution) are three such

---

[39] V Bader, 'Secularisms or Liberal-Democratic Constitutionalism?' in *The Oxford Handbook of Secularism* (Oxford, Oxford University Press, 2017) 334–35. V Bader, 'Constitutionalizing secularism, alternative secularisms or liberal-democratic constitutionalism? A critical reading of some Turkish, ECtHR and Indian Supreme Court cases on "secularism"' (2010) 6 *Utrecht Law Review* 8.
[40] C Taylor, *A Secular Age* (Cambridge, MA, Harvard University Press, 2007) 1.
[41] ibid 3.
[42] ibid 4.
[43] ibid 5.

goods that need to be balanced when they are in conflict with each other.[44] For Taylor, these three goals require that all beliefs (religious, nonreligious and those not failing within that dichotomy) are treated equally by the state.[45] Secularism is then concerned with the management of diversity. In his later work with Jocelyn Maclure, Taylor argues that secularism rests on two key principles, that is, equality of respect and freedom of conscience.[46] From this perspective, the separation of church and state and state neutrality enable the two principles of equal respect and freedom of conscience to be realised in practice.[47] Thus, Taylor and Maclure develop a framework based on a pluralistic political secularism supported by an ethics of respectful dialogue that they argue is ideal and necessary to adequately realise the right to freedom of conscience.

Other scholars offer a more stinging critique of notions of the secular and secularism. For Talal Asad, the 'secular' is not a fixed category. What constitutes 'the secular' is made possible by certain conditions.[48] The consequences of this are that secularism should not be assumed to be necessarily neutral, benevolent or inclusive. How secularism is interpreted in practice has in fact often resulted in unequal outcomes for religious adherents, as highlighted by the 'critical religion scholars' as shown in chapter two.[49] Claims of secularism's apparent neutrality have been widely discredited. But secularism is not synonymous with the absence of religion. It would be a mistake to assume that secularism is simply a product of the decline of public religious practice and/or the emergence of increasingly diverse modern societies. Rather, secularism is better understood as a doctrine, ideology or analytical category that itself shapes the role of religion in liberal states. In this way, discussions of secularism are inherently normative. Craig Calhoun argues that:

> For although secularism is often defined negatively – as what is left after religion fades – it is not itself neutral. Secularism should be seen as a presence. It is *something*, and it is therefore in need of elaboration and understanding. Whether it is seen as an ideology, a worldview, a stance towards religion, a constitutional framework, or simply an aspect of some other project – of science or a particular philosophical system – secularism is, rather than merely the absence of religion, something we need to think through.[50]

---

[44] C Taylor, 'The Meaning of Secularism' (2010) *The Hedgehog Review* 23, 23.

[45] ibid 27.

[46] J Maclure and C Taylor, *Secularism and Freedom of Conscience* (Cambridge, Massachusetts, and London, England, Harvard University Press 2011) 20.

[47] ibid, 20.

[48] T Asad, *Formations of the Secular: Christianity, Islam, Modernity* (Stanford, Stanford University Press, 2003) 25.

[49] See also T Fitzgerald, 'Encompassing Religion, Privatized Religions and the Invention of Modern Politics in Timothy Fitzgerald' in T Fitzgerald (ed), *Religion and the Secular: Historical and Colonial Formations* (London, Equinox Press, 2007) 211–40. Fitzgerald argues that non-European and non-Christian religious communities have been analogised in terms of what is basically a Christian understanding of religion. He points out that 'a notion of the secular as the non-religious, the natural, the rational, was generated as the superior ground from which to observe and order the world' at 235. The argument here is that our understanding of religion is itself constructed by certain assumptions that have exclusionary implications for certain religions.

[50] C Calhoun et al, 'Introduction' in C Calhoun and others (eds), *Rethinking Secularism* (New York, Oxford University Press, 2011) 5.

Secularism is, thus, constructed and context-specific, and a number of normative choices about its role in the constitution must be made, each with different consequences for the right to FORB. Veit Bader identifies no less than twelve versions of secularism that include the following: 'inclusive', 'passive', 'moderate', 'evolutionary', 'weak', 'tolerant', 'liberal', 'benevolent' or 'ameliorative' secularism, *laïcité plurielle*, *positive*, *de gestion*, *bien entendue*, in opposition to 'exclusive', 'assertive', 'aggressive', 'strong', 'intolerant', 'statist' or 'malevolent' secularism.[51] It is evident that secularism can be conceptualised in a number of ways. In order to construct a model of religious accommodation, it is necessary to limit the discussion to how secularism is interpreted in constitutional law. To that end, it can be divided into two broad categories: thin and thick versions of secularism. Although the distinction between thin and thick versions of secularism is not necessarily strict in that the variants of secularism are to be found on a spectrum, it is nevertheless useful for the purpose of clarity and for understanding the content of secularism as a constitutional norm.

A. Thin Versions of Secularism

Thin secularism include a range of versions whose content is not pre-determined. Moreover, and quite fundamentally, there is no necessary or *a priori* hostility between religion and the state.[52] Of course, thin forms of secularism also denote a degree of commitment to the separation of church and state, so that there are some clear cases that would constitute a breach of secularism such as the enactment of religious laws that would apply to all citizens. However, thin forms of secularism are not as *prescriptive* as thick forms of secularism. For example, procedural forms of secularism, that is, versions of secularism that focus on the need to implement certain institutional desiderata, are compatible with forms of Church establishment because religion is not *per se* considered a problem. Rather, the question is about the extent to which law and religion remain distinct. Procedural secularism can be understood to be primarily concerned with institutional design and the need to justify laws without appealing to religious or comprehensive reasons. It includes a range of specific requirements that institutions must adhere to. These might include the following: ensuring that institutions uphold the distinction between religious authority and political authority as well as the separation of religious reasons and political reasons within legal and political processes. What is, however, less clear, is when exactly thin forms of secularism, which include procedural secularism, are breached.

   Whilst procedural forms of secularism generate certain institutional and jurisdicational obligations for the liberal state to determine the scope of religion,

---

[51] See Bader 'Constitutionalizing secularism' (n 39).
[52] T Modood, 'Paul Hanly Furfey Lecture: Is There a Crisis of Secularism in Western Europe?' (2012) 73 *Sociology of Religion* 130, 130.

they do not prescribe a substantive *content* of secularism. In other words, secularism and the duty of neutrality is an open-textured requirement and there are a number of legitimate options that can be implemented. Procedural forms of secularism potentially permit the following types of religious accommodation: (i) religion is favoured through state official recognition and/or subsidies; (ii) religious symbols can be worn by state officials and in public; and (iii) religious exemptions are permissible. This does not mean that procedural forms of secularism *require* such forms of accommodation. Rather, procedural secularism permits a range of options that are not always permissible under specific versions of substantive secularism, as outlined in the next section. Therefore, there remains a conceptual and practical distinction between thin forms of secularism and thicker substantive versions.

To a lesser or greater degree, thin forms of secularism that include institutional and procedural secularism are upheld in liberal states such as the UK and Germany, although it is important to note that fundamental constitutional differences exist between both jurisdictions. For example, England has an established Church, whilst in Germany, it is possible for certain religious organisations to be registered as public corporations.[53] The respective differences mean that the application of the duty of state neutrality differs considerably. Yet, the advantages of thin procedural forms of secularism are that religion is not favoured or disfavoured, but instead there is a separation of state and religion in the decision-making processes of the core political institutions. Of course, the liberal state must remain secular – and crucially this can be realised at a minimum through the enactment of specific procedures. Procedural forms of secularism uphold liberal values in the sense that they require certain institutional mechanisms and safeguards to protect moral pluralism and the separation of the law making functions from religion. However, while offering, at first glance, a rather straightforward way to implement the separation between church and state, it turns out to be more complex in practice. Procedural secularism can result in fundamental differences in outcomes for religious believers despite there being a general consensus at the level of principle about the necessity of upholding the 'sub-principles' of equality and neutrality. Moreover, abstract notions of equality of individual citizenship are problematic, ambiguous, and in practice have not protected minorities, including religious claimants.[54] Thus, procedural, procedural or 'thin' conceptions of secularism can be misleading in terms of the extent to which they accommodate religion or religious beliefs. For Rajeev Bhargava, the institutional separation of church and state cannot be the distinguishing feature of a secular state.[55] Whilst he argues that church–state separation is a necessary condition, he identifies further ways

---

[53] See Art 140 of the Basic Law.

[54] Asad (n 48) 173.

[55] R Bhargava, 'Multiple Secularisms and Multiple Secular States' in A Berg-Sørensen, *Contesting Secularism: Comparative Perspectives* (Farnham, Ashgate Publishing, 2013) 22.

in which a secular state 'disconnects' from religion, which includes, at the level of ends, institutions, law and policy. Accordingly, procedural and thin versions of secularism require further choices to be made in order to decide how and when exactly comprehensive or religious reasons (used to support or not support laws and policy) and religious claims can be accommodated.

B. Thick Versions of Secularism

Thick versions of secularism can be placed on a spectrum ranging from 'hostile' to 'ethical/inclusive'. Thicker versions of secularism constitute substantive visions of the state as they are grounded in a comprehensive understanding of what the state's relationship towards religion ought to be. Substantive forms of secularism seek to entrench a particular worldview or political doctrine. Secularism has been enshrined as a constitutional principle in a number of countries such as France, Turkey and India; however, the application of secularism in each case has led to different outcomes.[56] In its more hostile version, secularism is based on the premise that religion constitutes a problem. Hostile forms of secularism such as in some former Communist states adopt a sceptical attitude towards religion and treat it, at best, with suspicion or, at worst, as a threat to the state. The starting assumption, therefore, is that religion must be carefully regulated.

Hostile secularism can be codified in a variety of forms. In its softest form, it accommodates religion in a very limited range of public spaces. Although both substantive and procedural secularism seek to limit the role of religion, they do so to different degrees and for different reasons. Hostile secularism focuses less on the equal treatment of religions than it does on ensuring that the boundaries of religion are carefully defined and policed. Hostile forms of secularism might, for example, seek to limit the role of religion in the public sphere; the visibility of religious symbols; and the visibility and practices of minority religions. According to Rowan Williams, such forms of secularism are informed by the deep suspicion that 'any religious or ideological system demanding a hearing in the public sphere is aiming to seize control of the political realm'.[57] In fact, hostile secularism is often premised on the claim that religion is inherently political. Harder forms of hostile secularism either seek to ban religion or strictly limit its role through privatisation. Thus, certain versions of hostile secularism are contrary to liberal values since they fail to uphold moral pluralism. Secularism is not merely an organising framework in such cases; it is a moral/political ideal.

---

[56] See J De Roover, *Europe, India, and the Limits of Secularism* (New Delhi, Oxford University Press, 2015).
[57] R Williams, Rome Lecture: 'Secularism, Faith and Freedom' (23 November 2006) http://rowanwilliams.archbishopofcanterbury.org/articles.php/1175/rome-lecture-secularism-faith-and-freedom, accessed 17 March 2022.

The entrenchment of hostile forms of secularism has obvious problematic implications for the right to FORB. For some scholars, the French conception of secularism, which is constitutionally codified via the principle of *laïcité*, exemplifies such a hostile version.[58] For others, *laïcité* is inherently indeterminate[59] and politically controversial. *Laïcité* can be interpreted in a number of ways, each interpretation having different consequences for religious freedom. *Laïcité* is, at times, equated with the need to protect the Republican nature of the state; at others, it is used to refer to the common secular education provided by the state. Moreover, the concept of *laïcité* is often invoked to press home the point that religion should be 'privatised'.[60] For some, *laïcité* represents a secular comprehensive ethic that is a conception of the good[61] akin to a 'civil religion' constituted through concepts and rituals such as reliance on founding heroes, texts, symbols, holidays and commemorations.[62] If *laïcité* is a thick conception of the good, its application is not exclusively a theoretical question since it places more limits on the interpretation of the right to FORB.

However, substantive secularism does not have to be hostile towards religion or view religion as a threat. It can be inclusive and can even support religion. What has been called an 'ethical' version of secularism, for example, requires the liberal state to adopt an equal and fair approach towards different religions and conceptions of the good. More than that, it positively promotes the existence of different conceptions of the good in the public sphere. As such, ethical secularism is distinguishable from procedural secularism since the former does not merely provide a framework for managing moral pluralism. For example, Lorenzo Zucca proposes a version of ethical secularism that treats all religions equally and, more specifically, one that 'rids itself of its Christian bias and treats minorities with more respect'.[63] In this way, his ethical secularism does more than simply manage pluralism by implementing a regulative framework; it considers minority religious rights to be important and in need of recognition and protection. It is thus a comparatively more accommodative approach. Zucca criticises the application of secularism in liberal states and at the European supra-national level, arguing, for instance, that the ECtHR has been inconsistent in its reasoning as evidenced in the cases *Lautsi v Italy* and *SAS v France*.[64] He justifies his version of ethical secularism by appealing to the need to create a 'free marketplace of religions' as this, arguably,

---

[58] Critics of French secularism include: Asad (n 48) 175–77, S Mahmood, *Religious Difference in A Secular Age* (Princeton, Princeton University Press, 2015); Modood (n 52).

[59] JR Bowen, *The Indeterminacy of Laïcité: Secularism and the State in France in Contesting Secularism: Comparative Perspectives* (Farnham, Ashgate Publishing, 2013).

[60] Blandine Chelini-Pont, 'Is Laicite the Civil Religion of France?' (2009–2010) 41 *George Washington International Law Review* 765, 766.

[61] *SAS v France* App no 43835/11 Grand Chamber Judgment [2014] ECHR 695 (1 July 2014).

[62] Chelini-Pont (n 60).

[63] Zucca, 'A Secular Manifesto for Europe' SSRN (2015), https://papers.ssrn.com/sol3/papers.cfm?abstract_id=2574165, accessed 13 December 2016.

[64] ibid.

best promotes free thought.[65] However, whether 'free thought' should be afforded more weight, as compared to other competing values, is disputed. The value of free thought is *one* value amongst others. For those who favour hostile secularism, the creation of a free market of religion is unnecessary and perhaps even dangerous. Zucca certainly offers an interesting version of ethical secularism, although it is far from universally accepted as desirable.

To sum up, 'thick' forms of secularism differ from 'thin' forms because they offer a comprehensive worldview. Thicker, substantive forms of secularism go further than providing an over-arching framework of principles; rather, they identify the goals to be pursued. Thick versions of secularism are problematic to the extent that they seek to entrench a certain conception of the good. State neutrality and equal treatment of religions are subordinated as these are not the key goals. Given that there is no consensus about the extent to which religion should be accommodated in liberal states, substantive forms of secularism are controversial since they can add to ongoing disagreements about the role of religion.

It is also evident that secularism itself can be a competing conception of the good. Michel Rosenfeld, for example, proposes a constitutional model that treats secularism as one conception of the good amongst many.[66] Rosenfeld's proposal is controversial as it does not treat secularism as a fundamental ideal. In practice, the liberal state and the courts, however, *do* treat secularism as a constitutional norm or as a synonym for neutrality. Appeals to neutrality and secularism in the case law across jurisdictions have not yet produced a consistent and principled approach to the right to FORB, as I argued in chapter three. This is partly because decision-makers across liberal jurisdictions have different outcomes in mind: for some, secularism is a strict requirement;[67] for others, it is concerned with accommo-dating diversity;[68] while for others still, secularism is a tool for treating religions equally.[69] Since secularism is itself subject to reasonable disagreement, additional criteria are necessary for devising a workable model of religious accommodation.

III. Secularism and Religious Autonomy

As set out above, different versions of secularism generate different normative obligations. Consequently, secularism as a constitutional norm is not necessarily fixed or neutral, as is evident from its inconsistent application in the case law. Here,

---

[65] ibid.

[66] S Mancini and M Rosenfeld, *Constitutional Secularism in an Age of Religious Revival* (Oxford, Oxford University Press, 2014).

[67] As in *Dahlab v Switzerland* (2005) 42393/98 – Admissibility Decision, [2001] ECHR 899.

[68] See the dissenting opinion in *Francesco Sessa v Italy* App no 28790/08 (ECtHR, 3 April 2012).

[69] As in the German conception of 'open neutrality': see Ludin, [BVerfG] [Federal Constitutional Court] Sep 24, 2003, 108 Entscheidungen des Bundesverfassungsgerichts [BVerfGE] 282, (283–84) (FRG).

I argue that the relationship between the liberal state, secularism and religion should be framed in a way that upholds personal autonomy. The purpose of secularism as a constitutional norm is then not to eliminate or be hostile towards religion, nor is it about upholding the bare minimum needed for church-state separation; rather, it should be considered as an integral aspect of determining the limits of the right to FORB in its various dimensions.

Religious freedom in liberal theory is linked to the ideals of autonomy, equality, and moral pluralism. Whilst there are different justifications for the right to FORB – including historical, religious as well as good instrumental reasons such as toleration to preserve peace and harmony[70] – the debates on religious freedom in liberal theory centrally focus on individual conscience and autonomy. As Carolyn Evans points out, 'it is clear that choice in matters of religion and conscience are an essential component of versions of autonomy as found in the theories of Joseph Raz (explicitly through autonomy), Ronald Dworkin (through equal respect) and John Rawls (through justice)'.[71] The key goals that are considered by these leading liberal thinkers as buttressing religious freedom are inter-related. The commitment to moral pluralism is a distinguishing characteristic of a liberal state and an ongoing goal. As part of this, the importance of individual autonomy in shaping the boundaries of religious freedom is undoubtedly normatively significant.

The malleability of secularism as a constitutional norm means that it does not always protect religious autonomy. Procedural secularism might or might not uphold religious autonomy given that the content of secular neutrality is not predetermined. At best, ethical versions of substantive secularism seek to maximise religious autonomy; at worst, hostile versions of substantive secularism seek to eliminate, severely reduce, and curtail religious autonomy. Accordingly, autonomy is upheld to differing degrees depending on how secularism as a constitutional norm is interpreted and entrenched. Yet, autonomy is central to the right to FORB in liberal states. This section argues that secularism as a constitutional norm *should* protect autonomy by upholding moral pluralism and creating the conditions necessary to enable citizens to choose and change their beliefs.

Procedural secularism as a thinner version of secularism might not 'entrench' secularism, but ensure that certain procedures are institutionalised to guarantee equality and neutrality between different conceptions of the good. Institutionalised in this way, secularism, by maintaining a distinction between the political democratic processes and religious conceptions of the good, upholds autonomy by ensuring that laws are not grounded in one set of comprehensive reasons. The requirement of justificatory neutrality guarantees that citizens can hold different sets of beliefs which in turn upholds moral pluralism. To that end, procedural forms of secularism guarantee a degree of fairness, neutrality, and equal treatment.

---

[70] C Evans, *Freedom of Religion under the European Convention on Human Rights* (Oxford, Oxford University Press, 2001).
[71] ibid 29–32.

However, as argued in chapter three, the principle of neutrality has at times been applied in a manner that undermines personal autonomy. The numerous cases concerning the Islamic headscarf are illustrative of this. Likewise, some substantive forms of secularism provide the conditions necessary for realising individual autonomy. For example, ethical secularism[72] seeks to create a level playing field for different conceptions of the good and, accordingly, enables individuals to choose from a wide range of ideas and beliefs. The right to FORB is realised through the creation of a 'marketplace of ideas' since individuals are given the option to change their opinions, beliefs and religion. The value placed on one's ability to revise and change one's beliefs distinguishes liberal states from non-liberal and theocratic states. Thus, some substantive forms of secularism such as ethical secularism can protect individual autonomy.

By contrast, religious autonomy is undermined by entrenched versions of *hostile* secularism as the latter do not aim to maximise the autonomy of *all* citizens. It singles out religion as inherently problematic. A hostile version of secularism that views religion as a threat is bound to lead to a narrow interpretation of the right to FORB. For example, it is widely argued that French *laïcité* reduces the autonomy of religious minorities.[73] An ideologically entrenched version of secularism thus risks unequal treatment and fails to protect the right to FORB.

Secularism as a constitutional norm should be interpreted in a way that upholds and protects individual autonomy. The interpretation of secularism within my model does not purport to be strictly neutral as it draws on Joseph Raz's perfectionist liberalism as the most appropriate approach for the regulation of religion. Raz criticises conceptions of strict political neutrality;[74] instead, he favours a perfectionist version of liberal theory that commits itself to a comprehensive liberalism, as outlined earlier. The status of religion in liberal states requires the state to set out the framework of principles within which religion can operate. The limits of the right to FORB should be defined within the framework of a comprehensive liberalism that upholds certain values, and in particular, personal autonomy.

Substantive secularism that upholds autonomy offers a framework for interpreting the right to FORB in a way that incorporates a legal duty or policy approach in favour of religious accommodation. Furthermore, the extent to which autonomy is put centre stage helps to differentiate between versions of secularism. It has already been demonstrated that secularism can be a good itself[75] and sometimes finds itself in conflict with other comprehensive worldviews. Autonomy as an evaluative criterion provides a useful guide as to when secularism is hostile and tends to limit the autonomy of religious believers and/or minorities. Autonomy is not merely an instrumental goal, *but an end in and of itself.* It provides essential criteria

---

[72] Zucca (n 63).
[73] See C Hancock, 'Spatialities of the Secular, Geographies of the Veil in France and Turkey' (2008) 15 *European Journal of Women's Studies* 165, 176.
[74] Raz (n 1).
[75] Mancini and Rosenfeld (n 66).

to guide the evaluation of secularism as a norm that is central to the balancing of competing interests and to determining the appropriate limits of the right to FORB. However, autonomy itself is complex and requires further clarification in the context of religious accommodation.

A. Religious Accommodation and the Dimensions of Autonomy

The right to FORB is universal: it applies to 'religious believers, atheists, and agnostics'.[76] Each person is endowed with the mental faculties to reason and to hold sincere beliefs that provide 'ultimate meaning' to human life, whether that is realised through monotheistic beliefs, philosophical beliefs, or an attitude of general scepticism. The right to FORB is centrally concerned with the autonomy, choices and religious practices of individuals. To claim that the right to FORB is intimately linked to autonomy is banal but necessary in order to highlight how different *dimensions* of autonomy are protected by religious accommodation. Religious accommodation goes much further than just offering minimal protection of the right to FORB; rather, it ensures that that right has practical and effective application in a wide range of contexts. Religious accommodation, ultimately, can better realise personal religious autonomy.

The key textual sources for religious freedom codify the importance of individual autonomy both explicitly and implicitly. Article 18 of the ICCPR provides for the basic right to freedom of thought, conscience and religion, the right to change one's beliefs as well as freedom from coercion. Moreover, the Human Rights Committee, General Comment 22, outlines:

> 5. The Committee observes that the freedom to 'have or to adopt' a religion or belief necessarily entails the freedom to choose a religion or belief, including the right to replace one's current religion or belief with another or to adopt atheistic views, as well as the right to retain one's religion or belief. Article 18.2 bars coercion that would impair the right to have or adopt a religion or belief, including the use of threat of physical force or penal sanctions to compel believers or non-believers to adhere to their religious beliefs and congregations, to recant their religion or belief or to convert. Policies or practices having the same intention or effect, such as, for example, those restricting access to education, medical care, employment or the rights guaranteed by article 25 and other provisions of the Covenant, are similarly inconsistent with article 18.2. The same protection is enjoyed by holders of all beliefs of a non-religious nature.[77]

The General Comment emphasises that any sanctions, policies, and practices that have the effect of restricting or punishing individuals for their beliefs, or for

---

[76] *Kokkinakis v Greece* App no 14307/88 (1994) 17 EHRR 397, para 31.
[77] Human Rights Committee, General Comment 22, Article 18 (Forty-eighth session, 1993). Compilation of General Comments and General Recommendations Adopted by Human Rights Treaty Bodies, UN Doc HRI/GEN/1/Rev.1 at 35 (1994).

changing their beliefs, constitute a breach of Article 18. In essence, the right to FORB protects a range of personal choices: the choice to change one's belief or revise one's beliefs.

Accordingly, the right to FORB is, in numerous ways, centrally concerned with autonomy. Jane Norton states that 'autonomy is an important liberal normative justification for religious freedom' because 'if we value personal autonomy then we must value autonomy in relation to religious matters too'.[78] Similarly, Carolyn Evans argues that choice in matters of religion and conscience is an essential component of versions of autonomy.[79] Raz's account of autonomy, which represents one of the most authoritative and comprehensive accounts of autonomy in the body of liberal political philosophy, is particularly illuminating in that respect.[80] Crucially, the link between Raz's work on autonomy and religious freedom is clearly spelt out by Norton, who states that commitment to personal autonomy *necessarily* entails a commitment to religious freedom.[81] This is because personal autonomy often engages one's conscience or deeply held personal beliefs.

Raz's perfectionist liberalism, with its emphasis on autonomy, is directly related to the right to FORB. His version of liberalism seeks to uphold autonomy – a core value that goes to the heart of liberal theories. It is uncontroversial to claim that the right to FORB in liberal democratic states is joined to individual autonomy in *at least* a nominal way. In non-democratic and non-liberal states, the link between religious freedom and personal autonomy is tenuous at best, if not altogether non-existent.[82] Non-liberal states might rely on other justifications for religious freedom, ranging from various ideological and/or theological reasons to pragmatic reasons such as minimal toleration. That is not to say that non-liberal states do not uphold some form of personal autonomy; rather, the claim here is more specific: that is, autonomy has a different normative status in liberal democracies. In liberal democracies, individual autonomy is a central tenet of political liberalism and provides a way of measuring how liberal a state is in practice. Political autonomy, in fact, forms the basis of constitutional rights[83] such as the rights to FORB and freedom of expression.

---

[78] JC Norton, *Freedom of Religious Organizations* (Oxford, Oxford University Press, 2016), 16.
[79] It is found in the different theories of Joseph Raz (through autonomy), Ronald Dworkin (through equal respect), and John Rawls (through justice) in Evans (n 70) 29–32.
[80] Norton (n 78) 17.
[81] ibid.
[82] See JL Neo, 'Secularism without Liberalism: Religious Freedom and Secularism in a Non-liberal State' (2017) *Michigan State Law Review* 333.
[83] See K Möller, *The Global Model of Constitutional Rights* (Oxford, Oxford University Press, 2012) 73–95. Möller defends a general right to personal autonomy: a right to anything, which according to the agent's self-conception, is in his or her interest. The consequences of this right are that every act by a public authority that places a burden on a person's autonomy requires justification. If we take a broad conception of religious freedom, it follows that the state and other actors should justify their actions where they limit the right to religion.

Raz persuasively argues that in western industrial societies, the ideal of personal autonomy is particularly applicable to the conditions of the modern industrial age and the fast-changing technologies it has spawned.[84] Autonomy, in this context, enables individuals to make far-reaching, life-changing choices and become 'part authors' of their life.[85] This concern for authorship of one's life is central to the right to religious freedom in *liberal* states. Of course, religious freedom in other contexts and religious traditions might not *necessarily* be couched in terms of self-authorship but instead might be more about doctrine, rituals, obedience and so forth.[86] Religious freedom in liberal states, however, necessarily involves the freedom to choose one's personal beliefs and conception of the good life.

A commitment to political autonomy necessarily entails a commitment to constitutional rights. As I have pointed out in chapter one, a generous approach to religious accommodation is the necessary precondition for religious freedom to become *meaningful* and have practical value.[87] There are at least three reasons, then, that highlight the importance of autonomy in the context of the right to FORB: first, autonomy is a goal *in and of itself* and is a centrally important value in liberal states. Second, autonomy can help to achieve substantive equality by recognising that religious practices are important to the identity and the practical life of religious believers. Third, autonomy can be given normative content through Raz's conception of the harm principle and, therefore, provide the basis for deciding limitations to the right to FORB. Moreover, the dimensions of autonomy are best captured through a legal duty or policy approach in favour of religious accommodation.

B. Religious Accommodation as Creating Adequate Options

As mentioned earlier, the right to FORB is geared towards ensuring that individuals have the option to choose and change their religion. It follows an obligation for the liberal state to guarantee that the option to choose between different beliefs is available. These options must also be *adequate*, otherwise they would not be options in any meaningful sense. Raz argues that certain conditions must be met in order to realise autonomy, which include the following: (i) individuals must possess relevant mental capabilities to form intentions and complex plans; (ii) the existence of pluralism, which entails the need for an adequacy of options; and (iii) freedom from manipulation and coercion.[88] Crucially, for Raz the availability of 'adequate options' is a necessary condition for the attainment of moral pluralism, which, in turn, is essential for personal autonomy. As Raz points out, 'Autonomy is exercised through choice, and choice requires a variety of options to choose

---

[84] Raz (n 1) 369.
[85] ibid.
[86] See Asad (n 48).
[87] K Alidadi, *Religion, Equality and Employment in Europe* (Oxford, Hart Publishing, 2017).
[88] Raz (n 1) 369.

from. To satisfy the conditions of the adequacy of the range of options the options available must differ in respects which may rationally affect choice.'[89] Moreover, Raz further elaborates on the adequacy of options:

> the options must include a variety of morally acceptable options. So the morally acceptable options must themselves vary in the reasons which speak in favour of each of them. There are, in other words, more valuable options than can be chosen, and they must be significantly different or else the requirements of variety which is a precondition of the adequacy of options will not be met.[90]

This means that the liberal (perfectionist) state must facilitate autonomy by ensuring the adequacy of options. Raz states that 'moral pluralism is the view that there are various forms and styles of life which exemplify different virtues and which are incompatible'.[91] The right to FORB also protects a range of religious beliefs that are incompatible with each other to at least *some degree*.[92] For example, (most forms of) monotheistic religions are incompatible with polytheistic or atheistic beliefs. Thus, the right to FORB, as a liberal constitutional right, can be interpreted in a way that upholds Raz's conception of autonomy and also protects the co-existence of a variety of opinions, beliefs and conceptions of good.[93]

Religious accommodation protects and upholds autonomy because it expands the scope of the right to FORB in order to create further options for individuals in different areas such as at the workplace, etc. Religious accommodation aims at maximising the contexts in which religious or other beliefs can be practised. Moreover, religious accommodation applies to a range of protected beliefs. Farrah Ahmed points out that religious autonomy does not have value only for religious individuals since religious choice inherently involves the choice to reject or change one's beliefs.[94] Whilst Ahmed also invokes Raz's definition of autonomy,

---

[89] ibid.

[90] ibid.

[91] ibid 395.

[92] It is not my aim here to identify which religious beliefs are in conflict with one another; rather, the claim is more generic and limited.

[93] Raz's describes the autonomous person as '(part) author of his own life' in Raz (n 1) 369. I have somewhat glossed over the complexities of Raz's theory due to limitations of space, but see in particular chs 14 and 15 of his book. Raz's posits three necessary conditions to realise autonomy, which include the following: (i) individuals must possess relevant mental capabilities to form intentions and complex plans; (ii) the existence of pluralism which entails the need for an adequacy of options; and (iii) independence/freedom from manipulation and coercion (at 372). In J Raz, 'Autonomy, Toleration and the Harm Principle' in S Mendus (ed) *Justifying Toleration* (Cambridge, Cambridge University Press, 1988), Raz argues that the autonomous person must have options to develop his/her abilities and these options must include a variety of morally acceptable options. According to Raz, 'if the government has a duty to promote the autonomy of people the harm principle allows it to use coercion both in order to stop people from actions which would diminish people's autonomy and in order to force them to take actions which are required to improve people's options and opportunities' (at 172). For critical engagement with Raz's conception of the harm principle, see J Quong, *Liberalism without Perfection* (Oxford, Oxford University Press, 2010). I rely on Raz in a specific way: to justify the normative foundations of my typology of harms.

[94] F Ahmed, *Religious Freedom under the Personal Law System* (New Delhi, Oxford University Press, 2016) 55.

she makes a distinction between personal and professional autonomy to address cases where a person lacks agency in the former realm but remains autonomous in their professional life.[95] Religious autonomy is considered to be a central part of *personal* autonomy.[96] Ahmed argues that a person might be autonomous in one sphere of life but not necessarily in others. Autonomy is a matter of degree.[97] Yet, in many cases the line of demarcation between personal and religious autonomy is blurry and impossible to draw. Personal and professional lives cannot always be neatly separated into different domains. It is arguable that, at times, personal autonomy is influenced or shaped by religious beliefs and/or professional life. Such influence is not unidirectional. An individual's professional autonomy might be limited by their religious beliefs, as demonstrated by key employment cases.

Even if there is disagreement about the extent that personal autonomy is achievable and realised in different spheres of life, autonomy in making choices about one's religious or ethical beliefs remains important and is highlighted by the different aspects of the right to FORB which include everything from places and time of worship, fasting, dietary requirements to clothing. These choices are concerned with personal, private and public autonomy. Religious accommodation facilitates personal autonomy in a myriad of ways. Religious accommodation implemented through a legal duty or a policy approach which is in favour of trying to fulfil the right to FORB to the fullest extent possible protects autonomy in the aforementioned spheres. Religious accommodation, therefore, creates a presumption in favour of protecting religious views as well as (non-religious) sincerely held beliefs that fall within the scope of the relevant legislation. If employers and institutions are encouraged to take steps to attempt to balance competing interests in a more nuanced fashion, this upholds personal autonomy and maximises religious freedom by creating adequate options.

C. Religious Accommodation and Freedom from Religious Coercion

Raz's second necessary condition for the realisation of autonomy includes the requirement of freedom from coercion and manipulation. Freedom from coercion is crucial because the latter diminishes a person's choices and can pervert the way in which a person reaches a decision.[98] Coercion and manipulation are forms of interference with one's autonomy. The right to follow one's conscience and freedom from coercion are both protected by the right to FORB. However, freedom from coercion is a complex requirement, especially in our digital age that

---

[95] ibid 54.
[96] ibid 54.
[97] ibid 62.
[98] Raz (n 1) 377.

is characterised by the use of manipulative marketing strategies in a variety of contexts. Such techniques of manipulation are often employed by religious groups whose practices can undermine the autonomy and agency of individuals.[99] It is true that the right to FORB can be weaponised to limit other's rights and autonomy. In some cases, religious freedom is used to manipulate and coerce others into adopting certain practices or beliefs through proselytisation strategies. Further complexity arises because the right to proselytise is also protected by the right to FORB, although there are, again, limits to this. In the leading case of *Kokkinakis v Greece* the ECtHR stated:

> There were good reasons for laying down in Article 9 that freedom of religion includes freedom to teach one's religion: many religious faiths count teaching the faith amongst the principal duties of believers. Admittedly, such teaching may gradually shade off into proselytising. It is true, furthermore, that proselytising creates a possible 'conflict' between two subjects of the right to freedom of religion: it sets the rights of those whose religious faith encourages or requires such activity against the rights of those targeted to maintain their beliefs. ... In principle, however, it is not within the province of the State to interfere in this 'conflict' between proselytiser and proselytised.[100]

Another important case that touches on the issue of proselytisation and religious education is *Nasirov v Azerbaijan*. The ECtHR outlined the importance of the communal and practical dimensions of religious belief and stated: 'The manifestation of religious belief may take the form of worship, teaching, practice and observance. Bearing witness in words and deeds is bound up with the existence of religious convictions.'[101] However, it is difficult to determine the limits of the right to proselytise, educate or influence others. According to Farrah Ahmed, beliefs formed as a result of manipulation are not autonomous beliefs.[102] Ahmed argues that the autonomy rationale for religious freedom is undermined particularly in cases of 'resistant beliefs' and 'manipulative proselytism'.[103] Religious beliefs are often considered to be resistant beliefs and not subject to revision or choice. Ahmed notes that 'Holding resistant beliefs often leads individuals to hold discordant sets of beliefs and desires'. Moreover, she argues that 'under these circumstances it is harder for [these individuals] to act on beliefs and desires with which they identify and thus it is harder for them to act autonomously'.[104] If this is true, then the 'autonomy rationale' fails to explain the justification provided in many of the ECHR religious freedom cases according to Ahmed: that is, autonomy does not explain why religious freedom needs to be protected since in many cases the claimants are not acting in a truly autonomous way. This is an important

---

[99] See S Bruce, *Pray TV: Televangelism in America*, Routledge Library Editions: Sociology of Religion 1990 (Oxford, Routledge, 2020).
[100] *Kokkinakis v Greece* App no 14307/88 (1994) 17 EHRR 397, para 15.
[101] *Nasirov and others v Azerbaijan* App no 58717/10, para 60.
[102] Ahmed (n 94) 62.
[103] F Ahmed, 'The Autonomy Rationale for Religious Freedom' (2017) 80 *Modern Law Review* 238.
[104] ibid 247.

criticism of the autonomy rationale because it demonstrates that many religious freedom cases are either not grounded in autonomy or do not uphold autonomy. However, the need to uphold a degree or dimension of personal autonomy remains relevant to realising religious freedom. It is not necessary to rely on a substantive version of autonomy which requires an individual to be free from any form of persuasion and manipulation as this would set a very high threshold. Protecting the autonomy of the religious believer need not be the motivating factor in every case as long as autonomy remains relevant to some degree and significant in a sufficient number of cases. Religious belief and motivations are intimately tied with the need to make autonomous choices. Moreover, autonomy is not 'all or nothing'; a religious believer can be autonomous in some or parts of their life. Richer conceptions of autonomy, such as relational autonomy, emphasise the importance of our social relations in decision-making, and clearly highlight its multi-layered complexity. That is to say, autonomous individuals might want to make decisions with others or have decisions made by others since this is what they value or hold to be important. Another analogous example is the relationship between married couples who might consult or defer to one another without losing complete individual autonomy. Religious believers might reasonably hold resistant beliefs and be subject to 'manipulation' without this negating their autonomy in totality.

Ahmed acknowledges that the reason(s) for why some beliefs are 'resistant' (in that they are not subject to revision) is complex and multi-faceted. It could be that resistant beliefs are formed in childhood or are entangled with familial and cultural ties.[105] It is true that some people do not ever change their religious beliefs; but Ahmed goes further and argues that 'resistant beliefs' constitute a hindrance in that the latter prevent a person from doing what they *truly* want to do'.[106] Because these individuals find it harder to act on beliefs and desires with which they identify, she argues that it is more difficult for them to act autonomously.[107] Ahmed provides the fictional example of 'Sal', a climate change activist, who also holds a resistant religious belief that requires her to eat ritually slaughtered meat and frequently travel to a far-away country to perform pilgrimage – obligations that run counter to and make it difficult for her to act on her beliefs about climate change. Ahmed maintains that in such a case the resistant religious belief leads to a reduction of Sal's autonomy and ability to shape her life.

A number of issues are raised by this case study. For example, which set of beliefs – the environmentalist or the religious belief – is dominant? And which of these beliefs is resistant? Why cannot the environmental belief be considered resistant? It is difficult, if not impossible, to determine this. Perhaps, an alternative

---

[105] ibid.
[106] ibid.
[107] ibid.

way to analyse such a case is not to see it as manifesting a *conflict* as such but rather as illustrative of an instance in which the ordering or prioritisation of beliefs is at stake. From this perspective, holding discordant beliefs does not entail that 'Sal' is less autonomous. Does the religious belief obstruct the belief in environmental- ism or is it the other way around? How is it possible to draw a boundary between different beliefs since these boundaries are likely to be subjective in most cases? What is the difference between a religious belief and a desire? Individuals often act in conflicting ways on a daily basis: for example, let us draw on a fictional case of Mr Arthur who believes that a second slice of chocolate cake is not good for him but has another slice anyway. Does this mean that Mr A is less autonomous, and if so, compared to whom? Mr A's actions do not necessarily mean that he is less autonomous in any *meaningful* sense if Mr A knowingly chooses to take on the risks of his course of action. As these crucial questions are left unanswered, the claim that those who hold resistant beliefs are necessarily *less* autonomous has not been convincingly made.

Moreover, the concept or definition of a 'resistant belief' is not clear or readily apparent. For Ahmed, resistant beliefs are those not subject to revision. Yet, if a resistant belief is a dogmatic belief, it is perfectly possible that an individual can be autonomous *and* dogmatic at the same time. The claim that a person can choose to be dogmatic follows from the argument that autonomy works at different *levels*. Being confronted with a set of constraints and conflicting desires does not auto- matically undermine personal autonomy. To be sure, autonomy might *potentially* be undermined in such cases, but this is not a *necessary* conclusion.

Thus, the ability to be autonomous must include the choice to do things that one does not fully endorse or that one deems to be unwise. In other words, autonomy includes the choice or freedom to make bad choices and/or undesir- able decisions. This also includes acting on religious beliefs that are problematic or create barriers, say, in the context of employment. For example, many of the cases on religious freedom concern individuals who are well aware that their reli- gious belief will create a conflict of interest at the workplace. Autonomy is not all or nothing. Gerald Dworkin's characterisation of autonomy is particularly illu- minating in such cases as it sheds light on its complexity. Dworkin argues that even if a person decides to live in accordance with 'what their mother or priest tells them to do', that person must count as autonomous.[108] Autonomy does not necessarily require a particular content in the *substantive* sense.[109] This is because autonomy relates to other values and commitments such as loyalty, commitment and love.[110] Thus, weaker or thinner conceptions of autonomy are both instruc- tive and valuable. Dworkin's nuanced account highlights how autonomy is often a

---

[108] G Dworkin, *The Theory and Practice of Autonomy* (Cambridge, Cambridge University Press, 1988) 21.
[109] ibid.
[110] ibid.

relational concept in that our (inter-personal) relationships often define or shape our goals.[111] Moreover, in order to be considered an autonomous person, Dworkin argues, it is not mutually exclusive with following beliefs and desires that potentially generate conflict. Thus, the individual who chooses to adhere or defer to dogmatic religious authority continues to be autonomous even in the absence of the conditions of substantive autonomy being met. Dworkin notes that 'if someone chooses to follow their "mother's instructions", and if it is their decision, then they are living the type of life *they* think is worth living'.[112] If committing to one option over another reduces overall autonomy, then arguably the bar for being autonomous is set too high. In other words, one can defer or decide to follow a particular set of rules, institutions or persons and still be an autonomous agent. In fact, this is the case for most people on a daily basis in some form or another. Furthermore, for many religious believers, deference to a set of dogmatic rules or to an institution is part and parcel of religious practice. The 'revisability' of beliefs should not be taken as a central criterion for assessing autonomy for it is difficult to measure and perhaps impossible to determine with certainty.

Cases of 'manipulative and resistant beliefs' demonstrate that different conceptions and degrees of autonomy are at play in religious freedom cases. For the purposes of this chapter, it is sufficient to establish the importance and relevance of autonomy to religious freedom even if complex cases of religious coercion and manipulation undermine the realisation of autonomy in *some* sets of cases. In summary, Raz's persuasive account of autonomy highlights that religious commitments are worthy of protection. Autonomy is of central importance to the right to FORB notwithstanding the existence of cases in which a religious belief curtails autonomy or narrows down the range of options to choose from.[113] The right to FORB does not require justification as to why a religious believer chooses to submit to a religious leader, organisation or 'irrational' belief. What is important is that the right to FORB is protected in practice in a way that allows individuals to make decisions – even if that means deciding to defer to a religious authority. In fact, more often than not, religious beliefs are a product of influence and religious hierarchies, and in addition are often considered by some to be irrational. This is a part of the right to FORB. Finally, to reiterate, despite these complexities, religious accommodation can be a supple tool that can address the various dimensions of religious autonomy.

---

[111] An increasing amount of literature on autonomy outlines different accounts of autonomy and engages with the dimensions of autonomy: see TE Hill, *Autonomy and Self Respect* (Cambridge, Cambridge University Press, 2001), C McLeod, *Self-Trust and Reproductive Autonomy* (Cambridge, MA, MIT, 2002), and also MC Foblets et al (eds), *Personal Autonomy in Plural Societies* (London and New York, Routledge, 2017).
[112] Dworkin (n 108) 23.
[113] Ahmed (n 103).

IV. Conclusion

The preceding sections have clearly established that the principle of autonomy can assist us in distinguishing between different forms of secularism whilst being at the same time centrally linked to religious freedom in modern liberal states. The definition, meaning and scope of 'secularism' is unclear. Different 'formulae' are subsumed under the label of secularism. However, the consensus amongst leading scholars, such as Charles Taylor, Jürgen Habermas and, most recently, Cécile Laborde, is that secularism provides the legitimising framework within which the modern liberal state must operate. There is a broad consensus on the fundamental importance of secularism in the liberal constitution despite the significant differences in the methodologies and insights offered by these scholars. The liberal state's legitimacy depends on its secular normativity. Beyond this core, secularism as a constitutional norm and its role in shaping the boundaries of the right to FORB varies depending on whether the state adopts proceduralist and/or substantive versions of secularism. However, secularism as a constitutional norm should balance the principles of neutrality and equality in light of the core liberal value of individual autonomy. Religious accommodation is not necessarily intractable and unmanageable – a problem that can follow from too expansive and generous a reading of this right. Religious accommodation upholds autonomy by expanding the scope of the right to FORB and by creating options in different contexts. My model of religious accommodation seeks to protect religious freedom beyond its minimal core, whilst enabling conflicts to be resolved and balanced. The next chapter proposes an approach to limitations which is underpinned by autonomy, and synthesises a substantive form of secularism with the harm principle.

5

A Model of Religious Accommodation

This chapter sets out an original model of religious accommodation. I identify four broad categories of harm to the autonomy of others that justify non-accommodation of religious claims. In particular, I suggest that harms should be classified according to whether they (i) endanger other persons' health and safety; (ii) impede access to rights, goods and services; (iii) constitute violations of dignity; and (iv) pose excessive practical costs. Section I discusses existing approaches based on the harm principle and their use in the context of religious freedom. Whilst a number of approaches to limitations based on harm already exist, the model I propose differs from the former in that it systematises various kinds of harm and introduces definite evaluative criteria to determine when harm should be considered a strong-enough reason for non-accommodation. In section II I sketch out my own framework of religious accommodation, apply the four broad categories of harm to select case studies and summarise the key principles in the form of guidelines. Section III then addresses some of the complexities arising from the proposed model. My model is meant to act as an analytical guide to the task of determining the limits of religious claims by applying a normatively consistent method. It is designed to serve as a tool for decision-makers confronted with conflicting principles, rights and freedoms when assessing limitations to the right to FORB.

I. Approaches to Limitations Based on Harm

The recognition that religious practices can cause harm to others is a settled part of the jurisprudence on religious freedom. In the leading Canadian case of *Syndicat Northcrest v Amselem*, the Supreme Court stated: 'Conduct which would potentially cause harm to or interference with the rights of others would not automatically be protected.'[1]

Approaches to limitations to the right to FORB based on the harm principle share certain similarities, although they are often based on different conceptions of what constitutes harm. For example, Raymond Plant favours a normative

---

[1] *Syndicat Northcrest v Amselem* [2004] 2 SCR 551, 2004 SCC 47, para [62].

conception of the harm principle which he interprets in light of a duty of civic equality.[2] He argues that limitations of religious freedom should be grounded in 'the harm principle along with a defence of the idea that a liberal democratic society requires people to be treated with equal concern and respect and as civic equals, whatever their identity might happen to be and whatever normative requirements individuals might think arise from their identities'.[3] In other words, Plant's conception of harm is intrinsically conjoined to the need to treat individuals as civic equals. From his perspective, circumscribing religious freedom is justified under two key conditions: (i) if harm is caused to others and (ii) if such harm undermines the civil status of particular individuals.[4] There is support for this line of reasoning in the case law where refusals to provide a specific service on religious grounds have been interpreted as undermining civic equality. For example, in the UK case of *Catholic Care (Diocese of Leeds) v Charity Commission for England & Wales*, it was unlawful for a Catholic charity to deny the provision of adoption services to homosexual couples.[5] Whilst the case concerned more technical points of charity and equality law, the Court at the same time explicitly foregrounded the harm this refusal caused to the notion of the equal civic status of homosexuals:

> The fact that same sex couples could seek to have access to adoption services offered elsewhere tended to reduce somewhat the immediate detrimental effect on them, but it did not remove the harm that would be caused to them through feeling that discrimination on grounds of sexual orientation was practised at some point in the adoption system nor would it remove the harm to the general social value of promotion of equality of treatment for heterosexuals and homosexuals …[6]

The refusal to serve certain sections of society does not only constitute an instance of discrimination but also undermines the civic status of the affected individuals and groups, and such differentiation is bound to reduce equal opportunities. However, it is also important that religious institutional autonomy is protected, and it should be possible for religious organisations to offer their services in line with their values, as discussed later.

Robert Wintemute offers a different analysis of the relationship between harm and religious accommodation. He argues that religious beliefs and practices should be accommodated only if the following three conditions are met: (i) the manifestation of the religious belief in question does not cause *direct* harm to others; (ii) it involves minimal cost; and (iii) it does not cause *indirect* harm to others.[7] According to this analysis, Wintemute argues that Islamic headscarves worn by

---

[2] R Plant, 'Religion, Identity and Freedom of Expression' (2011) 17 *Res Publica* 7.
[3] ibid 15.
[4] ibid 15.
[5] *Catholic Care (Diocese of Leeds) v Charity Commission for England & Wales* [2010] EWHC 520.
[6] ibid para [66].
[7] R Wintemute, 'Accommodating Religious Beliefs: Harm, Clothing or Symbols, and Refusals to Serve Others' (2014) 77 *Modern Law Review* 223, 228.

Muslim women can generally be accommodated because they meet the three criteria identified above. However, cases where religious believers refuse to serve others on the grounds of a 'protected characteristic', such as sexual orientation and other characteristics enshrined in human rights and anti-discrimination law, should not be accommodated. This is because in the latter cases there is direct and indirect harm caused to others. For example, in *Ladele*, the claimant refused to serve gay couples by registering their civil partnerships, on the grounds that the registration of gay civil partnerships breached her religious beliefs.[8] Her claim was unsuccessful. Likewise, in the UK case of *Bull v Hall*, a refusal to offer accommodation in a guesthouse to a homosexual couple was deemed unlawful discrimination.[9] In both cases, Wintemute would argue that accommodation of the refusal to serve a particular customer 'behind the customer's back' would result in direct and indirect harm.[10]

Douglas NeJaime and Reva Siegel also offer a solution, grounded in the harm principle, to the challenge of the increase in conscience claims that require exemptions from generally applicable laws. They generally support exemptions provided that the following two conditions are met: exemptions should not (i) obstruct the achievement of major social goals and (ii) inflict targeted material harms or dignitary harms on other citizens.[11] They further elaborate that material harms include restrictions to access to goods and services and information about them, whilst dignity-based harms may be caused by refusals to provide certain services as this can either give rise to or further reinforce social stigma.[12] NeJaime and Siegel's approach is not dissimilar to Wintemute's analysis of direct and indirect harms; however, it further emphasises the normative values that should guide the harm analysis. Both conceptions highlight the strengths of a harm-based approach by offering normative criteria for limitations to FORB. The harm principle, therefore, is crucial to determining the limits of religious freedom. Before elaborating on how exactly instances of harm can be interpreted and classified, it is necessary to address some of the key criticisms of the harm principle.

A. Problems with the Harm Principle

This section briefly sketches some of the shortcomings of relying on the harm principle as a way of guiding decisions about limitations to the right to FORB. The harm principle is, arguably, deceptively simple as it conceals some of its

---

[8] *Ladele v London Borough of Islington* [2009] EWCA Civ 1357.
[9] *Ball and Another v Hall and Another* [2013] UKHL 73.
[10] Wintemute (n 7) 240.
[11] D NeJaime and R Siegel, 'Conscience Wars in Transnational Perspective' in S Mancini and M Rosenfeld (eds), *Conscientious Objection or Culture Wars?* (Cambridge, Cambridge University Press, 2018) 200.
[12] ibid 201.

conceptual complexities. Its application requires making value judgements and can be subjected to various criticisms such as the following: the harm principle, as elaborated by Mill, is a result of a utilitarian and liberal theory and is therefore overly individualistic;[13] harm is too vague a criterion;[14] it is non-neutral;[15] and it does not resolve complex conflicts. For example, the harm principle does not explain why and when harm matters.[16] It is, moreover, incapable of providing immediate answers to the pressing complexities raised by the right to FORB. Inevitably, harm is a complex concept with (often hidden) normative dimensions. Steven Smith goes so far as to argue that the harm principle 'is an empty vessel, alluring and even irresistible but without any inherent legal or political content, into which advocates can pour whatever substantive views and values they happen to favour.'[17] In particular, the 'base line problem' of harm raises the question of comparing relative harms[18] and the level of harm necessary to justify limitations.[19] The base line is a foundational problem which pertains to explaining just how a person is harmed or worse off as compared *to what?*[20] Casting into doubt its general usefulness, Georgia du Plessis, maintains that the sole use of the harm principle does not have a place in increasingly diverse societies and thus should be replaced by a politics of recognition.[21] In other words, the harm principle, according to its critics, does not provide satisfactory guidance or a sound basis for decisions on limitations. These are valid challenges that expose some weaknesses of relying on the harm principle as a method of resolving conflicting interests in the highly sensitive context of the right to FORB, where notions of harm are understood in a number of complex ways.

B. The Added-Value of Harm

Notwithstanding criticisms of the harm principle, there are several reasons as to why the harm principle is preferable and useful. First, the harm principle favours

---

[13] C Maris, 'Pornography is Going on-line: The Harm Principle in Dutch Law' (2013) 17 *Law Democracy & Development* 1, 4.

[14] D Dripps, 'The Liberal Critique of the Harm Principle' (1998) 17 *Criminal Justice Ethics* 3: '... the idea of harm is too vague, too dependent on baseline assessments of private rights, too open to long chains of causal speculation, and too catastrophic in its categorical judgments to give liberty much practical protection' (at 3).

[15] S Smith, 'The Hollowness of the Harm Principle' (2004) *University of San Diego Research Paper Series* 17.

[16] A Ripstein, 'Beyond the Harm Principle' (2006) 34 *Philosophy & Public Affairs* 215, 217.

[17] SD Smith, 'Is the Harm Principle Illiberal?' (2006) 51 *American Journal of Jurisprudence* 1.

[18] TS Petersen, 'Being Worse Off: But in Comparison with What? On the Baseline Problem of Harm and the Harm Principle' (2014) 20 *Res Publica* 199, 201.

[19] BE Harcourt, 'The Collapse of the Harm Principle' (1999) 90 *The Journal of Criminal Law and Criminology* 109, 113.

[20] N Holtug, 'The Harm Principle' (2002) 5 *Ethical Theory and Moral Practice* 35.

[21] G du Plessis, 'The Legitimacy of Using the Harm Principle in Cases of Religious Freedom Within Education' (2016) 17 *Human Rights Review* 349.

liberty over coercive measures. Mill's classic articulation of the harm principle has continued to influence law and policy in liberal states because it provides a simple and clear justification for deciding when interference with an individual's liberty can be regarded as either legitimate or illegitimate. The harm principle focuses on the individual and only permits limitations to liberty if harm is done to others. Thus, it is a non-paternalistic principle, allowing individuals to act freely up until the point where their actions result in a harmful effect on others. Second, the harm principle can be given further content in order to address questions raised by the base-line problem so that the value(s) that are sought to be protected – which is personal autonomy for the purposes of this book – are identified. Harm can be defined in a structured manner and also in an open-ended way to account for hard cases. Third, it is flexible enough to be adapted to different factual situations, which is appropriate in the context of religious freedom. Therefore, the harm principle facilitates and upholds personal autonomy whilst placing appropriate and justifiable limits on individual liberty by zeroing in on harm done to others. This is precisely why it provides a useful normative basis for my own model of religious accommodation.

Harm to another's interests has practical consequences. For Raz, 'one harms another when one's action makes the other person worse off than he was, or is entitled to be, in a way which affects his future well-being', and this includes depriving others of their options or frustrating the pursuit of their projects and relationships.[22] The harm principle *in this sense* can maximise individual autonomy whilst preserving moral pluralism by clearly structuring the process of balancing different interests. To be sure, the harm principle requires supplementary criteria or 'mediating maxims',[23] but the need for supplementary criteria does not render the harm principle useless in and of itself. The 'base-line' problem[24] of the harm principle can be overcome by adopting a fact-sensitive case-by-case approach in addition to further criteria on what exactly constitutes harm. The key normative underpinning of my proposed model of religious accommodation is provided by a modified version of Raz's perfectionist version of autonomy. By relying on a 'thick', perfectionist principle, the proposed categorisation of four key harms to autonomy can be applied in practice. Overall, there is support for harm as a normative basis for deciding limits in both the scholarly literature, legal sources and the case law.

---

[22] J Raz, *The Morality of Freedom* (Oxford, Oxford University Press, 1986) 413–15 and see J Raz, 'Autonomy, Toleration, and the Harm Principle' in S Mendus (ed), *Justifying Toleration* (Cambridge, Cambridge University Press, 1988).

[23] J Feinberg, *The Moral Limits of the Criminal Law Volume 1: Harm to Others* (New York, Oxford University Press, 1987) 187–90; J Feinberg, 'Wrongful Conception and the Right Not to Be Harmed' (1985) 8 *Harvard Journal of Law and Public Policy* 57.

[24] Steven Smith, 'The Hollowness of the Harm Principle' (2004) University of San Diego Research Paper Series 17, available at ssrn.com/abstract=591327, accessed 12 June 2022.

II. A Model of Religious Accommodation

There are two key aims of the model: protecting the autonomy of religious believers *and* protecting the autonomy and rights of others *from* religious claims. As the two aims sometimes are in conflict, the model includes four categories of harm that can act as a mediating guide for decision-makers. My model promotes reasonable accommodation by using a principled and pragmatic approach for managing conflicts arising from religious claims in liberal states.[25]

A. A Hierarchy of Different Harms

The model ranks in terms of seriousness of effect four broad categories of harm to the autonomy of others. Category 1 harms pose risks for health and safety. They thus provide the strongest reason for the non-accommodation of a religious claim and attract stricter scrutiny either from the judiciary or the decision-makers. There are obvious reasons for prioritising the health and safety of others such as the need to protect the life, bodily integrity and autonomy of others. For example, the intervention of the responsible authorities is justified in cases where parents make a choice that is likely to have life-threatening consequences for their child, such as refusing to agree to a blood transfusion. The harms subsumed under the second category emerge from the impairment of people's *access to constitutional rights, goods and services*. This type of harm affects the practical ways in which individuals exercise their rights. Accordingly, Category 2 harms to autonomy have a specific and practical content, for example, barring others from obtaining abortion or divorce services or preventing them from accessing specific goods. The focus here rests on cases in which others cannot exercise their *rights* to a sufficient degree or are unable to act upon their interests because of a specific religious claim. Category 3 harms include religious claims that undermine the dignity of others, which is intrinsically linked to individual autonomy. Dignity as autonomy relates to the need to protect the self-worth of others, in particular that of historically disadvantaged groups such as minorities. Category 4 harms relate to the impracticality or cost (financial or otherwise) of accommodating a particular religious claim. For example, non-accommodation is justifiable where a small employer cannot afford to adopt a flexible scheduling timetable for its religious employees or where a school cannot make arrangements to accommodate a religious claim because

---

[25] My model builds on the work of Joseph Raz, Raymond Plant and Robert Wintemute. In Plant (n 2), Plant offers a very persuasive theoretical account for why harm is a better way of addressing religious claims, as discussed in ch 4. I also build on Robert Wintemute's application of a harm-based analysis to two case studies of religious claims: (i) refusals to serve others based on religious belief and (ii) requests to wear religious symbols such as Islamic headscarves. (Wintemute (n 7)). My model can be distinguished from Wintemute's analysis as I focus on autonomy and develop a detailed account of categories of harm that can act as a guide to decision-making in a wider range of cases.

of the impracticality of doing so.[26] This hierarchy of harms is necessary so as to prioritise and weigh up different harms; otherwise, there is the risk that numerous parties can make superfluous claims about alleged harms to their autonomy. Moreover, a hierarchy of harms does not entail that, for instance, dignity-based harms are trivial; rather it means that health and safety remain a priority and that there is a need for any harm to reach a certain threshold of seriousness.

B. The Threshold Question

The four broad categories of harm must meet a certain *threshold of harm* to prevent them from being easily relativised and/or weaponised. Drawing on the works of John Stuart Mill and Joel Feinberg[27] is helpful in addressing this issue, as it is crucial to rule out the risk of opening a 'floodgate' of claims of harm in order to ensure the workability of my model. Mill's version of the harm principle can be broken down into five components in the following way: '(i) harm (ii) to others (iii) caused by a wrongdoer (iv) that permits the state to interfere with (v) the wrongdoer's liberty of action'.[28] These components point to the need for a chain of causation to be established between the religious claim, on the one hand, and the harm caused to the *autonomy* of others, on the other hand. Obviously, in some cases the chain of causation between a religious claim and an alleged harm is too weak and cannot be sufficiently established.

Religious claims can often cause minor inconveniences. However, my model excludes such 'trivial' cases since a certain threshold of harm must be met. Joel Feinberg points out that 'In its bare formulation, without further explanation, the harm principle is a mere convenient abbreviation for a complicated statement that includes, among other things, moral judgments and value weightings of a variety of kinds'.[29] Feinberg offers a classification of different interests which provides criteria to define a relevant threshold and thus helps to eliminate cases that fall outside the scope of my model of religious accommodation. Feinberg distinguishes between classes of interests which include:

(1) passing wants (eating an ice cream cone); (2) instrumental wants (to get exercise); (3) welfare interests (the congeries of conditions and goods, such as physical health and economic sufficiency, that make it possible for us to achieve our ulterior or ultimate or focal aims); and (4) focal aims (our ultimate aims, that is, what we see as our good, such as building a dream house, running a restaurant, seeking religious salvation, promoting a cause, raising a family).[30]

---

[26] ibid.

[27] J Feinberg, *The Moral Limits* (n 23).

[28] As cited in JK Lieberman, 'The Meaning of Harm Derived from Interests' in JK Lieberman, *Liberalism Undressed* (Oxford, Oxford University Press, 2012) 49.

[29] Feinberg, *The Moral Limits* (n 23) 31.

[30] Feinberg's rich discussion of interests is summarised by JK Lieberman in *Liberalism Undressed* (Oxford, Oxford University Press, 2012) 49.

Since welfare interests and ultimate aims can concern one's religious or philosophical beliefs, they should, accordingly, be subject to a higher level of constitutional protection. If a religious claim only causes minimal harm to the health and safety of another, as compared to a serious violation of another's dignity, then these harms should be weighed accordingly within the proportionality test. Thus, decision-makers must first identify the categories of harm relevant to a case before moving on to assess the threshold and degree of that alleged harm. The analysis will vary on a case-by-case basis, but the different kinds of harm to the autonomy of others provide the normative foundation and guide the balancing of different interests.

C. Multiple Harms and Conflicts

A key challenge for my model is posed by cases in which multiple parties make conflicting claims of harm. How are such claims to be dealt with? For example, let us assume that Mary, Neil and Olivia work in the same office. Mary requests a shelf for herself in the shared kitchen fridge so as to be able to observe her religious dietary and hygiene rules. Mary asks all users to ensure that their products do not mix and to follow specific cleaning rules. Neil does not find this harmful to his interests, but Olivia does. Mary and Olivia could potentially make a number of irreconcilable claims of harm against each other. Since my model seeks to protect the autonomy of all parties, there is a risk of facilitating an ongoing proliferation of competing claims of harm. To guard against this risk, my model is, as outlined earlier, based on a hierarchy of four broad categories of harm. With health and safety being placed at its top, this hierarchisation helps to order and rank different harms. Not all forms of harm are equal or have the same effect; therefore, an evaluative judgement is necessary. Moreover, each case is to be assessed in light of the key concept of autonomy, which provides the normative underpinning to the act of adjudicating competing claims and interests. In other words, 'autonomy' is the main yardstick against which each claim is to be measured.

Finally, the model, and its categorisation of harms, fits within the proportionality test, which assists in balancing between different harms and thus makes it possible to conduct an exacting analysis. For example, if Olivia argued that the accommodation of Mary's religious claim would expose her to one or more of the four categories of harm, the next step would be to make an assessment of each individual claim. Whilst Olivia can invoke the full range of harms, the assessment stage is meant to act as a filter to prevent individuals from making numerous counter-claims against a specific claim for religious accommodation. The crucial question here is whether each claim of harm reaches a certain threshold. The task is to winnow out claims that are aimed against religious accommodation tout court. To return to the above example, the non-accommodation of a religious claim cannot be justified *unless* Olivia's autonomy is at risk of being harmed. Therefore, the four categories of harm are not abstract as they require a substantiation of how precisely the autonomy of others would be infringed in practice by a particular religious claim. From the preceding discussion of the core principles and aims of my model, a number of general guidelines for the model can be distilled:

• Limitations should be based on one of the four key harms to the autonomy of others: (i) harms to health and safety; (ii) harms flowing from denying access to rights, goods and services; (iii) violations of dignity; and (iv) excessive practical costs.
• The model makes an evaluative judgement about different kinds of harms by ranking them to create a 'hierarchy of harms'.

• In order for non-accommodation to be justified the following criteria should be met:
  – the identification of one of the four key harms (categories 1–4);
  – causation to be established between the religious claim and the effect of the claim on the autonomy of others; and
  – a minimum threshold of harm (defined as 'welfare interests and focal aims').

These conditions combined allow for competing claims of harm to autonomy to be managed in a consistent way, thus opening up space for flexibility whilst excluding superfluous claims.

D. Four Categories of Harm to the Autonomy of Others

i. Category 1: Harm to Health and Safety of Others

The strongest reason for limiting a religious claim is because it causes harm to the health and safety of others. The jurisprudence on the right to FORB includes a number of key cases that raise such health and safety concerns. Harm to the health and safety of others includes both physical and mental health in the medical context; security concerns such as fraud and the need for identification for the purpose of official identity documentation as in the ECtHR case of *Mann Singh v France*;[31] and reasons concerned with maintaining health and hygiene standards as in the UK case of *Chaplin v Royal Devon & Exeter Hospital NHS Foundation Trust* in which a nurse wished to wear a necklace at work.[32] Individuals cannot exercise their autonomy if they feel unsafe or are put in a position where their health is at risk. For example, this is the case when parents refuse to consent to necessary medical treatments such as a blood transfusion or a mandatory vaccination on behalf of their children.[33] Religious claims that jeopardise the health and safety of

---

[31] *Mann Singh v France* App no 24479/07 (27 November 2008), Admissibility Decision.
[32] *Chaplin v Royal Devon & Exeter Hospital NHS Foundation Trust* [2010] ET 1702886/2009 (21 April 2010).
[33] J O'Neill, 'Case for Persuasion in Parental Informed Consent to Promote Rational Vaccine Choices' (2020) 48 *Journal of Medical Ethics* 1.

others clearly fall within the scope of the harm principle because causing someone physical harm or pain constitutes a serious interference with the autonomy of that person.[34] In other words, putting another's health and safety at risk is bound to undermine the conditions required to live an autonomous life.

Health and safety might be an important consideration even if the potential harm is not immediately apparent. A prime example is the ECtHR case of *Eweida and others v UK*, where one of the four cases heard concerned Ms Chaplin, who was employed as a nurse and was forbidden to wear her necklace with a cross pendant at work because it was deemed to breach the uniform policy of the hospital.[35] Ms Chaplin was requested to remove her necklace after a new uniform code was introduced. She refused to do so and was transferred to a non-nursing position – a position that subsequently ceased to exist. Ms Chaplin argued that she suffered direct and indirect discrimination, and after losing her case in the employment tribunal she appealed to the ECtHR, where she also lost her case. The employer submitted that the uniform policy was informed by health and safety considerations which included, amongst other aims, reducing 'the risk of injury when handling patients'.[36] The ECtHR agreed with the need to maintain hygiene and safety for *both* nurses and patients[37] and held that the authorities, such as the hospital managers, were better placed to make decisions about clinical safety and ought to have the final say on accommodating religious symbols in accordance with the margin of appreciation afforded to decision-makers.[38] The Court held that there was no violation of Ms Chaplin's rights under Article 9 of the ECHR. Notably, the employer did consider accommodating Ms Chaplin's request in a way that would minimise risks to health and safety.[39] A risk assessment to determine whether it is possible to eliminate or minimise harm to a negligible degree to the health and safety of others should be conducted in order to seriously consider if accommodating a religious claim is possible.

Moreover, in the sensitive context of healthcare, there often exists a range of options that are worth exploring before non-accommodation should be considered. For example, religious symbols worn creatively and safely, such as surgical hijabs, can comply with strict health and safety regulations. Thus, the advantage of my model of religious accommodation is that it upholds the autonomy of both the religious believer and the other parties involved in a given case, whilst at the same time directing the analysis towards the question of which harms are preventable. By doing so, my model encourages supple, balanced negotiation between different claims.

---

[34] See V Bergelson, 'Autonomy, Dignity and Consent to Harm' (2008) *The David J Stoffer Lecture: Rutgers School of Law–Newark* 723.
[35] *Eweida and others v UK* App nos 48420/10, 59842/10, 51671/10 and 36516/10 [2013] ECHR 37 (ECtHR, 15 January 2013).
[36] ibid para 19.
[37] ibid para 98.
[38] ibid para 99.
[39] ibid para 93.

Harms to health and safety should not merely be discussed in the abstract but should be assessed in accordance with the likelihood of the risk materialising. For example, carrying or wearing a religious symbol or item that could potentially cause harm to others should be subject to a full risk assessment. In *Multani v Commission scolaire Marguerite-Bourgeoys*[40] the Supreme Court of Canada adopted a carefully balanced approach to the possibility of harm being caused in a case concerning a Sikh schoolboy who wished to carry a *kirpan* (a holy blade) at school. Charron J held that 'Given the evidence in the record, it is my opinion that the respondents' argument in support of an absolute prohibition – namely that kirpans are inherently dangerous – must fail.'[41] The Canadian Supreme Court's reasoning in *Multani* considered both religious freedom and the interests of the health and safety of others. The Court conducted a carefully reasoned analysis that ruled out a blanket ban,[42] thereby leaving scope for appropriate limitations.

Harms to health and safety exist on a spectrum and not all risks to the health of others justify the non-accommodation of a given religious practice. Risks must be *more than trivial*,[43] substantiated by evidence, and balanced against competing interests of autonomy. For example, some religious practices, especially the wearing of religious clothing, have prompted a range of health and safety arguments. One such argument revolves around the need for identification for security purposes. Security concerns have been engendered in particular by the full face veil worn by a minority of Muslim women, but also by turbans worn by some Sikh men. In *Mann Singh v France*, the ECtHR upheld a rule that required a Sikh man to remove his turban when taking a photograph for a driving licence[44] as the relevant French law required people to appear bareheaded on official photographs.[45] The applicant refused to remove his turban and his application for the licence was subsequently refused. The ECtHR held that 'the requirement of having a bare head for photographs pursued the legitimate aim of minimising the risk of fraud or falsification of driving licences' and held that the interference with the applicant's Article 9 rights was justified.[46] In particular the Court stated 'identity photographs for use on driving licences which showed the subject bareheaded were needed by the authorities in charge of public safety and law and order'. In this case, the interest of minimising fraud (and thereby enhancing the safety of others) outweighed the interests of the claimant. However, the ECtHR's decision can be criticised for interpreting safety restrictions too imprecisely in this case: the link between Sikh men wearing turbans and preventing fraud was by no means clearly established.

---

[40] *Multani v Commission scolaire Marguerite-Bourgeoys* [2006] 1 SCR 256, 2006 SCC 6.
[41] ibid 67.
[42] ibid.
[43] Feinberg, *The Moral Limits* (n 23).
[44] *Mann Singh v France* (n 31).
[45] ibid.
[46] ibid.

Mann Singh then appealed to the United Nations Human Rights Committee (UN HRC). The decision of the ECtHR stands in stark contrast to the decision of the UN HRC, which held that 'the state party had not shown why the limitation was necessary'. After all, it had not been demonstrated *why* the turban would make the process of identification more difficult, nor had it been established that there exists a link between people who appear with their heads covered and a somehow increased 'risk of fraud'.[47] Whilst harm to the health and safety of others is a strong reason for non-accommodation, options to minimise and reduce the risk of harm should be explored so as to maximise the autonomy of all parties to the greatest extent possible. The UN HRC's reasoning is more precise than that of the ECtHR as the latter failed to explain why an uncovered head would make the identification of Mann Singh more difficult. Such an explanation was all the more necessary given that the applicant would ordinarily be wearing a turban in any event. *Mann Singh v France* illustrates that limitations based on health and safety must meet a certain threshold of harm and be subjected to a proportionality test so that less restrictive measures can be considered that might make the complete non-accommodation of a particular religious practice unnecessary.

In an Employment Tribunal case on religious symbols at the workplace in the UK, the claimant was a Roman Catholic employed as a Theatre Practitioner by the respondent NHS Trust. The claimant wore a necklace with a small cross pendant both at the workplace and outside of work. This was deemed to breach a newly implemented uniform policy. Due to a series of subsequent decisions and events, the claimant eventually resigned from her job and brought a case against her former employer. The claimant succeeded in part. The Tribunal emphasised that there was no explanation as to why some items of jewellery had been permitted but a 'fine necklace with a small pendant of religious devotional significance is not'.[48] The Tribunal stated that:

> In order to properly analyse the balance it is necessary to set the risks posed by the Cross-Necklace in context. That context includes a consideration of how other items, that posed comparable risks, were treated, and, where there was a difference of treatment, the quality of the explanation for it.[49]

The Tribunal emphasised the need for the employer to ensure equal treatment between different religious groups. It follows that workplace policies ought to aim for consistency at the outset rather than only after there is a challenge to the policy, as this would improve decision-making processes overall.

Harms to the health and safety of others should be the primary focus when assessing whether or not a given religious practice is to be accommodated. It follows that a person should be able to take reasonable risks to their health and safety as this is consistent with the classic non-paternalistic interpretation of the

---

[47] *Shingara Mann Singh v France* [2013] UNHRC CCPR/C/108/D/1928/2010, 9.4.
[48] *Mrs Onuoha v Croydon Health Services NHS Trust* [2021] ET 2300516/2019, para [271].
[49] ibid para [269].

harm principle. For example, Sikh men who prefer to wear a turban instead of a safety helmet when riding a motorcycle should be able to do so. The burden is, or should be, borne by the wearer.[50] Another example relates to the right to refuse medical treatment, such as in the case of an adult Jehovah Witness who refuses a blood transfusion. Adults take such personal risks as autonomous individuals capable of choosing their ultimate life goals. At times, however, interference with individual religious autonomy might be justified in cases that also fall within the remit of criminal law or, as will be discussed in chapter six, where a person lacks capacity. Overall, harms caused by religious claims that result in the reduction of the autonomy of others because of health and safety concerns constitute serious reasons for non-accommodation. There is, nevertheless, a need for a balanced and careful approach when assessing the kinds and degree of harm. The points and questions raised in the guidelines on Category 1 harms should be considered.

Guidelines

Category 1 Harms to Health and Safety of Others
• (Potential) harm to the health and safety of others is the strongest reason for non-accommodation.
• Harms to the health and safety of others exist on a spectrum.
• Health and safety might be a relevant consideration even if the harm is not readily apparent, for example, if it affects mental wellbeing.
• Harms to the health and safety of others should not be merely abstract.
• Harms must be more than trivial, substantiated by evidence, and balanced against competing interests of autonomy.
• Employers should consider carrying out a risk assessment to determine whether it is possible to eliminate or minimise harm to a negligible degree to the health and safety of others in order to consider seriously whether accommodating a religious claim is possible.
• Public bodies, employers and institutions should justify non-accommodation with well founded and consistent reasons and reference to specific harms and not by appeals to generic health and safety concerns.

ii. Category 2: Harms to Access to Rights, Goods and Services

Category 2 harms are in evidence in a range of complex cases where religious beliefs restrict *access to rights, goods and services*. There has been considerable litigation, and debate about, conflict of rights and access to goods and services

---

[50] See ss 11 and 12 of the Employment Act as amended by the Deregulation Act 2015, s 6.

in the context of the right to FORB. 'Refusals to serve' customers on religious grounds have made the headlines and pose a number of difficult questions for limitations.

In the UK Supreme Court case of *Bull v Hall* Christian hotel keepers refused to offer, in keeping with their religious beliefs, a double room to a gay couple who were unmarried.[51] The couple had entered into a civil partnership. At the time, marriage was not yet an option available to gay couples.[52] The hotelkeepers argued that they did not discriminate against Mr Hall and Mr Preddy on the grounds of their sexual orientation, but rather because they were not married. In fact, they pointed out that they applied the same policy of refusing a double bedroom to unmarried heterosexual couples.[53] At the same time, the hotel owners accepted that there had been indirect discrimination since same sex couples could not get married, which put same sex couples at a particular disadvantage.

The question of whether there had been direct discrimination divided the Court. Was the criterion of marriage dissociable from sexual orientation? The majority argued that there had been direct discrimination. Lady Hale held:

> I would therefore regard the criterion of marriage or civil partnership as indissociable from the sexual orientation of those who qualify to enter it. More importantly, there is an exact correspondence between the advantage conferred and the disadvantage imposed in allowing a double bed to the one and denying it to the other.[54]

Lords Kerr and Toulson agreed. However, Lord Neuberger and Lord Hughes believed that this was not a case of direct discrimination, but instead, amounted to unjustifiable indirect discrimination. Notwithstanding the fact that equality and discrimination legislation across liberal jurisdictions varies in scope, the central question is when discriminatory private choices and preferences become 'public' and are in need of regulation. The boundary is not easy to draw and therefore gives rise to litigation.

The Supreme Court, moreover, adopted a narrow approach in the UK case of *Lee v McArthur*[55] in which the owners of a bakery – a devout Christian family – sincerely believed that marriage should be between a man and a woman only. Mr Lee, a gay customer, placed an order for a custom-made cake with the message 'Support Gay marriage'. The owners of the bakery believed that it would be against their conscience to complete the order and accordingly cancelled it. Subsequently, Mr Lee complained to the Equality Commission for Northern Ireland about the cancellation and brought a claim for both direct and indirect discrimination on grounds of sexual orientation, religious belief or political opinion. The UK Supreme Court acknowledged the 'dignitarian' harm that is

---

[51] *Bull and Another v Hall and Another* [2013] UKSC 73.
[52] ibid paras [26]–[27] and para [29].
[53] ibid para [17].
[54] ibid.
[55] *Lee v McArthur and others* [2016] NICA 39.

caused when a religious belief leads to a refusal to serve others on the grounds of a protected characteristic:

> It is deeply humiliating, and an affront to human dignity, to deny someone a service because of that person's race, gender, disability, sexual orientation or any of the other protected personal characteristics. But that is not what happened in this case and it does the project of equal treatment no favours to seek to extend it beyond its proper scope.[56]

The Court arrived at this decision since it held that 'the objection was to the message and not to any particular person or persons'.[57] In the US case of *Masterpiece Cakeshop Ltd v Colorado Civil Rights Commission*,[58] Mr Phillips, a devout Christian baker, refused to prepare a wedding cake for a same-sex couple as he claimed this would contravene his religious beliefs. The customers complained to the Colorado Civil Rights Commission pursuant to the Colorado Anti-Discrimination Act. For Mr Philips, 'creating a wedding cake for a same-sex wedding would be equivalent to participating in a celebration that is contrary to his own most deeply held beliefs'.[59] The Commission did not accept Mr Philip's claim that to bake a cake with that message would be tantamount to compelling him to use his artistic talent to express a message he profoundly disagreed with, and thus, would violate his right to free speech and free exercise of religion. However, the US Supreme Court held that the Commission's decision violated Mr Philips' First Amendment rights. Sandra Fredman argues that in the 'cake cases' an express hierarchy of values is necessary since tolerance does not assist us in deciding how to resolve such disputes. She bases her proposed solution on her multi-dimensional model of substantive equality via the proportionality analysis.[60]

These cases give rise to profound disagreements about the very scope of religious exemptions and raise the question as to whether religious believers can, or should be able to, refuse to provide a particular service to customers by invoking reasons of conscience or religious beliefs. Yet limiting access to rights, goods and services can constitute a significant harm because it can result in severely circumscribing the autonomy of others. According to Raz, 'respect for the autonomy of others largely consists in securing adequate options, i.e. opportunities and the ability to use them, and therefore, to deprive a person of opportunities or of the ability to use them, is a way of causing them harm'.[61] When these options include fundamental rights, there is a stronger reason for protecting the autonomy of others over accommodating a religious claim.

---

[56] ibid para [35].
[57] *Lee v Ashers Baking Company Ltd and others* [2018] UKSC 49.
[58] *Masterpiece Cakeshop, Ltd v Colorado Civil Rights Commission* 138 S Ct 419 (2018).
[59] ibid.
[60] S Fredman, 'Tolerating the Intolerant: Religious Freedom, Complicity, and the Right to Equality' (2020) 9 *Oxford Journal of Law and Religion* 305.
[61] Raz, *The Morality of Freedom* (n 22) 413.

Category 2 harms require that courts consider a range of factors such as the *nature* of the good or service in question as well as *adequate* access to it. Moreover, courts have to evaluate whether denying access to the good or service ultimately constitutes a violation of dignity. To strike an appropriate balance between the rights of religious believers and the rights of others to access certain goods and services, Category 2 harms relate to the *practical* ways in which individuals are prevented from pursuing their interests. If a religious claim would prevent or limit access to key services to which women are legally entitled, such as abortion services or divorce,[62] then non-accommodation is justified as it would directly infringe the rights of *others*. Crucially such claims are not solely concerned with maximising the individual's right to exercising their religious freedom(s) – but because some of these claims are primarily about curtailing the choices available to others.

The *nature* of the right, good or service in question is an important consideration in balancing the various interests in a case. Key services can include registration of marriage or civil partnerships as in *Ladele*;[63] abortion and related treatments;[64] and services for obtaining a divorce.[65] A constitutional right, which includes the right to equal treatment, should not be easily overridden. That is, all individuals have a right to certain goods. The question, therefore, is whether there ought to be some discretion which enables a religious claim to limit the access to certain sets of goods and services. In general, the possibility should be ruled out for a religious claimant to be able to refuse to 'serve others', for example, on the basis of their sexual orientation or gender, as equality law protects all individuals from discrimination. In other words, there are limitations to the right to FORB in the context of discrimination law.

However, there are cases where it is not necessarily clear that equality law has been breached and a religious claim or exemption can be accommodated, provided it does not impede *adequate* access to goods and services. According to Nehushtan, the 'content' of a conscience claim is important in that morally repugnant beliefs should not be accommodated by the liberal state.[66] This is problematic since many religious beliefs can be considered as morally repugnant by some sections of society. Focusing on the likely consequences of a religious claim is more productive as it avoids thick evaluations of different comprehensive views. Carving out exceptions to equality law is obviously problematic and raises a number of difficult questions. However, it is possible to avoid a conflict of rights and

---

[62] See S Bano, 'Muslim Family Justice and Human Rights: The Experience of British Muslim Women' (2007) 2 *Journal of Comparative Law* 38.

[63] *Ladele* (n 8).

[64] *Greater Glasgow Health Board v Doogan and another (Scotland)* [2014] UKSC 68.

[65] See RC Akhtar, R Probert and A Moors, 'Informal Muslim Marriages: Regulations and Contestations' (2018) 7 *Oxford Journal of Law and Religion* 367–75 and see Bano (n 62).

[66] Y Nehushtan and J Danaher, 'The Foundations of Conscientious Objection: Against Freedom and Autonomy' (2018) 9 *Jurisprudence* 541.

viewpoints – something that is inevitable in the context of increasing plural-ism – by following an approach that, first, takes a religious claim seriously, and second, by scrutinising the practical effects this claim has on the autonomy of others. Therefore, in the context of specific religious services, it might be possible to uphold beliefs and norms that are nevertheless discriminatory; their effects are confined to the remit of religious organisations and institutions and, as such, they fall within the scope of religious autonomy.

To be sure, there are cases where limiting access to a service also harms the health and safety of others in a broader, more expansive sense as the effects of such a practice can, ultimately, ripple far beyond the remit of the religious organisations. For example, in cases concerning abortion services, religious claims are likely to result in harm to the health and safety of women in an immediate and direct sense. This emerges clearly from the UK case of *Greater Glasgow Health Board v Doogan*, which dealt with two Roman Catholic midwives who worked in the Labour Ward of Greater Glasgow Health Board. The midwives held a conscientious objection to taking part in the termination of pregnancy, believing, more specifically, that 'any involvement in the process of termination renders them accomplices to and culpable for that grave offence'.[67] Abortion in the UK is regulated by the Abortion Act 1967. Section 4 of that Act provides for a 'conscience-based exemption' for those who do not wish to be involved in procedures resulting in the termination of pregnancy.[68] Section 4(1) of the Act reads:

> Subject to subsection (2) of this section, no person shall be under any duty, whether by contract or by any statutory or other legal requirement, to participate in any treatment authorised by this Act to which he has a conscientious objection.

Apprehensive that more abortions would be carried out by the Labour Ward in light of the reorganisation of maternity services, the midwives had sought assurances from their manager.[69] They objected to 'delegating, supervising and/or supporting staff to participate in and provide care to patients throughout the termination process'.[70] The hospital took the view that this did not constitute one-to-one care. The question for the Supreme Court was the meaning of 'to participate in any treatment authorised by this Act to which he has a conscientious objection'. Lady Hale pointed out that section 4(1) could be narrowly or broadly construed:

> The more difficult question is what is meant by 'to participate in' the course of treatment in question. The employers accept that it could have a broad or a narrow meaning. … a broad meaning might cover things done in connection with that treatment after it had begun, such as assigning staff to work with the patient, supervising and supporting such staff, and keeping a managerial eye on all the patients in the ward, including any

---

[67] *Doogan & Anor v NHS Greater Glasgow & Clyde Health Board* [2013] ScotCS CSIH 36, at para [12].
[68] Abortion Act 1967, s 4.
[69] *Doogan* (n 67) para [19].
[70] ibid.

undergoing a termination. A narrow meaning would restrict it to 'actually taking part', that is actually performing the tasks involved in the course of treatment.[71]

For Lady Hale a narrow construction was overall consistent with Parliamentary intent: '"Participate" in my view means taking part in a "hands-on" capacity.'[72] But should the midwives be exempt from 'ordinary duties' during the course of their employment too? The Court went on to evaluate the agreed list of various responsibilities given to midwives and held that tasks such as the management of resources and the allocation of staff did not fall under the conscience clause, whilst providing guidance and responding to requests for assistance might, in certain cases, be covered by it.[73] It would have been too impractical to schedule and assign tasks to the midwives in a way that would, at one and the same time, be in line with their conscience claim, safeguard patients and ensure the provision of an efficient service.[74]

Sandra Fredman acknowledges that 'allocations to marriage registrars might be sensitive to the latter's conscientious objection without the same-sex couple being aware of how allocations are made. However, this would not work if there was widespread refusal to provide the service, as in abortion cases.'[75] She argues that therefore 'finding an accommodation depends, not on principle, but on how widespread the objection is. The dividing line in normative, as against practical, terms, is not clear.'[76] There might be a small number of instances where access to abortion-related services would not be affected by the accommodation of a religious claim where medical staff and services are readily available without hardship and delay. However, such accommodation depends on the institutional capabilities necessary to achieve the dual goal of providing services and care to patients and accommodating medical professionals. As the boundaries between 'public' and 'private' domains are in constant flux,[77] decision-makers might legitimately assess whether *adequate* access to a good exists, thereby leaving some room for the accommodation of a religious practice if the context allows. For example, alternatives might exist that do not disadvantage or cause any 'dignitarian' harm to others. Focusing on adequate access and options potentially allows courts to 'fudge' a conflict of rights scenario, but this might sometimes be a sensible option in liberal democratic states so that one position is not automatically favoured as a hard rule.

For some legal scholars, the juridification of conflicts marks a shift in the way religious freedom is understood and litigated. Raymond Plant argues that by making liberal principles explicit in law and regulation, the scope for 'easy fudging

---

[71] ibid para [37].
[72] ibid para [38].
[73] ibid para [39].
[74] ibid para [39].
[75] Fredman (n 60) 316.
[76] ibid 317.
[77] See T Kahana and A Scolnicov, *Boundaries of State, Boundaries of Rights: Human Rights, Private Actors, and Positive Obligations* (Cambridge, Cambridge University Press, 2016).

and compromise is significantly reduced'.[78] He points out that in the context of the UK,

> The Human Rights Act has been important in what might be seen as a transition from ethos to rules – a move from seeing liberal democracy as a matter of practice and habit to one of explicit rules, principles and laws such as those embodied in the HRA and the 2010 Equality Act.[79]

The risk is that diversity and conflicts can very quickly become legal issues reducing the room for compromise and negotiation. Whilst Category 2 harms provide strong reasons for non-accommodation, appropriate and flexible use of discretion should be encouraged. The harms that fall under Category 2 are potentially numerous because of the many ways in which access can be limited by religious claims. Religious beliefs are inherently limiting since by definition a religious belief limits the options of the religious believer, which, in turn, can affect others. There is a need to ensure consistency and to take seriously the various needs and interests of different parties. In order to ensure consistency and balance, the following guidelines are suggested.

Guidelines

Category 2 Harms to the Access to Rights, Goods and Services

- Category 2 harms are concerned with how a religious claim might limit the autonomy of others by preventing or significantly reducing access to rights, goods and services.
- The nature of the right, goods or service is a weighty consideration since protection of access to core rights, goods and services strongly justifies the non-accommodation of a religious claim.
- Where a religious claim would result in the complete prevention of access to core rights, goods and services, it should not be accommodated.
- A religious claim, therefore, should not impede the rights of others to adequate access to a right, good or service.
- Where alternative adequate access to a good exists, there is discretion for the accommodation of a religious practice if the context allows.
- The context will depend on the nature of the right, good or service in question; the feasibility of ensuring safe and efficient services; and whether appropriate and flexible use of discretion is possible.
- Category 2 harms relate to the practical ways in which others are prevented from accessing services because of a religious claim or belief.
- However, restricting access to rights, goods and services might, in some cases, result in dignitarian harm (category 3 harms).

---

[78] ibid 9.
[79] Plant (n 2) 8.

iii. Category 3: Harm to the Dignity of Others

There are cases in which accommodating a particular religious claim would result in harm to the dignity of others. In other words, the manifestation of *certain* religious beliefs or practices is likely to have effects that constitute 'more than an offence' to others. Such violations of dignity, which I subsume under the rubric of Category 3 harms, are, however, difficult to define. This is so since there is a lack of a general consensus on the precise meaning of the concept of dignity and a consequent uncertainty as to what dignity entails in practice. As Christopher McCrudden argues, beyond a minimum core, the meaning of dignity is contested.[80] Nevertheless, dignity features as a centrally important principle in the context of the right to FORB because it is at stake in a particular class of cases that are unified by their concern for the integrity of others. This section will first outline competing conceptions of dignity before offering specific guidelines that are illustrated through application to the case law.

Although dignity is a common foundational principle across common law and civil law jurisdictions, a basic question as to its normative consequences persists. Dignity has multiple connotations and relates to different goods. At the level of principle, a range of conceptions of dignity exists, encompassing theological, political, and legal meanings.[81] Samuel Moyn notes that the genealogy of the modern constitutional concept of dignity originated in Catholic debates, although today the concept of dignity has been unmoored from and has largely transcended its origins.[82] Dignity is closely related to equality, but it is not necessarily synonymous with the latter. Whilst dignity is extensively invoked in human rights cases, dignity goes at times beyond certain conceptions of equality.[83] Dignity, it has been pointed out, can be deceptive, 'weaponised' in ways that attack autonomy, and is sometimes drafted into serving anti-democratic purposes.[84] Moreover, dignity can be understood in objective or subjective terms.[85] As Feldman states, 'the law may

---

[80] C McCrudden, 'Human Dignity and Judicial Interpretation of Human Rights' (2008) 19 *European Journal of International Law* 655.

[81] Joseph Ratzinger's multidimensional conception of dignity rests on the belief that man is created in the image of God, but his conception is by no means simplistic or reductionist. See DG Kirchhoffer, 'Benedict XVI, Human Dignity, and Absolute Moral Norms' (2010) *New Blackfriars* 586. For Jeremy Waldron, dignity is related to recognition and must 'function as a normative idea: it is the idea of a certain status that ought to be accredited to all persons and taken seriously in the way they are ruled'. J Waldron, 'How Law Protects Dignity' (2012) *NYU Public Law and Legal Theory Working Papers No 317*, 3.

[82] S Moyn, 'The Secret History of Constitutional Dignity' in C McCrudden, *Understanding Human Dignity* (Oxford, Oxford University Press, 2013).

[83] F Klug and H Wildbore, 'Equality, Dignity and Discrimination under Human Rights Law' (2005) LSE Depository.

[84] M Rosenfeld, 'The Case Against Dignity' in C McCrudden (ed), *Understanding Human Dignity* (Oxford, Oxford University Press, 2013).

[85] D Feldman, 'Human dignity as a legal value: Part 1' (1999) Spr *Public Law* 682. Feldman points out that 'Human dignity can operate on three levels: the dignity attaching to the whole human species; the dignity of groups within the human species; and the dignity of human individuals. The legal implications of each kind of dignity are slightly different'.

subjugate a person's autonomy or physical integrity to a court's ideas about what is necessary to protect an objective view of the dignity of that person or of humanity generally, opening the way to principled paternalism or legal moralism'.[86] Dignity is considered a 'double-edged sword'.[87] Some liberals rely on the concept to justify the expansion of the scope of individual choice, whilst some conservatives invoke it to impose limits on personal choice.[88] Thus, dignity as a legal principle can be understood in terms of 'dignity-as-autonomy' or 'dignity-as-constraint'.[89] Two cursory points can be culled from this discussion about the concept of dignity: its origins are diverse, and it is subject to a wide range of interpretations.

Dignity, in the legal context, is concerned with how the law should treat individuals in certain circumstances. The law in different liberal jurisdictions recognises the importance of dignity, although there does not exist a universally accepted understanding of this concept. Some constitutions entrench dignity as a fundamental principle, whereas others recognise dignity albeit less systematically.[90] For example, in Germany, dignity is a key constitutional principle that centrally guides the interpretation of constitutional rights.[91] In the UK, by contrast, the concept does not figure as a lodestar of constitutional interpretation in the way that it does in Germany. However, the Racial and Religious Hatred Act 2006 creates an offence of inciting hatred against persons on racial or religious grounds. Moreover, the Equality Act 2010 protects individuals from harassment and victimisation. Specifically, Section 26 of the Equality Act 2010 provides that 'A harasses another (B) if s/he violates another's dignity or creates an intimidating, hostile, degrading, humiliating or offensive environment for B'. Thus, dignity has a crucial role in explaining why the law prohibits certain acts. This is the case in other various jurisdictions as well where dignity has played an important role in the development of equality and human rights norms.[92] My model of religious accommodation does not offer a comprehensive normative account of dignity but favours an interpretation in terms of 'dignity-as-autonomy'. Approaching harm through the lens of dignity-as-autonomy brings into view cases that undermine the 'self-worth' of others or exploit the weaker position[93] of minorities by stigmatising or ostracising them.

---

[86] D Feldman, 'Human dignity as a legal value: Part 2' (2000) Spr *Public Law* 61, 76.

[87] D Feldman, 'Human dignity as a legal value: Part 1' (1999) Spr *Public Law* 682.

[88] R Brownsword, 'Human Dignity from a Legal Perspective' in M Düwell et al (eds), *The Cambridge Handbook of Human Dignity* (Cambridge, Cambridge University Press, 2014) 1.

[89] See RJ Fyfe, 'Dignity as Theory: Competing Conceptions of Human Dignity at the Supreme Court of Canada' (2007) 70 *Saskatchewan Law Review* 1. See also C Henckels, R Sifris and T Penovic, 'Dignity as a Constitutional Value: Abortion, Political Communication and Proportionality' (2021) 49 *Federal Law Review* 554 discussing how the courts in Australia have relied on dignity-based arguments in cases concerning both abortion and free speech.

[90] D Bedford, 'Human Dignity in Great Britain and Northern Ireland' in P Becchi and K Mathis (eds), *Handbook of Human Dignity in Europe* (Cham, Springer International Publishing, 2019) 361.

[91] *Mr N Cherfi v G4S Security Services Ltd* Appeal No UKEAT/0379/10/DM, 24 May 2011.

[92] See the landmark judgment of *S v Makwanyane and Another* (CCT3/94) [1995] ZACC 3.

[93] Waldron (n 81).

Thus, Category 3 harms to dignity might arise in a variety of situations in which more than just access to goods and services is at stake.

In the case law, appeals to the concept of dignity have featured prominently in anti-discrimination and equality cases such as in *Ashers*, where Christian owners of a bakery refused to fulfil an order for a custom-made cake with a 'Support Gay Marriage' logo. In her judgment in the case, Lady Hale pointed out: 'It is deeply humiliating, and an affront to human dignity, to deny someone a service because of that person's race, gender, disability, sexual orientation or any of the other protected personal characteristics.'[94] However, the Supreme Court went on to find no direct discrimination on the facts of the case because 'the objection was to the message and not to any particular person or persons.'[95] Similarly, in *Masterpiece Cakeshop v Colorado Civil Rights Commission* the US Supreme Court stated: 'Our society has come to the recognition that gay persons and gay couples cannot be treated as social outcasts or as inferior in dignity and worth.'[96]

John Adenitire argues that the violation of dignity in *Ashers*[97] stems from the refusal to provide the service in question because this is bound to undermine the equal social standing of members of a certain section of the political community.[98] McCrudden disagreed with this argument, noting that the rights of religious believers and non-believers, in addition to moral pluralism, must be protected.[99] *Ashers* and its US 'counter-part'[100] *Masterpiece Cakeshop v Colorado Civil Rights Commission*[101] have prompted considerable debate about the proper scope of anti-discrimination law, religious exemptions and the hierarchy of rights. For Eugenio Ibarra, the Supreme Court in *Ashers* got it right,[102] whereas for Daphne Romney, the law has been left in a state of confusion.[103] In light of the often-clashing opinions that have characterised this debate, McCrudden concludes that 'the concept of human dignity invites openness to the posing of the question of what it is to be human in our public and communal discourse.'[104] He is right in that the normative

---

[94] *Lee v Ashers Baking Company* (n 57) para [35].

[95] ibid para [34].

[96] *Masterpiece Cakeshop* (n 58).

[97] *Lee v Ashers Baking Company* (n 57).

[98] J Adenitire, *A General Right to Conscientious Objection: Beyond Religious Privilege* (Cambridge University Press, 2020) 282.

[99] C McCrudden, 'The Gay Cake Case: What the Supreme Court Did, and Didn't, Decide in Ashers' (2020) *Oxford Journal of Law and Religion* 1.

[100] For differences between the two cases, see R Reyes, 'Masterpiece Cakeshop and Ashers Baking Company: A Comparative Analysis of Constitutional Confections' (2020) 16 *Stanford Journal of Civil Rights & Civil Liberties* 113 and Lady Hale's postscript to her judgment.

[101] *Masterpiece Cakeshop* (n 58).

[102] EV Ibarra, '*Lee v Ashers Baking Company Ltd and Others*: The Inapplicability of Discrimination Law to an Illusory Conflict of Rights' (2020) 83 *Modern Law Review* 190.

[103] Because whilst refusing a service on the grounds of a protected characteristic is unlawful, the scope of what constitutes a political/religious message is unclear in Daphne Romney QC, 'The Consequences of the Ashers Cake Judgment' (OxHRH Blog, 12 October 2018), available at ohrh.law.ox.ac.uk/the-consequences-of-the-ashers-cake-judgment.

[104] C McCrudden, *Litigating Religion* (Oxford, Oxford University Press, 2018) 163.

principles we select are continually open to contestation. There is no sidestepping the reality that different conceptions of dignity-based harms can promote different (often political) causes, no matter whether one thinks the balance should be tipped in favour of religious believers or not. There is no neutral ground and equality arguments do not necessarily offer a self-evident solution. Rather, dignity is a normative and dynamic concept that cannot be ignored when considering the limitations of religious freedom.

Within my framework of religious accommodation, dignity is given specific normative and practical content through the concept of autonomy. Moreover, when accessing goods and services their *nature*[105] is a relevant factor in determining where exactly the balance lies for finding a Category 3 violation of dignity. For example, access to commercial goods and services such as guesthouses are important (Category 2 harms), but access to marriage services and abortion have a higher significance because preventing access to the latter also entails an additional dignitarian harm due to the *nature* of the good (Category 3 harms). Access to the rights to marriage and abortion are not only constitutional in nature but also relate to 'ultimate life choices' and are 'identity-forming' as compared to access to commercial services.

In the UK case of *HM Chief Inspector of Education, Children's Services and Skills v The Interim Executive Board of Al-Hijrah School*, the issue was whether the segregation of male and female students, in an Islamic mixed-sex school, constituted direct discrimination contrary to Sections 13 and 85 of the Equality Act 2010.[106] Ofsted submitted that 'although the girls and the boys were taught the same subjects and to the same standard, they all suffered educationally from the restriction on social interaction'.[107] The Court of Appeal overturned the finding of no discrimination and held that *both* boys and girls suffered a less favourable treatment since both were denied the opportunity to mix with each other.[108] Lady Justice Gloster's partial dissent was persuasive because she discussed two related harms that resulted from the segregation policy.[109] The first was the 'practical' harm that followed from segregating females who, as the judge pointed out, remain 'the group with minority power in society'.[110] The second harm was an 'expressive' harm, which was based on Ofsted's finding that 'segregation constitutes less favourable treatment of girls because it cannot be separated from deep-seated cultural and historical perspectives as to the inferiority of the female sex, and

---

[105] For example, Ahdar and Giles distinguish between a customized wedding cake, photography or florist service with the hire of a hall since the former entails some artistic and creative skill in R Ahdar and J Giles, 'The Supreme Courts' Icing on the Trans-Atlantic Cakes' (2020) *Oxford Journal of Law and Religion* 1.
[106] *HM Chief Inspector of Education, Children's Services and Skills v The Interim Executive Board of Al-Hijrah School* [2017] EWCA Civ 1426, para [7].
[107] ibid para [25].
[108] ibid para [53].
[109] ibid para [130].
[110] ibid para [131].

which serves to perpetuate a clear message about that status'.[111] Whilst Lady Justice Gloster pointed out that the distinction between the two harms was not hard and fast,[112] the more important issue was that there was evidence of both practical and expressive detriments such as the girls having to wait for the boys to finish their meals first.[113] This evidence-orientated approach is to be welcomed as it moves beyond abstract harms. In particular, the attention paid to the dignity of women and their role in society highlighted that in some cases religious accommodation not only reduces the immediate autonomy of others but can also negatively affect autonomy via violations of people's dignity and self-worth, and therefore limit the opportunities available to certain groups such as female students. In other words, the case did not harm the health and safety of the students (Category 1 harms) nor prevent girls from accessing the same services (Category 2 harms). It did, however, perpetuate negative gender stereotypes of girls as unequal and of secondary status.

There is a risk that Category 3 harms are instrumentalised to significantly limit religious freedom because many religious beliefs are often considered problematic by the majority. An important set of cases in that regard are those that concern the visibility of religious symbols. In *Lautsi v Italy* it was argued that children should not be exposed to religious symbols and imagery in state schools.[114] Similarly, in *Dahlab v Switzerland*, a primary school teacher, who had converted to Islam during the course of her employment, started to wear a headscarf.[115] The ECtHR held that:

> it is very difficult to assess the impact that a powerful external symbol such as the wearing of a headscarf may have on the freedom of conscience and religion of very young children ... it cannot be denied outright that the wearing of a headscarf might have some kind of proselytising effect, seeing that it appears to be imposed on women ...[116]

The Court further held that the Islamic headscarf represented an intention to convey a strong religious message through a specific mode of communication.[117] Religious symbols, according to this line of argument, can cause offence or harm through the enforcement of 'gender discrimination', a case in point being the Islamic headscarf which is only worn by women. However, as Jeroen Temperman maintains, 'the ECtHR's reasoning contained little in the way of substantiation of how, *in this case*, the rights of others (*i.e.* the pupils) were undermined especially as no complaints had been filed'.[118] Therefore, it is important to guard against the risk of positing the existence of a harm to dignity mainly because there exists

---

[111] ibid para [114].
[112] ibid para [138].
[113] ibid para [140].
[114] *Lautsi v Italy* App no 30814/06 (ECtHR, 18 March 2011) Grand Chamber.
[115] *Dahlab v Switzerland* App no 42393/98 (ECtHR, 15 February 2001).
[116] ibid.
[117] ibid.
[118] J Temperman, 'State Neutrality in Public School Education' (2010) 32 *Human Rights Quarterly* 865, 894.

a majoritarian bias against a certain religious belief or practice. The concept of dignity, in fact, is to be given content through autonomy so as to curtail the risk of interpreting dignity-based limitations too broadly or limiting other rights.

Category 3 harms to dignity are at risk of being 'over-inflated' and also conflict with the right to freedom of expression. The extent to which controversial views should be permitted is subject to heated public debate and beyond the scope of this book. However, the 'inflation' of dignity-based claims can work both ways. In the 1994 case of *Otto-Preminger-Institut v Austria* the screening of a satirical and controversial film about Christian beliefs was banned. The film was based on a play written by a playwright who had been convicted of blasphemy in 1895. The announcement for the screening of the film read: 'Trivial imagery and absurdities of the Christian creed are targeted in a caricature mode and the relationship between religious beliefs and worldly mechanisms of oppression is investigated.'[119] The Innsbruck Diocese of the Roman Catholic Church had initiated criminal proceedings against the Institute, which led to the banning of the film. The Institute eventually challenged the ban on the grounds that it violates freedom of expression as protected by Article 10 of the ECHR. The ECtHR, however, held that there had been no violation of Article 10 and stated:

> In seizing the film, the Austrian authorities acted to ensure religious peace in that region and to prevent that some people should feel the object of attacks on their religious beliefs in an unwarranted and offensive manner.[120]

The Court connected the religious sentiments of others to their personal dignity and held that this constituted a weighty reason for limiting expression. It is doubtful whether this case would be decided the same way today.

In the UK case of *Core Issue Trust v TFL*, Transport for London (TFL) refused to place an advertisement across its network that read 'NOT GAY! EX-GAY, POST-GAY AND PROUD. GET OVER IT!'[121] TFL submitted that its decision was legitimate as it was based on the need to protect sections of the public who might be offended or harmed by the message of the proposed advert.[122] The Core Issue Trust, a Christian organisation, argued, on the other hand, that TFL's refusal was inconsistent with latter's earlier approach which had allowed adverts that caused offence to many Christians.[123] These included a poster by the British Humanist Association that read 'There's probably no God' and another by Stonewall that proclaimed that 'SOME PEOPLE ARE GAY. GET OVER IT!'[124] The Court,

---

[119] *Otto-Preminger-Institut v Austria* App no 13470/87, para 10.
[120] ibid para 56.
[121] *Core Issue Trust v TFL* [2013] EWHC 651.
[122] ibid para [94].
[123] ibid para [96].
[124] ibid.

however, upheld TFL's decision. The case demonstrates that it is sometimes necessary to protect groups who have suffered past discrimination.

For Andrew Koppelman the conflict between gay rights and religious liberty is, at times, inflated and unnecessary.[125] It is possible to find balanced solutions even if these are somewhat uncomfortable. Whilst hate speech laws should guide limitations in the context of the right to FORB, the values of freedom of expression and pluralism can be protected by ensuring that Category 3 harms are primarily identified at the level of the practical effects of a religious claim so that abstract appeals to self-worth and identity do not automatically trump religious views. Rather, the effects of singling out or excluding a protected characteristic (such as sexual orientation or sex) are to be balanced against competing claims to autonomy. As *Core Issue Trust v TFL* and *Al-Hijrah School* demonstrate, the autonomy of LGBTQ+ persons and female students was at risk of being harmed in practice through stigma and segregation, respectively. Dignity, evidently, is a valuable but deeply contested principle in law. Its importance in religious freedom cases cannot be ignored, yet, it ought not to be over-stretched and expected to solve cases that concern a basic, irresolvable clash of worldviews. Instead, dignity within my model helps us to decide cases in which autonomy is harmed due to the effect of a religious belief as follows:

Guidelines

Category 3 Harm to the Dignity of Others

- Religious claims sometimes result in harming the dignity of others.
- Dignity remains an important albeit contested concept.
- Dignity is to be defined as dignity-as-autonomy.
- A harm to dignity is not necessarily the same as unequal treatment, although the two can overlap.
- Dignity is violated if a religious claim undermines:
  - the self-worth of others; or
  - exploits the weaker position of minorities by stigmatising or ostracising them. This is important because stigma, in turn, limits the autonomy of others since it can limit the adequacy of options available to those who are stigmatised.
- Dignity as a harm should not be 'inflated' so as to undermine the right to freedom of expression.
- A contextual approach is necessary since there is always a risk of seepage of social, moral and political biases into the process of identifying what constitutes dignitary harm.

---

[125] Koppelman is not convinced by the 'racism' analogy in A Koppelman, *Gay Rights vs. Religious Liberality: The Unnecessary Conflict* (New York, Oxford University Press, 2020).

iv. Category 4: Harms Caused by Practical Costs

Finally, Category 4 harms arise from the *impracticality or cost*, financial or otherwise, of accommodating religious claims. Category 4 harms constitute the weakest reasons for non-accommodation because the presumption of my model is clearly in favour of accommodation, and, accordingly, practical burdens are generally not deemed to be weighty enough reasons to withhold it. Harm as practical cost is to be found where accommodation imposes a high burden on, for instance, an employer or educational institute. Cases that address what might be classified as 'clear direct costs' include harm to economic interests or general administrative inconvenience.

Non-accommodation is justifiable where a small business or employer is unable to adopt a flexible scheduling timetable for its religious employees as in *Ahmad v United Kingdom*[126] or where a school cannot make arrangements to accommodate a religious garment because of impracticality as in *Azmi v Kirklees Metropolitan Borough Council.*[127] In the latter case, the applicant was a school assistant who wanted to wear the niqab to school. Her request was refused because an assessment of her teaching whilst wearing the niqab concluded that the niqab obstructed the education of the children. Moreover, the school held that it was too impractical and undesirable to timetable her teaching to ensure that she could avoid coming into contact with male teachers when without her face covering. In such cases, it might not be possible to accommodate a religious symbol primarily because of reasons of impracticality. Maleiha Malik points out that in cases of *conflict* between religion and gender or sexual orientation, it may not be possible to accommodate 'all' aspects of religious conscience because of the rights of others.[128] Nevertheless, it might be possible to accommodate some aspects. This is a sensible approach to religious accommodation because it leaves room for the possibility of devising workable solutions by identifying harms caused by an accommodation and then balancing the various interests.

In the UK case *Mr N Cherfi v G4S Security Services Ltd* a Muslim security guard made a request for an extended lunch break for weekly Friday prayers.[129] His request was refused on the basis that its accommodation would be a breach of contract and, moreover, result in heavy losses for the company.[130] Specifically, it was stated that 'it was not practicable to bring in another guard to cover the Claimant's lunchtime absences.'[131] It became too impractical for the company to accommodate the request even though the employer had previously accommodated the practice. In reality, some managers are more open to accommodation policies than others,

---

[126] *Ahmad v UK* (1982) 4 EHRR 126.
[127] *Azmi v Kirklees Metropolitan Borough Council* [2007] IRLR 434 EAT.
[128] M Malik, 'From Conflict to Cohesion' (2008) *Equality and Diversity Forum* 29.
[129] *Mr N Cherfi v G4S Security Services Ltd* Appeal No UKEAT/0379/10/DM, 24 May 2011.
[130] ibid.
[131] ibid, para [32].

which is why a general policy approach in favour of accommodation at work is preferable so as to generally enhance protection of religious freedom.

In the ECHR case *Francesco Sessa v Italy*, a Jewish lawyer was unable to attend his client's adjourned hearings on the proposed dates because these clashed with his religious holidays (Yom Kippur and Sukkot respectively).[132] The applicant argued that the refusal to re-schedule the adjourned hearings infringed his right to religious freedom and was contrary to the Law no 101 of 8 March 1989, which governs the relations between the State and the Union of Italian Jewish communities. The government argued that 'there had been no interference with the applicant's right to manifest his religion freely since he had never been prevented from taking part in Jewish festivals and practising his religion freely'. Moreover, 'the authorities had simply sought to ensure that the applicant did not hamper the smooth operation of essential State services in exercising his right to request that the hearing be adjourned'.[133] The ECtHR similarly held that there had not been a violation of the applicant's Article 9 rights.[134] However, the dissenting judgment argued that the inconvenience to the Court's administrative system should not have outweighed the harm the religious believer incurred. The dissenting opinion stated that:

> the requested adjournment might have caused some administrative inconvenience stemming, for instance, from the need to inform the parties involved of the new date for the hearing. But this seems to us to be minimal and should *perhaps be seen as the small price* to be paid in order to ensure respect for freedom of religion in a multicultural society.[135] [my emphasis]

Whether harm follows from excessive costs depended, in this case, on the difficulty of re-arranging the court hearing etc. This is not an abstract issue but, rather, an operational and resource-related one. Since employers are generally in the stronger position, the responsibility of clearly substantiating the cost or burden of accommodation should fall on them. In *Jakóbski v Poland*, the applicant requested that the prison authorities provide him vegetarian meals in accordance with his religious beliefs.[136] The state authorities argued that accommodating his beliefs would 'entail too many difficulties of a technical and financial nature'.[137] The ECtHR acknowledged that 'making special arrangements for one prisoner had financial implications for the prison and other inmates' but held that a fair balance needed to be struck between the interests of the institution, other prisoners, and the applicant.[138] Thus, Category 4 harms arise in cases where religious claims entail a practical burden if accommodated, even though there is no principled reason for non-accommodation. Therefore, the focus is on institutional, administrative and logistical concerns, as set out in the guidelines on Category 4 harms.

---

[132] *Francesco Sessa v Italy* App no 28790/08 (ECtHR, 3 April 2012).
[133] ibid para 31.
[134] ibid paras 32–38.
[135] ibid.
[136] *Jakóbski v Poland* App no 18429/06 (2012) 55 EHRR 8.
[137] ibid para 41.
[138] ibid.

Guidelines

Category 4 Harms caused by Practical Costs
• Category 4 harms arise from the impracticality or cost, financial or otherwise, incurred by accommodating a religious claim.
• Category 4 harms constitute the weakest reasons for non-accommodation because the presumption of the proposed model is in favour of accommodation and, accordingly, practical burdens should generally not be considered weighty reasons for non-accommodation.
• Harm as excessive practical cost is found where an accommodation imposes a high burden on another such as an employer or educational institute.
• Cases that address what might be classified as 'clear direct costs' include harm to economic interests or administrative inconvenience.
• Employers should substantiate the cost or burden of accommodation since employers are generally in a stronger position.

Taken together, this four-fold categorisation of harms upholds the autonomy of all parties to the greatest extent possible and offers guidelines on limitations to religious freedom for decision-makers. The four categories of harm are complimentary, and whilst they still require difficult decisions to be made, different categories of harm to the autonomy of others offer a stable, normative foundation from which competing interests can be negotiated and balanced.

III. Addressing Some Complexities of the Model of Religious Accommodation

This section addresses some of the complexities that arise from my model. These include how to distinguish relevant and irrelevant harms. In fact, within each category of harm, irrespective of the threshold, some 'harms' should be considered irrelevant. Moreover, since religious claims can be understood in terms of direct and indirect effects, my model needs to address the numerous ways in which harms can be analysed in practice. Finally, the proposed model is compatible with current legal frameworks and the proportionality test.

A. Relevant versus Irrelevant 'Harms'

Many religious practices are considered harmful by people outside the community of believers. After all, what constitutes harm is often based on subjective beliefs. The purpose of this section is to outline why objections to some common religious claims, such as wearing religious symbols, should generally be considered irrelevant claims of harm. My model requires limitations to be justified: that is, in order for a religious claim to be limited it must have negative consequences for the autonomy of others in practice.

For example, religious symbols have been litigated across liberal and non-liberal jurisdictions. The principle of neutrality might reasonably require the state to not endorse any official religious symbols, although the display of religious symbols does not necessarily breach secularism as a constitutional norm which does not require a blanket ban of religious symbols in all contexts. A religious symbol worn by an individual generally does not affect the rights and autonomy of others. Yet, the public visibility of the Islamic headscarf and niqab worn by a minority of Muslim women has been disproportionately targeted and subject to controversial litigation in various jurisdictions. Unfortunately, the courts have hesitated to adopt a consistent and robust approach to the issues raised.

There are a range of objections to religious symbols such as the niqab. Cases concerning face veils raise a set of complex considerations that put my model to the test. Crucially, the question revolves around whether the niqab is offensive and whether wearing it communicate anti-liberal values in and of itself. How does my model of religious accommodation deal with this apparent 'harm'? Martha Nussbaum analyses the various arguments advanced in favour of banning the niqab, which she groups together under the following headings: (i) security; (ii) transparency; (iii) objectification; (iv) coercion; and (v) health risks to the wearer. She argues that each argument undermines the principle of equality[139] since women who choose to wear the niqab or headscarf should be permitted to exercise their autonomy irrespective of whether others think this is a choice that is unwise or patriarchal.

The niqab has caused a lot of controversy because it impeded identification and communication. In Australia, a request by a woman who wanted to wear a niqab whilst giving evidence in court was refused.[140] This contrasts with the Canadian case of *Ishaq v The Minister of Citizenship and Immigration* where a rule that required the applicant to remove her niqab when taking the official oath for obtaining Canadian citizenship in public was held to be unlawful.[141] The applicant in that case claimed that the requirement of removing her niqab would compel her to 'temporarily abandon' her religious practice.[142] The Canadian Supreme Court sought to uphold the 'greatest possible freedom' approach which contrasts with the decisions of the ECtHR on Islamic symbols. The jurisprudence

---

[139] M Nussbaum, 'New Religious Intolerance: The Burqa Debate and the Demands of Equality' *ABC* (3 October 2014), available at www.abc.net.au/religion/new-religious-intolerance-the-burqa-debate-and-the-demands-of-eq/10098952.

[140] 'Niqab Ruling: The Australian Judge's Decision in Full Australia' *The Guardian* (December 2016), available at www.theguardian.com/world/2016/dec/01/niqab-ruling-the-australian-judges-decision-in-full.

[141] *Ishaq v The Minister of Citizenship and Immigration* 2015 FC 156.

[142] ibid para [22].

of the ECtHR emphasises that not every religious manifestation is protected by the Convention[143] but has failed to offer a nuanced analysis of religious symbols. The Canadian approach demonstrates that it is possible to accommodate religious practices in cases in which the risk of causing obstruction or inconvenience is minimal.

Relevant harms include those I have set out in my model. A harm should be considered irrelevant where it is based on subjective or majoritarian bias, does not impact others in practice, is purely ideological or political, or where there is little substantiated evidence of harmful effects on others.

B. How to Weigh Different Harms: Direct and Indirect Harms

Whilst my model frames harm in terms of broad categories which capture a number of sub-categories within each general, superordinate category, other scholars and legal practitioners have instead focused on the direct and indirect effects of a religious claim. For Robert Wintemute it is possible to accommodate a religious claim provided that three conditions are met: (i) a manifestation of a religious belief causes no direct harm to others; (ii) it involves minimal cost; and (iii) it causes no indirect harm to others.[144] Claims to wear the Islamic headscarf, Wintemute argues, should generally be accommodated because (assuming that the woman consents to wearing it) others cannot claim a legitimate interest in seeing those parts of her body.[145] Furthermore, Wintemute contends that in such cases there is no direct or indirect harm caused to others because the wearer should not be held responsible for other people's belief that the headscarf sends out a negative political message or because others might feel pressure to wear the headscarf.[146] According to Wintemute, the woman who wears the Islamic headscarf should be able to exercise her independent choice and cannot be held responsible for the feelings of others.

In another set of cases, Wintemute maintains that 'direct harm to the customer provides the strongest case for non-accommodation'.[147] For example, resort to religious claims in order to defend the refusal to serve a customer constitutes discrimination on the grounds of protected characteristics as in *Ladele v London Borough of Islington*. In such a case, non-accommodation of a religious claim is therefore justifiable. In *Ladele*, as discussed in chapter three, the employee was a registrar of marriages in the UK, who held that the registration of gay marriages was against her Christian beliefs. On that basis, she requested an exemption from

---

[143] ibid para [54].
[144] Wintemute (n 7) 228.
[145] ibid 234.
[146] ibid.
[147] ibid 241.

serving gay couples as part of her job.[148] However, UK anti-discrimination law protects individuals against refusals of service where that refusal is based on a protected characteristic. As this case demonstrates, there is a conflict of interests or harms between religious freedom and the freedom from discrimination on the grounds of sexual orientation. Three options are available to decision-makers in such cases: (a) non-accommodation; (b) semi-accommodation; or (c) full accommodation of the religious claim. Wintemute rejects the option of semi-accommodation as that would entail timetabling staff so that service users would not know which employees are exempted from serving them.[149] This form of accommodation is arguably akin to permitting customers to say that they do not want to be 'served by someone of a particular colour'. Wintemute argues: 'Because accommodation causes indirect harm to customers when it is kept secret, and direct harm to co-workers (if not eventually also to customers) when it is revealed, the fact that it involves minimal cost, disruption or inconvenience to the employer is irrelevant.'[150] However, Maleiha Malik argues that various non-legal options can be explored in such cases to minimise conflicts between religion and sexual orientation, although she maintains that generally the religious adherents must accept the priority of equality law over the need for religious accommodation.[151]

Wintemute's analysis of direct and indirect harm is useful as it sets out the degrees of harm that can be caused by the accommodation of certain religious claims. However, a claim of indirect harm can be made by numerous parties who might seek to limit the rights of others based on their conception of the good. Steven Smith points out that there is a risk involved in using secondary or indirect harms as relevant classifications. This is so since some claims of indirect harm are disingenuous as they are nothing but calls for restricting the freedom of others based on 'moralistic motivations'.[152] In other words, indirect harm can be instrumentalised in a way that, in practice, reduces the personal autonomy of others. This constitutes one good reason for adopting a categorisation of harms as opposed to analysing harms solely in terms of their direct and indirect effects.

An important example that demonstrates the problematic nature of claims of indirect harm is *Burwell v Hobby Lobby Stores*, a case that concerned Christian employers who objected to paying into a mandatory health insurance scheme that included contributions to cover certain abortive medicines.[153] The US Department of Health and Human Services issued regulations under the Patient Protection and Affordable Care Act 2010, requiring specific employers to provide health coverage for its employees that included a range of contraceptives. The owners of Hobby Lobby objected to four types of contraceptives and argued that the requirement to

[148] *Ladele v London Borough of Islington* (n 8).
[149] Wintemute (n 7) 242.
[150] ibid 242.
[151] Malik (n 128).
[152] Smith (n 15) 2.
[153] *Burwell v Hobby Lobby Stores, Inc*, 134 S Ct 2751 (2014).

provide cover for these was contrary to their religious beliefs, although they were not responsible for directly supplying the contraceptives in question. The claim of the employers was based on an alleged indirect harm. The Supreme Court held in favour of Hobby Lobby, albeit on narrow grounds, arguing that 'closely held corporations' could benefit from an exemption to the general requirement of offering cover provided there was an alternative way for the employees to access the necessary contraceptives.[154] *Hobby Lobby* highlights that claims of indirect harm are very complex and can be made by various parties. The problem is that these claims of indirect harm can be difficult to manage especially when made by an employer in a stronger position than its employees. The effect of this is that employers could potentially make several claims of indirect harms in order to limit the scope of religious claims at the workplace. In some form or another, this has been seen in the case law, as discussed in chapter three. My model starts with the presumption in favour of accommodation and requires an articulation of exactly how the religious claim in question would harm the autonomy of others by specifying the relevant categories of harm before evaluating the threshold question.

Claims of indirect harm are potentially very broad and can limit the rights of others. Moreover, such claims are not to be conflated with indirect discrimination. For example, in *Hobby Lobby* the Christian employers were not discriminated against; rather, the employers used a claim of indirect harm to limit the autonomy of others. Another example of the potential over-reach of indirect harm, in the European context, are cases in which employers have limited the personal autonomy of Muslim women wearing the Islamic headscarf. In *Dahlab v Switzerland*, as discussed in chapter three, the government sought to uphold a ban on Islamic headscarves in the school classroom and argued that the sight of a headscarf could have a negative influence on children.[155] The government did not prove this claim by, for example, substantiating how exactly the harm of 'negative influence' would materialise in practice. In both *Hobby Lobby* and *Dahlab v Switzerland*, indirect harm was invoked by the employers and had the effect of limiting the rights of others. Indirect harm, is, therefore, potentially too broad a concept and does not tell us which *categories* of harm count as a legitimate reason for limiting religious claims.

Furthermore, the distinction between direct and indirect harm is not always clear-cut, and, as a result, framing harms in this way does not provide guidance on what the outcome in a particular case should be. For example, in *Dahlab v Switzerland* it was alleged that the schoolchildren were indirectly harmed by the mere sight of an Islamic headscarf. It was difficult to claim that the sight of the headscarf causes a direct harm unless there would be a claim that children were directly harmed by the 'non-neutrality' of the teacher (but this alone would not suffice since teachers are not entirely 'neutral' in appearance). Yet, at

---

[154] ibid.
[155] *Dahlab* (n 115).

the same time the schoolteacher was directly harmed as she was made to choose between either removing her headscarf or losing her job. The schoolteacher could also claim that she is *indirectly* harmed by the implementation of a neutral rule (that is, through indirect discrimination). The point is that *both parties* can make claims of direct and indirect harm, meaning that what constitutes a direct or indirect harm is not a value-free exercise, nor does it guide limitations since it is usually possible to identify some sort of harm. The question is what kinds of harm matter and to what degree. In cases such as *Ladele* and *Hobby Lobby*, where a conflict between two fundamental rights is at stake, there is a pressing need for a more principled method for deciding between cases. In particular, the direct/indirect distinction focuses on the *effect* of the harm but does not spell out which categories of harm are relevant to the balancing test.

Moreover, different harms affect people in different ways and to varying degrees. Dennis Baker argues that a key problem with harm is that it affects different people in different ways.[156] A further weakness with the conceptualisation in terms of direct and indirect harm is that harms are more complex and varied in degree and character than this dichotomy can capture. For example, as Dennis Baker asks, 'is physical assault worse than causing someone economic harm? And what if the physical harm is minor and the economic harm is great?'[157] I propose a possible solution to this conundrum of how to weigh different harms: my model sets out first the different broad *categories* of harm that could justify the non-accommodation of a religious claim. The second stage of the analysis is dedicated to a consideration of the *effects* of the harm to the autonomy of others, which could include direct or indirect harms. Overall, the distinction between direct and indirect harms has three problems: it does not tell us *what* categories of harm count as legitimate reasons for non-accommodation; the distinction is not clear-cut; and, finally, appeals to indirect harm are potentially too broad. To conclude, the distinction between direct and indirect harms is relevant to the balancing stage of the proportionality test *once* the broad category of harm is identified.

C. The Proportionality Test

My model of religious accommodation is compatible with the existing use of the proportionality test in human rights and anti-discrimination law cases across jurisdictions.[158] The proportionality test sets out the framework for how

---

[156] DJ Baker, 'Constitutionalizing the Harm Principle' (2008) 27 *Criminal Justice Ethics* 3, 17.
[157] ibid 17.
[158] There is a vast range of literature on proportionality and its use in human rights cases, which is beyond the scope of this book. Leading works include R Alexy, *A Theory of Constitutional Rights* (Oxford, Oxford University Press, 2002) and A Barak, *Proportionality: Constitutional Rights and their Limitations* (Cambridge, Cambridge University Press, 2012). Barak emphasises that the proportionality test is widely used by Constitutional Courts globally. This book agrees that the proportionality analysis is useful and should be used in human rights cases that raise conflicting interests. See also P Sales,

fundamental human rights are to be limited and balanced. The proportionality test requires that the decision-maker to take step A before B and C etc, thereby structuring the balancing of rights and interests in human rights cases.[159] Specifically, although there are slightly different formulations of the proportionality test,[160] the analysis proceeds in the following stages: (1) the identification of a legitimate goal that the restrictive measure seeks to achieve; (2) the suitability of that restrictive measure; (3) the necessity and whether there are less restrictive means; (4) the final balancing stage where different interests must be weighed against each other. The structured analysis is a key advantage as it ensures consistency in decision-making. However, the proportionality test is subject to various criticisms, for example, for not being able to address the deep moral conflicts raised by some human rights cases.[161] The proportionality test does not guide the analysis of competing claims, for example, by setting out whether value X is more important than Y. Let's take the example of two workplaces that enforce a rule that prohibits religious symbols. Workplace A (a department store) does so on the grounds of neutrality and workplace B (a bakery) on the grounds of health and safety. The proportionality analysis requires the stages of the test to be followed but does not prescribe how the balancing of different interests ought to take place. My model of religious accommodation compliments the existing use of the proportionality test because it guides the application of the test to religious claims. It does so by suggesting that the *balancing* stage of the proportionality analysis should be guided by harms to autonomy. The proportionality test requires the identification of a legitimate ground for limitation before the balancing test is carried out. This means that generic claims of

---

'Rationality, Proportionality and the Development of the Law' (2013) 129 *Law Quarterly Review* 223 and A Barak, 'Proportionality and Principled Balancing' (2010) 4 *Law & Ethics of Human Rights* 3.

[159] See K Möller, Proportionality: Challenging the Critics (2012) 10 *International Journal of Constitutional Law* 709, 711–16 for an explanation of the step-by-step proportionality analysis.

[160] See *Bank Mellat v Her Majesty's Treasury* [2013] UKSC 39: 'the question depends on an exacting analysis of the factual case advanced in defence of the measure, in order to determine (i) whether its objective is sufficiently important to justify the limitation of a fundamental right; (ii) whether it is rationally connected to the objective; (iii) whether a less intrusive measure could have been used; and (iv) whether, having regard to these matters and to the severity of the consequences, a fair balance has been struck between the rights of the individual and the interests of the community. These four requirements are logically separate, but in practice they inevitably overlap because the same facts are likely to be relevant to more than one of them' (at para [20]).

[161] A key criticism of proportionality is advanced by Grégoire Webber who argues that proportionality purports to be neutral and avoids moral issues: 'The structure of proportionality analysis itself does not purport (at least explicitly) to struggle with the *moral* correctness, goodness or rightness of a claim but only with its *technical* weight, cost or benefit. The principle of proportionality – being formal or empty – itself makes no claim to correctness in any morally significant way': see GCN Webber, *The Negotiable Constitution: on the Limitation of Rights* (Cambridge, Cambridge University Press, 2009) 90. Another key criticism of proportionality holds that proportionality necessarily gets moral questions wrong: see S Tsakyrakis, 'Proportionality: An Assault on Human Rights?' (2009) 7 *International Journal of Constitutional Law* 468, 488. However, K Möller defends proportionality on the basis that sometimes the balancing process does indeed require moral reasoning and that judgments handed down by Courts that are not carefully reasoned or justified with reference to proportionality do not necessarily prove that proportionality itself is flawed: Möller (n 159) 717–18.

harm ought to be excluded from the analysis, and that competing claims of harm must be balanced in light of the principle of autonomy. Thus applied to the above example, we would ask whether the restriction to the religious believer wanting to wear a religious symbol at work harms the autonomy of others (employees or customers) at the department store. Previous chapters have already confirmed that neutrality policies are problematic and should generally not constitute a relevant harm that legitimises non-accommodation, whereas there might be good reasons for a bakery to limit the wearing of religious symbols for hygiene reasons etc., although the proportionality test will require the employer to demonstrate alternatives / less restrictive means. Therefore, my model is relevant at the balancing stage of the test since it offers a way of balancing different interests by identifying what ought to count as harm in order to justify non-accommodation and limitations to the right to FORB.

IV. Conclusion

This chapter has introduced a model of religious accommodation that takes the autonomy of all interested parties in religious claims seriously. The model includes four broad categories of harm to the autonomy of others. The guidelines I have offered provide cues on how the different categories of harm are to be interpreted. The various harms can overlap, but in order for them to justify the non-accommodation of a specific religious claim they must meet a certain threshold. The aim of my model is not to propose a mathematical formula that automatically produces the 'right or wrong answer' in every case. Rather, it is meant to serve as an analytical guide that provides decision-makers with a precise and normatively clear method to help them decide when religious claims should be limited. This represents an improvement over current approaches to religious accommodation, which often fail to make their normative assumptions explicit.

6

Harm in the 'Hard' Cases

This chapter will address the right to FORB in a number of 'hard' cases that raise multiple challenges. Conceptions of harm inevitably draw on social, moral, and political values, thus making harm to the autonomy of others a multi-faceted phenomenon. Simon Gardner emphasises that any understanding of 'harm' must have intelligible limits:

> The process of discerning these limits is laborious and eventually frustrating, because in fact we properly understand the concept of 'harm' in a way that is context-relative. While in one context the description 'harm' only extends to physical injuries, in another we might include intense irritations, demoralizations, emotional manipulations and so on.[1]

In 'hard' cases of religious freedom, an individual conception of autonomy is not necessarily the most appropriate or desirable approach to determining the limitations to the right to FORB. Harm to the autonomy of others often requires the interests of various parties to be balanced. Hard cases demonstrate the limits of relying on a notion of harm when trying to resolve conflicts and bring to the fore the challenge of regulating religion through legal techniques alone. Section I addresses the definitional question of 'what makes a hard case'. In particular, I discuss cases that involve persons who lack the mental capacity to make decisions as well as cases where there are multiple conflicting interests such as those that involve religious organisations. Section II assesses religious claims in the medical context, whilst section III looks at religious claims that involve children. The focus of the latter rests on two case studies that concern education and non-therapeutic male circumcision. These case studies are particularly instructive as they raise different, multi-faceted problems for liberal conceptions of individual autonomy. Finally, section IV critically discusses the vexing problems that accommodating religious organisations poses. In short, this chapter outlines how my model of religious accommodation deals with hard cases whilst at the same time acknowledging the limits of the notion of harm itself. By tackling these issues head-on, I argue that the limits of my model overlap with the general limits of using the law as a central tool for managing conflicting claims. Thus, the most appropriate way to resolve a case might sometimes require a non-legal solution or a political decision

---

[1] J Gardner, 'Liberals and Unlawful Discrimination' (1989) 9 *Oxford Journal of Legal Studies* 1, 1.

where a flexible notion of autonomy can be applied that takes into account the various dimensions of autonomy.[2]

I. What Makes a 'Hard' Case?

There are numerous reasons why a religious freedom case might qualify as a 'hard' case. In one sense, all of the cases discussed in chapter five raise difficult questions. Religious claims are inherently complex, often concern multiple parties, and require value judgements. In another sense, defining a hard case is a normative question. My proposed model offers a set of principles and guidelines in light of a particular understanding of the right to FORB. However, some categories of cases raise particular challenges for my model and, therefore, ought to be discussed in detail. It bears emphasising at this point that my model of religious accommodation is centred on the individual as it conceives harm through the lens of the individual's autonomy. Whilst it is the autonomy of various parties that the model seeks to protect, the right to FORB is more layered, particularly in hard cases where multiple interests are at play. Individual autonomy does not, and should not, always trump other interests. Finally, it remains a valid question as to whether harm can or should be understood in exclusively legal, normative terms. For these reasons, this chapter assesses three categories of hard cases that encompass (i) the medical context; (ii) children; and (iii) religious organisations.

The medical context raises multiple specific issues not only because patients are vulnerable and sometimes lack capacity; there are additional factors that have to be taken into account such as the best interests of the patient, the role of health-care professionals, as well as the availability of resources, which impact what is logistically possible in practice. Capacity, in the legal sense, relates to the inability to make decisions for oneself. This category can include both adults and children, although different considerations apply in each case. Persons lacking capacity are vulnerable because their decision-making is entrusted to others. The clinical and legal determination of capacity and the giving of informed consent is complex and beyond the scope of this chapter.[3] Religious claims in the medical context can sometimes concern those who lack full or partial capacity and whose autonomy is thus being (partly) determined by others. Yet, autonomy must still be protected even if an individual currently lacks capacity; the latter's values, desires and potential choices are to be respected in any event. Moreover, a person might become

---

[2] J Herring, *Law and the Relational Self* (Cambridge, Cambridge University Press, 2019).
[3] In the UK, s 1(2) of the MCA 2005 defines capacity in the following way: 'A person must be assumed to have capacity unless it is established that he lacks capacity'. Section 1(5) of the MCA 2005 provides: 'An act done, or decision made, under this Act for or on behalf of a person who lacks capacity must be done, or made, in his best interests.' Moreover, s 1(6) of the MCA 2005 states: 'regard must be had to whether the purpose for which it is needed can be as effectively achieved in a way that is less restrictive of the person's rights and freedom of action.'

more or 'fully' autonomous in the future. The uncertainty regarding the notion of 'future' autonomy is a complicated one for the law to regulate. For example, in cases concerning the question of teenagers' consent to gender reassignment procedures, 'future' autonomy continues to be a contested issue.[4] In sum, the medical context raises issues about capacity, informed consent,[5] autonomy and institutional factors that affect the scope of religious accommodation thus creating hard cases.

Children's rights in the context of religious freedom give rise to several competing considerations. On the one hand, children lack capacity as they are not fully autonomous and are unable to take informed decisions on a wide range of issues. On the other hand, there exists nevertheless a spectrum of autonomy: that is, the older children are, the more they ought to be directly involved in decisions relating to their immediate interests. Religious freedom in education is a controversial issue since both the scope of state supervision and the parent's right to bring up their children according to their beliefs are subject to reasonable disagreement in public. For example, the promotion by the UK Department of Education of what it held to be 'Fundamental British Values'[6] as well as the so-called 'Trojan Horse Affair' which concerned the alleged Islamist infiltration of schools in Birmingham prompted heated debates about the need for collective public and civic values to be given priority over individualistic and private values as the guiding principles of public education.[7] Moreover, parents, who often wish to pass on to their children certain religious and cultural practices deemed inappropriate by the majority culture, face difficult choices. To that end, the right of the child to an 'open future',[8] and what is known as 'transmission of religious identity',[9] that is, the passing of the parent's religious beliefs to their children, is problematised and its proper scope is unclear.

The question of accommodation vis-à-vis religious organisations is challenging as multiple parties are involved and group rights are at stake. Religious organisations can be formal or informal in that they might be registered as an official religion or as a place of worship, charity, faith school, association or as a for-profit entity. They can compete with the state and other religious organisations for recognition and (political) power. The influence of such organisations

---

[4] For the US context see SM Shuster, 'Performing informed consent in transgender medicine' (2019) 226 Social Science and Medicine 190–97. See also K Gerritse et al, 'Decision-making approaches in transgender healthcare: conceptual analysis and ethical implications' (2021) 24 *Medicine, Health Care and Philosophy* 687.

[5] J Herring, *Medical Law and Ethics*, 8th edition (Oxford, Oxford University Press, 2020).

[6] H Starkey, 'Fundamental British Values and citizenship education: tensions between national and global perspectives' (2018) 110(2) *Geografiska Annaler: Series B, Human Geography* 149–62.

[7] J Arthur, 'Extremism and Neo-Liberal Education Policy: A Contextual Critique of the Trojan Horse Affair in Birmingham Schools' (2015) 63 *British Journal of Educational Studies* 311.

[8] F Dietrich, 'Liberalism, Neutrality, and the Child's Right to an Open Future' (2020) 51 *Journal of Social Philosophy* 104.

[9] See R Taylor, 'Responsibility for the Soul of the Child: The Role of the State and Parents in Determining Religious Upbringing and Education' (2015) 29 *International Journal of Law, Policy and the Family* 15 and *Re M (Children)* [2014] EWHC 667 (Fam).

varies greatly according to the context and the specific services they provide. Many religious organisations are internationally connected, thus making their reach not only local but cross-jurisdictional. My model is especially attuned to balancing conflicting interests in cases where there is a clash between two parties such as between a religious employee and the employer. However, cases involving religious organisations that seek exemptions from generally applicable laws or try to subject their employees to religious rules raise more challenging questions about the legitimate scope of 'harms to autonomy'. Religious organisations are diverse and thus pose a number of on-going and evolving challenges for the liberal state. To summarise, hard cases are characterised by the involvement of multiple parties and interests. In such cases, it is not always clear how harm to the autonomy of others should be interpreted. Inevitably, a prioritisation of interests and a context-specific notion of harm are necessary.

II. The Medical Context

In the medical context, the religious or ethical beliefs of healthcare professionals, patients, and their families play central roles in the decision-making process. Some beliefs might manifest themselves as a 'conscientious objection', which is based on a particular belief characterised by strong moral or ethical convictions. Conscientious objections in the medical sector often create conflicts between the right to religion and the right to the highest attainable standard of health. Such conflicts have, for instance, centrally included disputes over access to reproductive health services.[10] Moreover, claims for accommodation must be balanced in a generally tense and resource-limited context. A range of situations ultimately generate different kinds of accommodation claims. A distinction should be made, then, between religious or conscience claims by healthcare professionals, patients and those who lack (full) capacity. Different sets of issues are bound to arise in each case.

Harm to autonomy is multi-faceted in medical claims. For some critics, the principle of autonomy is 'overinflated' as it is unable to adequately address the complexities in medical cases.[11] The application of this principle in the medical context is particularly problematic since decision-making takes place at a moment when a patient is weak and vulnerable or without full capacity and when family members as well as healthcare professionals are under time constraints.[12]

---

[10] H Bielefeldt, 'Conscientious Objection in the Medical Sector. Towards a Holistic Human Rights Approach' in S Klotz et al (eds), *Healthcare as a Human Rights Issue: Normative Profile, Conflicts and Implementation* (transcript Verlag, Bielefeld, 2017).

[11] For an excellent critique of autonomy in the medical context see C Foster, *Choosing Life, Choosing Death: The Tyranny of Autonomy in Medical Ethics and Law* (Oxford, Hart Publishing, 2009).

[12] BJ Richards, 'Autonomy and the Law: Widely Used, Poorly Defined' in D Kirchhoffer and BJ Richards (eds), *Beyond Autonomy: Limits and Alternatives to Informed Consent in Research Ethics and Law* (Cambridge, Cambridge University Press, 2020).

Thus, autonomy is not the central issue at stake in many medical cases. These are valid criticisms. However, despite such qualifications, the autonomy of both healthcare professionals and patients remains *sufficiently* important in protecting their interests with respect to religious freedom. Therefore, attempts should be made to uphold their autonomy even if it is accepted that there are obvious limits to this. That is to say, religious autonomy, as a specific aspect of individual autonomy, remains crucial throughout and is, in some cases, even of central importance.

To begin with, medical professionals are under an over-riding obligatory duty to act in the best interests of the patient[13] – a duty that should, in theory, limit the scope of religious claims. Moreover, patients can refuse medical treatment even if this entails harm to themselves. The rationale for this is that patients should not be forced to adopt a particular course of treatment against their will. This line of reasoning follows the liberal principle of non-paternalism.[14] However, failure to accept treatment can sometimes negatively affect the rights of others, as in the following scenarios: a patient refuses a vaccination against a contagious disease; a parent with children refuses treatment; or a parent refuses treatment *on behalf of their children*.[15] A patient might or might not have religious reasons for choosing the preferred course of action; however, data confirms that religious and spiritual beliefs can influence how patients perceive risk and thus their treatment options.[16] Thus, medical professionals should engage positively with patients to try to understand their specific reasons, values, and motivations so as to ensure that patients are fully informed about the risks of different treatment options.[17] Accordingly, training and awareness of how to deal with different patient's personal religious/ethical beliefs and religious pluralism in healthcare is necessary.[18]

Religious claims made by healthcare professionals can be more problematic as they often entail more than just a one-off accommodation and instead require healthcare providers to devise solutions that would involve questions of resource distribution and overall policy. For Heiner Bielefeldt, conscientious objection is reserved for a small number of clearly circumscribed situations:

> Conscientious objection is not part of the general arsenal of voicing moral dissent. It must remain an exception reserved for specific dilemma situations when a person would otherwise feel torn between feelings of moral self-betrayal and the requirement to honour lawful obligations.[19]

---

[13] D Wilkinson et al, *Medical Ethics and Law* (Amsterdam, Elsevier, 2020) 42–46.
[14] ibid 47.
[15] K Greenawalt, *Exemptions* (Cambridge, Harvard University Press, 2016) 77.
[16] R Klitzman, 'Doctor, Will You Pray for Me? Responding to Patients' Religious and Spiritual Concerns' (2021) 96 *Academic Medicine* 349.
[17] See also the UK case of *Montgomery v Lanarkshire Health Board (Scotland)* [2015] UKSC 11.
[18] Klitzman (n 16).
[19] Bielefeldt (n 10). Bielefeldt proposes five criteria 'for qualifying conscientious objections that may warrant exemptions from lawful obligations: the gravity of the moral concern, the situation of a conscientious veto, the connectedness to an identity-shaping principled conviction, immediacy of involvement in the requested action and the willingness to perform an alternative service', at 214.

There are strong arguments against the accommodation of conscientious objection by healthcare professionals. For instance, a general accommodative approach is courting the risk of impeding access to healthcare services and burdening some doctors with inequitable workloads. Moreover, an argument can be made that the decision to join the medical profession is, after all, voluntary.[20] Some of these arguments have already been addressed in detail in previous chapters. The arguments about access to services and problems with workloads, in particular, relate to Category 4 harms which include harm as practical costs; and these are addressed by my model.

For some bioethicists, doctors should not have the right to refuse medical assistance in dying, abortion or contraception as a matter of principle.[21] However, such uncompromising approaches are insensitive and generally unsuitable in the medical context. Attempts to cleanse the medical sphere of religious claims or religious perspectives is bound to impoverish the debate and obstruct the search for solutions to the challenges posed by modern bioethics and new medical technologies.[22] Rather, the needs and voices of different parties should be taken seriously and balanced against institutional considerations. A conscientious objection to offering certain treatments should be, in principle, available to healthcare professionals. This includes exemptions from participating in abortion and end-of-life practices since these are issues on which a wide range of reasonable views exist.[23] The core question here is how expansive a scope ought to be given to exemptions or religious claims. For Mary Neal, 'the appropriate question is whether the action from which the individual seeks to be exempt would render her *morally responsible* for the outcome she perceives as immoral'.[24] Moreover, Neal argues that conscientious objection is based on an ethical position by its very nature and cannot be construed to exclude basic acts of care owed to vulnerable others. In this sense, religious and ethical claims are self-limiting in that they cannot extend to situations to exclude emergency care.[25]

Healthcare professionals are subject to a range of professional duties including, most centrally, a duty of care towards their patients. This duty enjoins the medical practitioner who refuses to participate in certain practices to refer patients to another professional who does not hold a similar objection on a particular issue. In the UK case of *Greater Glasgow Health Board v Doogan* two Roman Catholic

---

[20] U Schuklenk and R Smalling, 'Why Medical Professionals Have No Moral Claim to Conscientious Objection Accommodation in Liberal Democracies' (2017) 43 *Medical Ethics* 234.

[21] J Savulescu and U Schuklenk, 'Doctors Have no Right to Refuse Medical Assistance in Dying, Abortion or Contraception' (2017) 31 *Bioethics* 162.

[22] D Callahan, 'Religion and the Secularization of Bioethics' (1990) 20 *The Hastings Center Report* 2.

[23] RP George, 'Public Reason and Political Conflict: Abortion and Homosexuality' (1996) 106 *Yale Law Journal* 2475.

[24] M Neal, 'When Conscience isn't Clear: Greater Glasgow Health Board v Doogan and Another [2014] UKSC 68' (2015) 23 *Medical Law Review* 668, 678.

[25] ibid.

midwives objected to participating in procedures leading to the termination of a pregnancy.[26] In *Doogan*, the Supreme Court stated:

> Whatever the outcome of the objectors' stance, it is a feature of conscience clauses generally within the health care profession that the conscientious objector be under an obligation to refer the case to a professional who does not share that objection. This is a necessary corollary of the professional's duty of care towards the patient. Once she has assumed care of the patient, she needs a good reason for failing to provide that care. But when conscientious objection is the reason, another health care professional should be found who does not share the objection.[27]

Moreover, it is advisable that institutions adopt a balanced approach to religious claims in the medical context so that religious claims be given serious consideration within the framework of an appropriate policy that identifies the key issues, conflicts and desirable outcomes. Daphne Gilbert suggests that healthcare providers should avoid adopting an official stance on the most 'contested moral social issues' such as medical assistance in dying[28] which is preferable because healthcare providers have a duty to avoid or limit the potential to discriminate between patients. It follows that the individual patient's right of access to core healthcare services and medical treatment trumps other considerations. This does not preclude attempts to devise accommodative policies. In fact, the UK's General Medical Council guidelines neatly summarise key principles that healthcare professionals ought to follow in that regard:

> 13. If it's not practical for a patient to arrange to see another doctor, you must make sure that arrangements are made – without delay – for another suitably qualified colleague to advise, treat or refer the patient.
>
> 15. You must not obstruct patients from accessing services or leave them with nowhere to turn.
>
> 16. Whatever your personal beliefs about the procedure in question, you must be respectful of the patient's dignity and views.[29]

Thus, healthcare professionals may submit requests for religious accommodation under conditions that guarantee not only the patient's safety, access to treatment and to alternative therapy options but also uphold the patient's dignity and, generally, do not impose excessive practical costs. Thus, accommodating the beliefs and values of healthcare professionals need not necessarily result in a poorer provision of services or negligence, if appropriate frameworks and procedures are put in place.

---

[26] *Doogan & Anor v NHS Greater Glasgow & Clyde Health Board* [2013] ScotCS CSIH 36.
[27] ibid para [40].
[28] D Gilbert, 'Faith and/in Medicine: Religious and Conscientious Objections to MAiD' (2020) 43 *Dalhousie Law Journal* 657.
[29] *Personal Beliefs and Medical Practice* (GMC, 2013).

Moreover, there is the question of exemptions from vaccinations, which has become a pressing public health issue in light of the Covid-19 pandemic. Recently, a case in the UK concerned the dismissal of a care worker who refused to take the Covid-19 vaccine on religious grounds. The claimant, as a lifelong Roman Catholic, reasoned that the vaccine was prohibited because it 'involved the use of foetal blood' and might interfere with DNA in the nucleus of cells.[30] The Employment Tribunal accepted that the claimant's refusal was connected with moral concerns and was 'closely linked to the longstanding Catholic position on abortion and to the resulting opposition to the use of stem cells or foetal material in medical experiments of any sort' and were 'part and parcel of a fundamental view about the sanctity of human life'.[31] A range of arguments on mandatory vaccination exists, but the various debates about their respective validity fall outside the scope of this book. However, it is important to recognise that exemptions from vaccinations present an acute problem. The reasons for vaccine scepticism appear to arise from various 'religious' and 'nonreligious' sources. The stakes are high as the issues raised by the debates are multi-faceted and involve questions about state power, public health policy, and individual rights. One view on exemptions to mandatory vaccination is that objections should be reviewed by taking the *intensity* of a person's refusal against being vaccinated into account.[32] This overly subjective approach that prioritises an individual's perception is, however, problematic in the context of a public health emergency. Intensity alone – measured as it is in terms of subjective predispositions – is an insufficient criterion because harm caused to others is a crucial consideration at the balancing stage in the medical context. Nevertheless, calls for dialogue with groups holding different positions are welcome since issues raised in the context of public health policy are inextricably linked to a number of social and political issues.[33] More specifically, this area requires research, public campaigns and community engagement since an exclusive focus on individual autonomy is insufficient. Taking this into account, the medical context is highly sensitive, and hard and fast exclusionary rules should be avoided unless Category 1 or 2 harms are incurred. Otherwise, a flexible approach that is tailored to the patient's needs is preferable and should include at least the following points, as set out in the guidelines for the medical context.

---

[30] *Patrycja Wierowska v HC-One Oval Limited* Case Number: 1403077/2021 (2022), para 2.
[31] ibid para 23.
[32] M Navin, 'Prioritizing Religion in Vaccine Exemption Policies' in K Vallier and M Weber (eds), *Religious Exemptions* (Oxford, Oxford University Press, 2018).
[33] J King et al, 'Mandatory COVID-19 vaccination and human rights' (2022) 399 *The Lancet* 220. The authors conclude that 'exemptions for religious beliefs or freedom of conscience are not generally required by human rights law', thus glossing over the complexities of mandatory vaccination and conscientious objections.

Guidelines

---

(1) The Medical Context

- Religious accommodation in the medical context is dependent on who makes a religious claim or request for accommodation.
- As a starting point, both healthcare professionals and patients should be able to make requests for accommodation, although different considerations apply in each case.
- Patients reserve the right to refuse a specific course of treatment, and religious reasons might constitute legitimate reasons for the refusal.
- However, where a refusal based on a religious claim is made, healthcare professionals should engage with patients in a non-judgemental and non-confrontational way in order to understand the latter's reasoning, values and wishes and ascertain the extent to which accommodation is possible.
- Healthcare professionals should engage with the families of patients when it is appropriate to do so in order to improve the process of consent and treatment.
- The feasibility of claims should be tested against my model of four categories of harm.
- Claims made by healthcare professionals should be permissible, if:
- They are consistent with their professional obligations and duties. These duties can be interpreted in light of the four categories of harm where appropriate.
- The health and safety of others (primarily the patients) is priority and the strongest reason for non-accommodation.
- Access to health services should not be obstructed by a religious claim.
- The dignity of patients should be a consideration so that any claims that are accommodated are implemented with sensitivity and discretion.
- Category 4 types of harm are, ideally, to be mitigated by healthcare providers who should consider how they might devise accommodative policies so that certain kinds of exemptions might be granted to healthcare professionals.

III. Religious Accommodation and Contesting Children's Autonomy

It is not uncommon for religious freedom to be in conflict with what is deemed to be appropriate for realising the rights of children. In particular, limits to the right of FORB must be interpreted in light of the emerging children's right to an 'open future'.[34] Thus, the question of the autonomy of children is a topical issue that has increasingly moved to the centre of legal debates, as evidenced by the growing body of case law on children's rights. To what degree should children be considered (partially) autonomous individuals? Which values should legitimately shape the framework in which choices concerning children's welfare can be made? A nuanced account of autonomy is necessary in this case: one that takes into consideration the larger familial, cultural, religious and social context in which the child lives. My model of religious accommodation can be applied to the autonomy of children subject to specific modifications. Whilst the categories of harm remain relevant, the difference here lies in the way interests are balanced, as will be demonstrated in this section. In other words, a more nuanced and contextual approach to interpreting harms to autonomy is necessary in the case of children.

The central role that parents play in determining what they deem the 'best interests' of their children means that protecting the latter's rights and their autonomy is a multi-faceted task. As pointed out in previous chapters, prohibiting certain religious practices is often intrinsically linked to the need to respect the autonomy of the individual. Whilst Mill's harm principle focuses on individual liberty, its application to cases concerning children can be problematic as such cases engage the limits of parental rights that are themselves undergoing a process of evolution in accordance with larger changes in social values. An additional challenge is posed by the fact that *some* religious practices might result in a *future* harm by limiting the child's ability to make certain choices later in life. It is not always clear, then, whether it is the religious freedom of the parents, the autonomy of the children or some other (cultural) interest that is in need of legal protection. The religious and/or cultural beliefs of one or both parents can result in potential harm to children's autonomy. Examples come readily to mind, and these include requiring or encouraging children to wear religious clothing, participate in religious ceremonies, or receive a religious education. In some cases, parents might disagree between themselves about the religious upbringing of their child(ren). Assessing two controversial case studies that include (i) religious education and (ii) non-therapeutic male circumcision, this section will outline possible solutions to the conflicting interests at stake. These case studies have been selected not only because they are controversial and are the subject of litigation, but also because they raise key questions about what counts as 'harm for autonomy of others'. Education is an ongoing process which requires cooperation and coordination between different parties, whilst male circumcision is a one-time, limited invasive procedure. Thus, what exactly constitutes 'harm to autonomy' is in need of further elaboration.

There are a number of legal sources for the protection of children's rights. International human rights law guarantees the right of FORB of both parents

---

[34] DM Weinstock, 'How the Interests of Children Limit the Religious Freedom of Parents' in C Laborde and A Bardon, *Religion in Liberal Political Philosophy* (Oxford, Oxford University Press, 2017).

and children. The importance of spiritual development is codified in the Geneva Declaration on the Rights of the Child 1924: 'The child', it states, 'must be given the means requisite for its normal development, both materially and spiritually ...'[35] The right of parents to bring up their children in accordance with their religious beliefs is, moreover, protected by Article 18(4) of the ICCPR:

> The States Parties to the present Covenant undertake to have respect for the liberty of parents and, when applicable, legal guardians to ensure the religious and moral educa- tion of their children in conformity with their own convictions.[36]

The UN Convention on the Rights of the Child 1989 (UN CRC) creates an obliga- tion on states to protect the 'best interests' of the child. Article 2 of the UN CRC protects children from discrimination on the grounds of protected characteristics including religion. Parents also have the right under international law to raise their children in accordance with their religious and philosophical beliefs. Moreover, Article 14 of the UN CRC provides:

(1) States Parties shall respect the right of the child to freedom of thought, conscience and religion.
(2) States Parties shall respect the rights and duties of the parents and, when applica- ble, legal guardians, to provide direction to the child in the exercise of his or her right in a manner consistent with the evolving capacities of the child.

Parent's rights are not unlimited and must be balanced against the child's best interests and the legitimate interests of the state in governing family and private life. Whilst John O'Neill argues that children have been largely missing in liberal individualistic theories, there has been a recent shift towards involving children in decisions.[37] Article 5 of the UN CRC states:

> States Parties shall respect the responsibilities, rights and duties of parents or, where applicable, the members of the extended family or community as provided for by local custom, legal guardians or other persons legally responsible for the child, to provide, in a manner consistent with the evolving capacities of the child, appropriate direction and guidance in the exercise by the child of the rights recognized in the present Convention.

There is now more attention paid towards how children are treated by the law and the justice system.[38] The notion of 'Child Friendly Justice' has been coined for the purpose of developing and fostering an approach that views children as active

---

[35] Geneva Declaration of the Rights of the Child of 1924, adopted 26 September 1924, League of Nations.
[36] International Covenant on Civil and Political Rights (ICCPR), adopted and opened for signature, ratification, and accession by General Assembly Resolution 2200A (XXI) of 16 December 1966 and entered into force on 23 March 1976 (999 UNTS 171).
[37] J O'Neill, *The Missing Child in Liberal Theory: Towards a Covenant Theory of Family, Community, Welfare and the Civic State* (Toronto, University of Toronto Press, 1994).
[38] See H Stalford and K Hollingsworth, '"This case is about you and your future": Towards Judgments for Children' (2020) 83 *Modern Law Review* 1030.

participants in decision-making processes. For instance, the Council of Europe has issued explicit Guidelines on Child Friendly Justice which include the following five core principles: child-friendly justice is accessible, age-appropriate and allows the child to participate in the proceedings; it has the child's best interests as its main focus; it safeguards the child's integrity and dignity; it offers protection from discrimination; and, finally, it is in general compliance with the rule of law.[39] The recent UK case *Re A: Letter to a Young Person* has been hailed as a landmark judgment for its open and accessible approach to decisions affecting children.[40] Thus, there is a legal, policy, and social shift towards involving children both at different stages of decision-making processes and in different kinds of decisions. However, the issue as to whether simply a more 'individualistic' notion is applied to children whereby they have increasing autonomy, or whether their autonomy is limited and/or considered to be rooted within their familial and cultural context remains unresolved.

A. Religious Claims in Education

This section addresses key issues raised by requests made by parents to exempt their child from specific classes at school. Exemptions in education and from classes at school have recently garnered considerable public attention. The school has become a hotly contested 'battlefield' for ideological claims in the 'culture wars'.[41] A recent report on religion and belief in schools in the UK recommended, amongst other things, that the 'right of parents to withdraw their children from the Religion, Belief and Values part of the curriculum should be removed'.[42] Such calls for prohibiting exemptions are partly based on the view that the scope of parental authority in educational institutions and decision-making should be narrow(er). The educational context is doubly important because (a) it concerns the limits of parents' autonomy vis-à-vis their children; and (b) it concerns the proper role of the state in the educational process, that is, in a matter that straddles the private/public divide. The debates about religion and education in recent years have centrally revolved around the question of home schooling, the kind of religious education provided (whether it pervades the entire syllabus or not), as well as the appropriateness of granting exemptions to pupils from studying certain topics

---

[39] Council of Europe, Guidelines of the Committee of Ministers of the Council of Europe on child-friendly justice (Strasbourg, Council of Europe, 2010).

[40] *Re A: Letter to a Young Person* [2017] EWFC 48.

[41] See M Gordon, *Education in a Cultural War Era: Thinking Philosophically about the Practice of Cancelling* (New York and London, Routledge, 2022).

[42] C Clarke and L Woodhead, 'A New Settlement Revised:Religion and Belief in Schools' (July 2018) Westminster Faith Debates, available at https://d3hgrlq6yacptf.cloudfront.net/615b4ef7da3cc/content/pages/documents/re-newsetrevised-pdf-2018.pdf., at 48.

such as evolutionary theory or attending sex education classes. It is not readily clear what a child's bests interests are in such cases.

i. Exemptions from School Attendance and State Supervision of Education

The desire to entirely remove a child from the jurisdiction of state education is highly controversial. Home schooling is permissible in some jurisdictions such as the UK,[43] and prohibited in others such as in Germany. In the ECHR case of *Konrad v Germany*, the applicants challenged Article 7 of the German Constitution, referred to as the Basic Law 1949 (*Grundgesetz*), which requires the state to supervise the education of all children. The applicants were Christians, who emphasised the centrality of the Bible to their worldview and therefore argued that 'their children's attendance of a primary school would inevitably lead to grave conflicts with their personal beliefs as far as syllabus and teaching methods were concerned'.[44] The applicants pointed out that 'by teaching their children at home, they were obeying a divine order'.[45] On the one hand, Article 4 of the Basic Law protects the religious freedom of the parents whilst Article 6(2) provides that 'the care and upbringing of children is the natural right of parents and a duty primarily incumbent upon them'. On the other hand, Article 6(2) of the Basic Law requires the State to supervise parents in the upbringing of their children. Moreover, Article 7 of the Basic Law places schooling and the formal education process under state control. The issue, therefore, was whether home-schooling was consistent with Article 7 of the Basic Law. The Federal Constitutional Court opined that attending primary school was mandatory and in the children's best interests especially as mingling with children from other backgrounds in school is essential for gaining a first experience of society and to acquire basic social skills.[46] The Court further reasoned that young children would be unable to foresee the consequences of home-schooling.[47] After the Federal Constitutional Court had refused to consider a constitutional complaint, the applicants decided to appeal to the ECtHR but were ultimately unsuccessful. The ECtHR pointed to the lack of a general consensus on compulsory attendance of primary schools amongst contracting states, and was satisfied that the need for acquisition of knowledge and the goal of societal integration were justifiable reasons for mandatory state supervision of education.[48]

---

[43] See www.gov.uk/home-education. The conditions for home-schooling are, comparatively speaking, not stringent. Section 7 of the Education Act 1996 merely states the following: 'It shall be the duty of the parent of every child of compulsory school age to cause him to receive efficient full-time education, suitable to his age, ability and aptitude and to any special educational needs he may have either by regular attendance at school or otherwise.'

[44] *Konrad v Germany* (2007) 44 EHRR SE8, at 6.

[45] ibid.

[46] ibid 7.

[47] ibid 2.

[48] ibid 7.

Konrad v Germany can be contrasted with the earlier US case *Wisconsin v Yoder*, which also revolved around a challenge to compulsory school education.[49] In *Wisconsin v Yoder* members of the Amish community were convicted for violating a law enacted in the State of Wisconsin that required children to attend school up to the age of 16. The parents refused to send their children to a public or private school once they had graduated from the eighth grade, that is, when the children were aged 14–15. The Supreme Court held that the State's interest in providing universal education was not free from a balancing process, in particular if it risked infringing other constitutional rights, for example, the right of parents to raise their children in accordance with their religious beliefs. The Supreme Court therefore held in favour of the Amish community and granted an exemption.[50]

Justice Douglas's dissenting opinion in *Wisconsin v Yoder* was, however, closer to the reasoning of the judges in *Konrad v Germany* as he argued that children's rights should have been afforded more weight than the religious beliefs of the parents.[51] Justice Douglas favoured an approach that prioritised the children's (current and future) autonomy over the parents' beliefs and autonomy. In cases such as *Konrad v Germany* and *Wiscon v Yoder*, it is not only the rights and autonomy of the interested parties that are at stake: there is a broader question about the form and level of education that the state is expected to provide to all children. The state has a social interest in children's education, as is emphasised in *Wisconsin v Yoder*:

> ... courts must move with great circumspection in performing the sensitive and delicate task of weighing a State's legitimate social concern when faced with religious claims for exemption from generally applicable educational requirements.

There a number of relevant considerations when it comes to determining social concerns. Autonomy, as a principle, can be invoked to justify both giving permission for home-schooling *and* prohibiting it. Arguably, education is a 'semi-reversible process', and, therefore, home-schooling does not *permanently* undermine the autonomy of the children since the latter can acquire knowledge later on in life, although the lack of a well-rounded education is likely to put them at a disadvantage vis-à-vis other children. If home-schooling is permitted, however, it does not follow that all state supervision is bound to be suspended. Appropriate safeguards and review processes can be implemented subject to available resources. Moreover, the opinion and views of the children about their own education gain in significance as they become older and might want to enter into the school system. Whilst parents remain the primary decision-makers of their children's education, Rachel Taylor argues that 'the outer limits of that discretion are increasingly constrained by a secular vision of responsible religious parenting'.[52] What this entails exactly

---

[49] *Wisconsin v Yoder* (406 US 205 (1972) at 213–15.
[50] ibid.
[51] ibid para 242.
[52] RE Taylor, 'Responsibility for the Soul of the Child: The Role of the State and Parents in Determining Religious Upbringing and Education' (2015) 29 *International Journal of Law, Policy and the Family* 215.

is subject to litigation and public debates. In this context, a conception of harm inevitably has cultural and social dimensions that inform what is considered to be an 'over reach' on the part of the state or the parents respectively. To effectively address such issues, ultimately requires public debate and an informed state level policy. To be sure, caution should be exercised when devising policies that allow home-schooling since the risks of a lower standard of education due to a lack of state supervision are high.

ii. Exemptions from Specific Classes and Topics

Exemptions from specific parts of the school curriculum are less problematic than a wholesale attempt to evade the state's supervision of education. In cases concerning specific exemptions, the religious beliefs of the parents must be balanced against the children's right to a comprehensive and well-rounded education. Specific exemptions are more manageable as they are narrow and limited. In the ECHR case of *Folgerø v Norway*, the applicants were members of the Norwegian Humanist Association who requested that their children be exempted from the Christianity, Religion and Philosophy class (KRL).[53] Norway had implemented educational reforms in the years 1993 to 1997, during the course of which it was decided that both the topics of religion and philosophy should be taught together whilst Christianity should be the central focus of the class.[54] The Norwegian Parliament had been advised that exemptions should be limited to certain aspects of the subject such as the participation in religious rituals.[55] Therefore, there existed an option for parents to request a *partial* exemption. The Norwegian Humanist Association, however, requested a *full* exemption from KRL,[56] a claim that was unsuccessful in the domestic courts. Eventually, the ECtHR held by a narrow majority of 9–8 that there had been a violation of Article 2 of Protocol 1 (the right to education) of the ECHR. The Court reasoned that 'non-Christian parents were faced with a greater burden than Christian parents, who had no reason for seeking an exemption from the KRL subject, which was designed in accordance with the premises of the majority'.[57] The ECtHR found that the state had not taken sufficient care to ensure that the information and knowledge which was part of the curriculum was conveyed in 'an objective, critical and pluralistic manner', thus going against Article 2 of Protocol 1.[58] The dissenting opinion, however, argued that Christianity was the state religion of Norway and an integral aspect of the history of the country.[59]

---

[53] *Folgerø v Norway* (2008) 46 EHRR 47.
[54] ibid paras 15–17.
[55] ibid para 15.
[56] ibid para 27.
[57] ibid para 52.
[58] ibid para 102.
[59] ibid.

Given the interest of the state in providing a holistic education, an exemption from a particular class or part of the school syllabus should not be granted solely on the grounds that an individual (or parent) dislikes or disagrees with a specific topic. The starting principle should be that all children should be taught the same syllabus. The syllabus itself should include a range of appropriate topics that include various religious and philosophical views. The teaching of controversial topics should not be equated with automatic indoctrination or as a form of coercion to believe or endorse specific disputed worldviews. Educational exemptions should be limited precisely because of the educational benefits children derive from learning about different views, as this best prepares them to make decisions and facilitates their future autonomy.

Folgerø v Norway contrasts with *Dojan v Germany*. In the latter case, Christian parents requested the ability to exempt their children from sex education classes.[60] The parents argued that 'their children had not attained the level of maturity necessary for sex education classes'.[61] Moreover, the parents deemed the textbooks used in class to be partly pornographic and, therefore, contrary to Christian sexual ethics.[62] The ECtHR held that the claim was inadmissible, thus agreeing with the previous decision of the courts [the District Court, Court of Appeal and the Federal Constitutional Court] in Germany:

> Sex education for the concerned age group was necessary with a view to enabling children to deal critically with influences from society instead of avoiding them and was aimed at educating responsible and emancipated citizens capable of participating in the democratic processes of a pluralistic society – in particular, with a view to integrating minorities and avoiding the formation of religiously or ideologically motivated 'parallel societies'.[63]

The ECtHR noted that the parents could still educate their children in line with their worldviews outside the school.[64] Compulsory sex education had already been addressed by the European Commission in *Kjeldsen, Busk Madsen and Pedersen v Denmark*, where the 'compulsory nature' of sex education and the 'manner of delivery' were unsuccessfully challenged by the applicants.[65] Exemptions from sex education should be limited because the health and safety of children should be accorded priority. However, it might be possible for schools to formulate flexible policies with input from parents in order to balance different interests to the extent possible.

---

[60] *Dojan v Germany* (2011) 53 EHRR SE24.
[61] ibid para 12.
[62] ibid.
[63] ibid para 65.
[64] ibid para 69.
[65] *Kjeldsen, Busk Madsen and Pedersen v Denmark* (1979–80) 1 EHRR 711 Series A, No 23.

The importance of a balanced syllabus was emphasised in *Hasan and Eylem Zengin v Turkey*. In this case, the applicant and his family being followers of Alevism, the father requested that his daughter be exempted from the religious culture and ethics classes. He argued that the compulsory religious class was incompatible with the principle of secularism.[66] The ECtHR held that whilst priority to Islam over other religions and philosophies was not in and of itself a breach of the principles of pluralism and objectivity,[67] it was essential that knowledge be disseminated in an 'objective, critical and pluralist manner'.[68] The Court held that there had in fact been a breach of Article 2 of Protocol 1 of the ECHR. Moreover, the Court found that the procedure for obtaining an exemption was flawed as it required those who did not adhere to majority Sunni Islam to disclose their beliefs during the process of obtaining an exemption.[69] Furthermore, in the ECtHR case of *Osmanoğlu and Kocabaş v Switzerland* a conflict of interests arose when parents objected to their daughters attending mixed swimming classes and an exemption was not granted.[70] The ECtHR held that the refusal of the state authority to exempt the children from swimming classes constituted an interference with applicants' right to their freedom of religion but that it did not constitute a breach of their rights. The Court emphasised the school's role in facilitating the integration of the students from various backgrounds and held that exemptions from certain lessons could be justified under exceptional, well-defined conditions.[71] However, rather than focus on the issues relating to ethnicity and identity, the Court could have grounded its reasoning in health and safety consideration given that swimming is a necessary life skill.

In sum, the importance of including both religious and non-religious views as part of school curricula should not be diluted as a general matter of principle[72] and the question of permitting exemptions and opt-outs should only be a secondary question. Some studies suggest, for example, as in the UK, the 2016 Casey Review that 'schools in certain areas face difficulties with reaching out to parents and in persuading them to not withdraw their children from school activities such as swimming or visiting the theatre'.[73] The reasons for why parents make exemption claims are varied. There is, therefore, a need for the feasibility and practicability of accommodation to be considered on a case-by-case basis and in accordance with

---

[66] *Hasan and Eylem Zengin v Turkey* (2008) 46 EHRR 44.
[67] ibid para 63.
[68] ibid para 64.
[69] ibid para 76.
[70] *Osmanoğlu and Kocabaş v Switzerland* App no 29086/12 (ECtHR, 10 January 2017).
[71] ibid.
[72] See S Juss, *High Court Ruling on Religious Education: Legal Guidance on What it Means for Local Authorities, Academies, Schools, Teachers, Agreed Syllabus Conferences, and SACREs* (2016).
[73] Dame Louise Casey, 'The Casey Review: A Review into Opportunity and Integration' (5 December 2016).

a more holistic vision of education codified in policy backed by empirical research on the relevant issues.

Additionally, there has been litigation concerning the admissions poli-cies of educational institutions including schools and university. The UK case *R (E) v Governing Body of JFS* concerned the admissions policy of a faith school that refused admission of an applicant (E) because the conversion of his mother (M) to Judaism was not recognised by the Office of the Chief Rabbi. Thus, M did not satisfy the Orthodox test of Jewish status. The UK Supreme Court had to decide whether the school's admission policy constituted direct or indirect discrimination on the grounds of race.[74] The Court held the 'JFS discriminates in its admission requirements on the sole basis of genetic descent by the maternal line from a woman who is Jewish, in the Mandla as well as the religious sense. I can see no escape from the conclusion that this is direct racial discrimination'.[75] Thus, the school policy was reviewed for its compatibility with anti-discrimination and equality law. Likewise, *Trinity Western University, et al v Law Society of Upper Canada* concerned religious freedom, the rights of LGBTQ+ students, and equality.[76] Trinity Western University (TWU) is a private Christian university in Langley, British Columbia, that wanted to enact a Code of Conduct that prohibited sexual intimacy except within marriage between a man and a woman. The Code would apply to both students and faculty on and off campus. The Supreme Court of Canada held that the decision of the Law Society of British Columbia to not accredit Trinity Western University's proposed law school were reasonable and represented a proportionate balance between the Charter rights of equality and religious freedom. Specifically, the majority held that the Law Society of Upper Canada was entitled to conclude that equal access to the legal profession, diversity within the bar, and preventing harm to LGBTQ+ law students were all within the scope of its duty to uphold the public interest. Admissions policy in the context of education should attract higher scrutiny since education is a fundamental public good that ought to be accessible to as many as possible. Due to this, religious autonomy should be curtailed in favour of the educational autonomy of others. This argument could also be developed in the direction of supporting the need to protect 'the adequacy of options'.

The above issues demonstrate that, as the harms to autonomy in this area are complex and multi-faceted, an *individual* conception of autonomy does not offer ready answers, although that does not mean that autonomy is not an important value. Accordingly, guidelines in this area ought to be subject to periodic review and revision since this area depends on wider educational

---

[74] *R (E) v Governing Body of JFS* [2009] UKSC 15.
[75] ibid para [46].
[76] *Trinity Western University et al v Law Society of Upper Canada* [2018] 2 SCR 453.

policies too. However, some core principles can help to anchor and fashion a coherent approach:

Guidelines

(2) Children's Rights
(a) Education
<ul><li>Full exemptions from school attendance and from state supervision of education should generally not be permitted because they risk harming a child's future autonomy since it is difficult to guarantee a home-schooling education that is holistic and of a high quality.</li><li>Home-schooling should only be permissible if certain strict conditions are met. These should include the following: state supervision; adherence to a standard syllabus; and periodic review and scrutiny of home-schooling practices.</li><li>The education curriculum should be delivered in 'an objective, critical and pluralistic' manner as is required by the jurisprudence of the ECtHR.</li><li>Specific exemptions from classes should be considered on a case-by-case basis and be limited in scope.</li><li>Exemptions from specific classes or topics should not be granted where they would undermine a child's right to a holistic education.</li><li>The child's best interests should be a guiding principle.</li><li>Exemptions from controversial topics such as sex education and evolutionary theory should not be permitted, especially if the exclusion causes harm such as in the case of sex education.</li></ul>

B. Non-therapeutic Male Circumcision

Non-therapeutic male circumcision, also referred to as religious or ritual circumcision, is a prime example of a hard case where balancing the rights of the parents and the rights of the child is difficult. Male circumcision raises questions about the current and future decision-making capacities of the child. Whilst parents are responsible for making ongoing choices about the welfare of their children, the rights of parents are not absolute and are subject to restrictions and state supervision. Increasingly, male circumcision has come under scrutiny. Arguments against male circumcision include that it is unnecessary, invasive and, at worst, a harmful form of mutilation. Parallels are drawn between the practice of Female Genital

Mutilation (FGM) and male circumcision.[77] Whilst FGM is unlawful in most jurisdictions, male circumcision remains lawful in some liberal states.[78] There are several issues at stake: is male circumcision unsafe *in and of itself* or is harm contingent upon how the circumcision is carried out, for example, by medically untrained staff? Should the familial and cultural context determine the extent to which male circumcision undermines the autonomy of a child? This section will survey select key arguments defending and criticising male circumcision before proposing a way forward that is based on a more holistic and contextual notion of harm that takes into account cultural and religious sensitivities without devaluing the all-important 'best interests' of the child.

Male circumcision can be characterised as both an individual *and* a familial and cultural practice. Generally, it is only carried out if the family decides in favour of it. This is usually for religious purposes as male circumcision is widely practised amongst Jewish and Muslim communities. Male circumcision raises questions about the moral and social dimensions of harm which feed into notions of autonomy.[79] Susan Mendus points out that infant male circumcision is peculiarly problematic for liberals because it brings together issues on which liberalism is itself conflicted and uncertain on.[80] The extent to which the parents should be able to decide to circumcise their male child centrally turns on how much autonomy should be ascribed to the interested parties. Different areas of law tend to characterise the individual differently – with family law accommodating more embedded constructions of the individual.[81] It is evident that there is no immediate correct answer provided by the notion of 'harm to the autonomy of others' on how exactly to regulate male circumcision. After all, it is disputed whether any harm occurs in the first place, whether autonomy is important enough a principle to justify banning such a practice and whether the 'others', that is, the children, can be appropriately engaged.

Male circumcision potentially engages a number of human rights including the following: Article 8 of the ECHR (right to respect for private and family life); Article 9 of the ECHR (right to religion or belief); and, to some extent, also Article 3 of the ECHR (freedom from torture and inhuman or degrading treatment or punishment). For some critics, both FGM and male circumcision result in significant harm(s). Kai Möller, for instance, argues that cutting children's genitals

---

[77] See K Möller, 'Male and Female Genital Cutting: Between the Best Interest of the Child and Genital Mutilation' (2019) *Oxford Journal of Legal Studies* 1.

[78] FGM is a crime in EU Member States: https://ec.europa.eu/commission/presscorner/detail/en/ QANDA_21_402. Male circumcision is lawful in many jurisdictions globally, see for example 'Neonatal and child male circumcision: a global review' UNAIDS/10.07E – JC1672E, available at https://www. malecircumcision.org/sites/default/files/document_library/Neonatal_child_MC_global_review.pdf.

[79] S Baum, 'Religious Circumcision: Free from Interference?' (1999) *UCL Jurisprudence Review*.

[80] S Mendus, 'Infant Male Circumcision in the Public Square: Applying the Public Reason of John Rawls' (2013) 3 *Global Discourse* 230.

[81] PW Edge, 'Male Circumcision after the Human Rights Act 1998' (2000) 5 *Journal of Civil Liberties* 320, 337.

is always wrong as the principle of personal freedom requires certain intimate decisions that relate to bodily integrity to not be made by parents.[82] Yet, this view is far from universal, as is shown by systematic studies on male circumcision from medical perspectives.[83] Moreover, some scholars criticise how European states have framed the practice of Non-therapeutic male circumcision through the use of secularisation and 'analogising strategies' that have led to a misrepresentation of this practice and hence to a further stigmatisation of already marginalised religious communities.[84] Members of the Jewish and Muslim communities by and large voluntarily 'choose' to practise infant male circumcision, but this argument of voluntary choice exercised by the community does not provide a sufficient reason in favour of either permitting or banning male circumcision on its own. The question for many liberals is whether family religious cohesion is enough to trump (the potential for) individual choice.[85] This section analyses some of these complexities before outlining some recommendations.

i. International Practice, Guidelines and Select Cases

There are a number of cases and guidelines from across the globe that attempt to clarify the justification, permissibility and scope of male circumcision. Surveying these is useful to extrapolate some key emerging principles that can serve to better govern this area and ensure consistency across jurisdictions. As a starting point, Article 12 of the UN CRC 1989 highlights the need for children 'to be heard':

> States Parties shall assure to the child who is capable of forming his or her own views the right to express those views freely in all matters affecting the child, the views of the child being given due weight in accordance with the age and maturity of the child.[86]

This means that children who have reached an age by which they are able to express their views should be given information on any procedure that affects them and offered an opportunity to voice their opinions.[87] In the case of 'older' children, these principles are applicable. The problem in the context of male circumcision is that this procedure is very often carried out on babies and very young children.

The World Health Organization (WHO) has approved of the practice of male circumcision provided that it is carried out under strict medical and hygienic

---

[82] Möller (n 77).

[83] BJ Morris et al, 'Critical Evaluation of Arguments Opposing Male Circumcision: A Systematic Review' (2019) 12 *Journal of Evidence Based Medicine* 263.

[84] L Salaymeh and S Lavi, 'Religion is Secularised Tradition: Jewish and Muslim Circumcisions in Germany' (2021) 41 *Oxford Journal of Legal Studies* 431.

[85] A Scolnicov, *The Right to Religious Freedom in International Law Between Group Rights and Individual Rights* (London, Routledge, 2011).

[86] Convention on the Rights of the Child (CRC), adopted and opened for signature, ratification, and accession by General Assembly Resolution 44/25 of 20 November 1989 and entered into force on 2 September 1990 (1577 UNTS 3).

[87] UN Committee on the Rights of the Child (CRC) General Comment No 12 (2009) 'The right of the child to be heard' CRC/C/GC/12.

conditions.[88] More specifically, the WHO has since 2007, in conjunction with the Joint United Nations Programme on HIV/AIDS (UN AIDS), 'recommended voluntary medical male circumcision (VMMC) as an important strategy for the prevention of heterosexually acquired HIV in men in settings where the prevalence of heterosexually transmitted HIV is high.'[89] Despite such official WHO endorsement, the medical benefits of male circumcision are, however, still open to debate.[90]

Across jurisdictions, a range of approaches has been adopted to regulate non-therapeutic male circumcision. In the US, whilst the number of infant males being circumcised has decreased,[91] the American Academy of Paediatrics concluded that the health benefits of circumcision during the neonatal period outweigh the risks.[92] Thus, male circumcision, if it is to be performed, is best performed earlier rather than later, which means that the child's exclusion from the decision-making process on this issue is unavoidable.

In the UK, a specific statute regulating non-therapeutic male circumcision is absent. Rather, the common law suggests that male circumcision is lawful provided that both parents consent to it. For example, in *R v Brown* Lord Templeman stated:

> Even when violence is intentionally afflicted and results in actual bodily harm, wounding or serious bodily harm the accused is entitled to be acquitted if the injury was a foreseeable incident of a lawful activity in which the person injured was participating. Surgery involves intentional violence resulting in actual or sometimes serious bodily harm but surgery is a lawful activity. Other activities carried on with consent by or on behalf of the injured person have been accepted as lawful notwithstanding that they involve actual bodily harm or may cause serious bodily harm. Ritual circumcision, tattooing, ear-piercing and violent sports including boxing are lawful activities.[93]

There is no general principle that establishes that the religious beliefs of parents automatically prevail. The case law demonstrates that the rights of parents are qualified. For example, in the UK case of *R (on the application of Williamson) v Secretary of State for Education and Employment* the parents argued that their belief in corporal punishment was an aspect of their religious belief. The House of

---

[88] World Health Organization and Department of Reproductive Health and Research and Joint United Nations Programme on HIV/AIDS (UNAIDS), 'Male Circumcision: Global Trends and Determinants of Prevalence, Safety and Acceptability' (2007), available at www.who.int/publications/i/item/978-92-4-000854-0.

[89] ibid.

[90] BJ Morris et al, 'The Medical Evidence on Non-therapeutic Circumcision of Infants and Boys – Setting the Record Straight' (2022) *International Journal of Impotence Research: Your Sexual Medicine Journal.*

[91] See www.worldpopulationreview.com/state-rankings/circumcision-rates-by-state.

[92] See www.publications.aap.org/pediatrics/article/130/3/585/30235/Circumcision-Policy-Statement?autologincheck=redirected.

[93] *R v Brown* [1993] 2 All ER 75, HL, per Lord Templeman.

Lords held that the harm that resulted from corporal punishment against children outweighed the beliefs of parents.[94] Lady Hale stated:

> Children have the right to be properly cared for and brought up so that they can fulfil their potential and play their part in society. Their parents have both the primary responsibility and the primary right to do this. The state steps in to regulate the exercise of that responsibility in the interests of children and society as a whole. But 'the child is not the child of the state' and it is important in a free society that parents should be allowed a large measure of autonomy in the way in which they discharge their parental responsibilities. A free society is premised on the fact that people are different from one another. A free society respects individual differences.[95]

The beliefs and views of parents or professionals, accordingly, do not necessarily trump the interests of the children or the state.

Some case law suggests that both parents must consent to non-therapeutic male circumcision. In the UK case of *Re J* a non-practising Muslim father applied to the court for an order in favour of circumcising his son because of the opposition of the boy's non-Muslim mother.[96] The court held in favour of the mother and emphasised that both parents must give their consent to the intervention.[97] Wall J held that the child's 'essentially secular upbringing' meant that it was not necessary for the children to undergo circumcision in order for him to fit within his family and social life.[98] However, Suhraiya Jivraj and Didi Herman argue that the Court's analysis in *Re J* reveals a particular biased understanding of religion and identity and that the court failed to appreciate fully the broader cultural issues at stake.[99] The cultural context of the family thus remains an important factor in determining whether harm to autonomy is identified and to what degree.

In the UK, the British Medical Association (BMA) guidelines on male circumcision state that male circumcision is presumed to be lawful provided it meets the following conditions: the procedure is to be performed competently, in the best interests of the child, and is based on valid consent.[100] The guidelines are useful in that they outline some minimum requirements. The BMA recognises the inconclusiveness of current research on the health benefits of male circumcision.[101]

---

[94] In *R v Secretary of State for Education and Employment and others* [2005] UKHL 15 per Lady Hale at para [86]. Lady Hale emphasised the need for the state to uphold its positive obligation to protect children from inhumane or degrading treatment.
[95] *R (on the application of Williamson) v Secretary of State for Education and Employment and Others* [2005] UKHL 15, para [72].
[96] 'Non-practising' as cited in the case.
[97] *Re J* [1999] 2 FLR 678, FD; *affirmed* [2000] 1 FLR 571, CA.
[98] ibid.
[99] S Jivraj and D Herman, 'It is Difficult for a White Judge to Understand': Orientalism, Racialisation, and Christianity in English Child Welfare Cases' (2009) 21 *Child and Family Law Quarterly* 283: 'A focus on the child's lack of consent not only masks the impositions taking place on the child's body by virtue of a failure to circumcise; such arguments also *produce* western modernity by relegating circumcision to a pre-modernity practice of unreason and pain' at 296.
[100] British Medical Association, 'The Law and Ethics of Male Circumcision Guide' (2006).
[101] ibid.

Its guidelines hold that parental preference for circumcision alone is insufficient and that additional medical factors must be considered by doctors when deciding whether to perform this surgical procedure.[102] Among the additional factors, the BMA includes any potential health risks to the child, the views of parents and family, as well as the latter's religious and cultural background. Thus, doctors should try to understand the broader context in a given case before making a decision.[103] Matt Gibson and his colleagues find the BMA's somewhat 'neutral' stance surprising.[104] They rather argue for statutory regulation of ritual male circumcision, noting that the current lack of regulation in the UK is a cause for concern.[105] They propose a generic prohibition on non-therapeutic male circumcision and advocate for an approach that 'medicalises the procedure' so that it can *only* be performed by qualified medical professionals.

'Automatic' and blanket bans are likely to be unhelpful in achieving communal cohesion. In 2012, a case on male circumcision in Germany made global headlines. The case concerned a doctor who faced criminal charges for performing a circumcision of a four-year old boy.[106] The circumcision was carried out for non-medical reasons and in accordance with the religious and cultural beliefs of the parents. The child began to bleed heavily due to complications and was rushed to a hospital where the state authorities took charge of the case. The doctor who had performed the circumcision was subsequently charged under criminal law. The Cologne Court (*Landgericht Köln*) held that male circumcision that had not been medically indicated was unlawful under section 223 of the German Criminal Code (*Strafgesetzbuch*), which provides for the offence of causing bodily harm. The judgment by the German Cologne Court focused on the autonomy of the child. The Court held that the right of the child to bodily integrity and self-determination ultimately outweighed the rights of the parents to religious freedom.[107] Its reasoning reflected a particular conception of autonomy that was couched in *individualised* terms. In other words, male circumcision was construed to limit severely the child's current and future autonomy. In the aftermath of the case and its media repercussions, the German Parliament amended the law to include a specific legal exemption that permits male circumcision.[108] The law does not require parents to demonstrate a religious motivation for the procedure, but limits are placed on male circumcision where it would be against the child's best interests.[109] The term

---

[102] ibid.
[103] ibid.
[104] M Gibson et al, 'Ritual Male Circumcision in the United Kingdom' in V Fortier (ed), *La Circoncision Rituelle: Enjeux de Droit, Enjeux de Vérité* (Strasbourg, Strasbourg University Press, 2016).
[105] ibid.
[106] *Landgericht Köln*, 151 Ns 169/11, 7 May 2012.
[107] ibid.
[108] R Merkel and H Putzke, 'After Cologne: Male Circumcision and the Law. Parental Right, Religious Liberty or Criminal Assault?' (2012) 39 *Journal of Medical Ethics* 444.
[109] A Dutta, 'Between Openness and Restriction: German Family Law and Multicultural Challenges' in N Yassari and MC Foblets (eds), *Normativity and Diversity in Family Law Lessons from Comparative Law, Global Studies in Comparative Law* (Cham, Spring, 2022) 271–72.

'best interests' is subject to interpretation and has recently been understood in a way that takes a child's increasing independence into account.[110]

However, debates at the European supra-national level persist. For example, the Parliamentary Assembly of the Council of Europe passed Resolution 1952 on 'Children's Right to Physical Integrity' in October 2013. Cross-jurisdictional approaches only serve to illustrate the need for a balanced and negotiation-friendly approach. As Marie-Claire Foblets argues, 'a different approach is needed than simply asserting that one group is right and the other wrong, if we are truly to speak of sustainable accommodation of these differences'.[111]

ii. Mediating Conflicting Views and Interests

The practice of male circumcision is evidently grounded in various religious or cultural reasons and is subject to evolving notions of harm that, in turn, shape conceptions of autonomy. In other words, harm in this context is not neutral since harm to autonomy depends on how the 'best interests' of the child are interpreted. There is no one single answer that will satisfy all parties, and male circumcision will likely remain a controversial hard case. The scientific evidence is unable to supply a definitive answer. Not every risk to one's health and safety should pass the threshold needed to justify non-accommodation of a religious claim. The question is whether male circumcision causes a significant harm to a child's health; once the specific kinds of harms (to health and safety etc) have been identified. Currently, there is insufficient empirical evidence to conclude that circumcised males suffer significant harm and barriers in life. The potential harmful effects of circumci-sion include risks from the actual procedure itself; lack of autonomy deriving from non-participation in the decision; loss of bodily tissue; and mental harm as a long-term, traumatic side-effect of circumcision. Risks from the actual procedure can be minimised by ensuring that it is performed by medically qualified staff.

Moreover, many comparisons are made between FGM and male circumcision. Although there are some arguments that apply to both cases, there are also key differences that need to be highlighted. In the UK case *Re B and G (Children) (No 2)*, the court stated:

> It is at this point in the analysis, as it seems to me, that the clear distinction between FGM and male circumcision appears. Whereas it can never be reasonable parenting to inflict *any* form of FGM on a child, the position is quite different with male circumci-sion. Society and the law, including family law, are prepared to tolerate non-therapeutic male circumcision performed for religious or even for purely cultural or conventional reasons, while no longer being willing to tolerate FGM in any of its forms. There are,

---

[110] ibid 270.
[111] MC Foblets, 'The Body as Identity Marker: Circumcision of Boys Caught between Contrasting Views on the Best Interests of the Child' in M Jänterä-Jareborg (ed), *The Child's Interests in Conflict* (Cambridge, Intersentia, 2016) 127.

after all, at least two important distinctions between the two. FGM has no basis in any religion; male circumcision is often performed for religious reasons. FGM has no medical justification and confers no health benefits; male circumcision is seen by some (although opinions are divided) as providing hygienic or prophylactic benefits. Be that as it may, 'reasonable' parenting is treated as permitting male circumcision.[112]

The Court emphasised that society and the law influence notions of permissibility. The distinction is important since FGM is criminalised in many jurisdictions and the moralising, loaded language which applies to FGM tends to obscure the issues at hand with regards to male circumcision. Whilst the arguments made against each practice are inter-related, the key difference lies in the degree of harm they cause in reality.

Even where male circumcision is carried out by a suitable medical practitioner and with the consent of both parents, the question of whether the *autonomy* of the child is harmed remains pressing. After all, male circumcision is mostly carried out on babies. For example, for many Orthodox Jews, male circumcision is essential to identity formation and is often performed on the eighth day after birth.[113] Some maintain that male circumcision violates the child's dignity because it constitutes a violent and irreversible act. Arguably, the autonomy and dignity of children must be contextualised in light of their best interests, which would be counteracted by measures bound to alienate them from their religious and cultural community. As Bijan Fateh-Moghadam argues, the wellbeing of the child is not an objectively defined essentialist entity and is open to different interpretations.[114] She argues that many decisions are in fact taken on behalf of children, and these decisions often include practices that concern bodily interventions. She concludes: 'Male circumcision is a relatively simple intervention that, if performed by trained professionals, has no negative health consequences and only a small risk of relatively light complications.'[115] The accommodation of male circumcision should primarily be guided by medical evidence. If medical evidence proves that male circumcision is clearly significantly harmful to the health and safety of children, then this would be the strongest reasons for non-accommodation. Moreover, the best interests of the child should be paramount. Yet as Marie-Claire Foblets points out, there are two contrasting interpretations of the child's best interests that can be summarised in the following way:

> on the one hand, an approach that links these interests to the incorporation of the child within the religion, tradition and group to which his parents (or one of them) belong

---

[112] *Re B and G (Children) (No 2)* [2015] EWFC 3, para [71].

[113] JM Glass, 'Religious Circumcision: A Jewish View' (1999) 83 *British Journal of Urology International* 17–21 for why male circumcision is regarded as an obligation under Jewish Law. I acknowledge that there is a diversity of opinions on the issue in both Judaism and Islam, but, for the sake of simplification, I take as representative the general view of a sizeable majority Jews and Muslims who regard circumcision of boys as mandatory.

[114] B Fateh-Moghadam, 'Criminalizing Male Circumcision? Case Note: Landgericht Cologne, Judgment of 7 May 2012 – No. 151 Ns 169/11' (2012) 13 *German Law Journal* 1131, 1137.

[115] ibid 1138.

and, on the other, a more individual conception of those interests that would endow the child with the right to make his own decision as soon as he has attained the necessary maturity to do so.[116]

Whilst the 'best interests' of the child is a central and over-arching principle, it can, nevertheless, be interpreted in opposing ways, and so cannot provide a holistic guide. The normative dimension in interpreting best interests and harms to autonomy are evident. Thus, different forms of mediation might be an appropriate option to resolve the issues raised by hard cases such as male circumcision. This is because mediation adopts a less adversarial approach that can be conducive to achieving relational autonomy in the medical context concerning children. Adam Shehata argues that in complex medical cases, bioethicists and mediators can assist parents and healthcare teams in finding a solution that works for everyone involved.[117] Mediation allows different parties to participate collectively, and in private, in order to arrive at non-legal solutions.

Evidently, there are limits to mediation, which include cases that would involve significant harm to the health of a child. In the Canadian case of *Hamilton Health Sciences Corp v DH*, a mother decided that her child should not receive chemotherapy and instead opted for traditional medicine in line with her First Nations' beliefs and rights.[118] The Ontario Court found in favour of the mother's rights, as protected by the Canadian Constitution, and held that the child did not need legal protection.[119] The child subsequently died. In such cases, religious and cultural rights that clearly harm the health and safety of others by endangering life or leading to death should not be accommodated.

The rights of the parents do not automatically trump children's rights, since treating doctors and the court also have jurisdiction over determining the child's best interests. In the headline-grabbing UK case *GOSH v Yates and Gard* the doctors believed that further medical treatment of a severely ill newborn was no longer of benefit. The Court held that it was in the best interests and lawful for artificial ventilation to be withdrawn and for the treating clinicians to offer palliative care only. The Court reiterated its jurisdiction and the limits of the powers of both the hospital and parents in such cases. The High Court emphasised the role of the courts in adjudicating on such complex cases: 'It is precisely because the hospital does not have power in respect of that child that this hospital makes an application to the court, to an independent judge, for a determination of what is in that child's best interests.'[120]

In summary, male circumcision is controversial because it is usually carried out before the decision-making capacity of children has been fully formed.

---

[116] Foblets (n 111) 126.
[117] A Shehata, 'Newfound Aboriginal Right to Pursue Traditional Medicine' (2016) 94 *University of Toronto Medical Journal* 38, 40.
[118] *Hamilton Health Sciences Corp v DH*, 2014 ONCJ 603 (CanLII).
[119] Shehata (n 117) 39.
[120] *GOSH v Yates and Gard* [2017] EWHC 1909 (Fam) para [18].

The case study of male circumcision highlights that competing conceptions of autonomy generate different outcomes. Male circumcision can be accommodated if the medical evidence does not demonstrate that the child's health and safety are compromised. Additional suggestions for moving forward include constructive debates within the framework of a deliberative model that takes seriously the various interests at stake.[121] The principles on non-therapeutic male circumcision set out in the guidelines ought to be incorporated within a dialogic framework that prioritises the best interests of the child, but placed within the context of that child's family.

Guidelines

(b) Non-therapeutic Male Circumcision

- Male circumcision is an example where relational autonomy that locates autonomy in its appropriate familial and cultural context is more important than individual autonomy since it usually concerns children whose best interests need to be assessed within their religious, social and cultural context.

- Risks to the health and safety of the child can be minimised if there is an over-arching framework that guides the procedure according to the following two key criteria: (i) the procedure is to be legally regulated; and (ii) it is to be carried out by a suitably qualified medical practitioner.

- A decision to circumcise a male child is inherently one that concerns the autonomy of several parties including the child and both parents.

- Both parents should agree and consent to male circumcision before it is carried out whether it be on the grounds of religious or cultural reasons.

- Male circumcision should always be carried out by a suitable and appropriately qualified medical practitioner.

- The best interests of the child override the interests of parents. This means that other factors aside from religious and cultural factors might need to be taken into consideration in a specific case when determining whether non-therapeutic circumcision should go ahead.

- However, the best interests of the child also include religious and cultural interests.

- The negotiation of competing interests is a preferable option for balancing relevant factors.

- In the case of conflicts between individuals, institutions or rights, mediation should be considered as the first best option as a way to come to an agreeable solution.

---

[121] R Cohen-Almagor, 'Should Liberal Government Regulate Male Circumcision Performed in the Name of Jewish Tradition?' (2021) 1 *SN Social Sciences* 21.

IV. Religious Organisations

This section briefly surveys select issues raised by the accommodation of religious organisations. Thus far, the focus has been on individuals, whereas religious organisations raise the question of whether it is group rights or individual rights that are in need of protection. The arguments relevant to the exemptions debate, such as the need to ensure equality and the rule of law, as discussed in chapter two, apply to religious organisations since many would argue that religious organisations should not be exempt from generally applicable laws. Arguments in favour of institutional autonomy are controversial since, in the case of organisations, an exemption can have far-reaching consequences. Critics have cast doubt on the argument that the interests of religious should benefit from exemptions since the claim that such organisations protect individual autonomy is not empirically proven across the board.[122] Using the example of *Ashers Bakery*, Stephanie Collins argues that religious organisations and individuals do not automatically converge. She argues that even 'if it is true that – to respect and protect individuals' autonomy or identity – individuals should be free not to endorse messages they disagree with, this individual freedom is not infringed upon when an organisation of which they are a member endorses a message'.[123] Accordingly, she argues that cases like *Ashers* that concern a religious organisation or business do not justify exemptions from discrimination law on the grounds that it is the individuals/employees who need to be protected.

Tarunabh Khaitan points out that the 'right against religious discrimination' is separate from the right to religious freedom.[124] Inevitably, there are a number of normative approaches to the question of conflicting rights (religion vs freedom of expression and religious freedom vs freedom from discrimination). The issue, however, is about the limits of accommodating religious organisations in *different* spheres. To what extent should religious organisations be permitted to proselytise, granted legal exemptions, and be able to require their members to adhere to specific moral codes? This section will briefly survey key examples and offer some guidelines.

A. A Multitude of Types of Accommodation

The institutional accommodation of religious organisations in liberal states takes many different forms. There are at least four layers of accommodation: the *first* is

---

[122] S Collins, 'Are Organizations' Religious Exemptions Democratically Defensible?' (2020) 149 *Dædalus, the Journal of the American Academy of Arts & Sciences* 105.
[123] ibid 109.
[124] T Khaitan, 'Two Facets of Religion: Religious Adherence and Religious Group Membership' (2021) 34 *Harvard Human Rights Journal* 231.

the formal constitutional establishment of religion. This constitutes official recognition of a state church. The *second* is a form of 'informal' or weak establishment that grants to some religions or religious organisation limited state recognition and attendant legal privileges. For example, certain religions can register as public law corporations in Germany and, as a consequence, can collect taxes from their respective constituencies.[125] This kind of arrangement represents a form of constitutional recognition, but it falls short of full constitutional entrenchment of religion. The *third* layer includes examples of specific official state accommodation within clearly defined limits such as religious charities or faith schools. Finally, the *fourth* layer encompasses a range of religious organisations, which might include associations and for-profit organisations. In light of their multi-layered integration into the fabric of civil society in liberal states, religious organisations thus constitute a hard case for my model of accommodation. These layers are not 'set in stone' and might differ across jurisdictions depending on the legal regulations. It is instructive to first reference the ECtHR's guiding principles since these are fairly well developed, although its jurisprudence could benefit from a more coherent approach.

i. The European Court of Human Right's Guiding Principles

Whilst the ECtHR has established a number of key principles to regulate the accommodation of religious organisations, there remains confusion as to the conceptual basis of some of its key decisions. The jurisprudence of the Court confirms that formal Church establishment does not in and of itself violate the rights guaranteed in the ECHR. As has been noted, whilst 'public authorities are under no obligation to provide an identical legal status to each community, the Court will control with severity the conformity with the Convention of advantages granted exclusively to one religious community which must rest on a legitimate justification and remain proportionate'.[126] However, establishing religious law would breach the ECHR as was held in *Refah Partisi (Welfare Party) v Turkey*.[127] Beyond these core norms, the ECtHR has developed a number of principles on Article 9 and religious organisations which include the following: state neutrality, moral pluralism, and institutional autonomy.

Neutrality towards religions and internal matters is a key principle that has been formally entrenched in many decisions handed down by the ECtHR, and specifically, in the context of religious organisations. For instance, *Hassan and Chaush v Bulgaria* concerned an internal dispute about the validity of leadership within the

---

[125] See also J Gesley, 'The Relationship Between Church and State in Germany Library of Congress' (6 December 2016), available at https://blogs.loc.gov/law/2017/12/the-relationship-between-church-and-state-in-germany.

[126] Ovey and White quoted in F Tulkens, 'The European Convention on Human Rights and Church-State Relations Pluralism vs. Pluralism' (2008–2009) 30 *Cardozo Law Review* 2575, 2585.

[127] *Refah Partisi (Welfare Party) and others v Turkey* App Nos 340/98 (2002) 35 EHRR 3.

Muslim community in Bulgaria. The ECtHR found a breach of Article 9 because the government recognised and supported one leader over another and thus failed to remain neutral.[128] The application of neutrality has already been discussed in chapter three. Relatedly, pluralism is another core principle informing the ECtHR's jurisprudence regarding Article 9. Conceptually complex, pluralism can be defined in religious, philosophical, legal and political terms.[129] It is not entirely clear which category of pluralism the Court upholds and to what degree. Religious legal pluralism has been explicitly rejected by the ECtHR in *Refah Partisi (Welfare Party) v Turkey*[130] because the enactment of Islamic law is deemed to be 'incompatible with democracy and human rights – in particular because sharia law defines the political regime'.[131] Moreover, religious organisations are not to be accommodated where they seek to change the democratic order. Arnout Nieuwenhuis argues that the ECtHR's case law on pluralism will continue to be interesting since pluralism is used to reconcile individual liberties with group interests.[132]

The ECtHR also protects the institutional autonomy of religious organisations. In *Obst and Schüth v Germany*, two employees of the Church were dismissed from their positions because they had extra-marital affairs and thus breached the Church's moral code. In *Siebenhaar v Germany* an employee of a nursery that was run by a Protestant parish was dismissed for being a member of another religious organisation named the Universal Church/Brotherhood of Humanity.[133] The ECtHR affirmed in both cases that religious organisations have the right to require their employees to adhere to their respective religious rules and principles.[134] Moreover, the ECtHR has held that states might be subject to positive duties to protect religious groups. In *Members of the Gldani Congregation of Jehovah's Witnesses v Georgia* a violent group of Orthodox Christians attacked a congregation of Jehovah's Witnesses.[135] In particular, the Court found the case investigator to be biased and noted that there had been a lack of proper investigation into the incident. These procedural failings constituted a violation of Articles 3 and 9 of the ECHR.

The ECtHR has also sought to protect minority Christian groups from state interference. The Court found a violation of Article 9 of the ECHR in *Association for Solidarity with Jehovah Witnesses v Turkey* where private premises

---

[128] *Hasan and Chaush v Bulgaria* App no 30985/96 (2002) 34 EHRR 55, para 78.

[129] See A Nieuwenhuis, 'The Concept of Pluralism in the Case-Law of the European Court of Human Rights' (2007) 3 *European Constitutional Law Review* 367, 367.

[130] *Refah Partisi* (n 127) para 43.

[131] ibid para 72.

[132] Nieuwenhuis (n 129) 384.

[133] *Obst v Germany* App no 425/03 (ECtHR, 23 September 2010); *Schüth v Germany* App no 1620/03 (ECtHR, 23 September 2010) and *Siebenhaar v Germany* App no 18136/02 (ECtHR, 3 February 2011).

[134] L Vickers, *Freedom of Religion or Belief and Employment Law*, 2nd edition (London, Hart Publishing, 2016).

[135] *Members of the Gldani Congregation of Jehovah's Witnesses and others v Georgia* App no 71156/01 (ECtHR, 3 May 2007).

used by a group of Jehovah witnesses were closed down by state authorities.[136] Similarly, in *Jehovah's Witnesses of Moscow v Russia* state authorities were found to have breached Articles 9 and 11 of the ECHR because they had dissolved the applicant community.[137] The Russian government argued that the dissolution of the association had been necessary since the 'Jehovah's Witnesses alienated their followers from their families, intimidated believers, controlled the minds of the believers, and incited civil disobedience and religious discord'.[138] However, the ECtHR held that there was insufficient evidence to support these claims.[139]

The accommodation of religious organisations is further complicated by the fact that it is sometimes necessary to interpret Article 9 in light of Article 11 (freedom of assembly and association). In *Metropolitan Church of Bessarabia v Moldova*, the Metropolitan Church of Bessarabia applied for official state recognition, but its application was refused by the government.[140] The government alleged that the case actually concerned an ecclesiastical conflict within the Orthodox Church in Moldova which could be resolved only by the Romanian and Russian Orthodox Churches.[141] The government argued that the application for recognition, and the administrative issues, were concealing the political conflict between the Churches in Romania and Russia.[142] In a letter dated 20 July 1999 the Prime Minister refused recognition on the grounds that the Metropolitan Church of Bessarabia was not a religious denomination in the legal sense but a schismatic group within the Metropolitan Church of Moldova.[143] The government submitted that it was bound by the duty of neutrality to not interfere with the dispute, and moreover, that if recognition were to be granted it would 'be detrimental to the independence and territorial integrity of the young Republic of Moldova'.[144] However, the ECtHR held that the Moldovan government's decision was not proportionate and held that there had been a breach of Article 9 of the ECHR.[145] The ECtHR stated 'since religious communities traditionally exist in the form of organised structures, Article 9 must be interpreted in the light of Article 11 of the Convention, which safeguards associative life against unjustified State interference'.[146]

Moreover, in the case of *Moscow Branch of the Salvation Army v Russia*, the Salvation Army had officially operated in Russia from 1913 onwards before it was dissolved on the grounds that it was an 'anti-Soviet organisation' in 1923.

---

[136] *Association for Solidarity with Jehovah Witnesses and others v Turkey* App nos 36915/10 and 8606/13 (ECtHR, 24 May 2016).
[137] *Jehovah's Witnesses of Moscow v Russia* App no 302/02 (ECtHR, 10 June 2010).
[138] ibid para 22.
[139] ibid paras 128–29.
[140] *Metropolitan Church of Bessarabia and others v Moldova* App no 45701/99 (2001) para 96.
[141] ibid para 23.
[142] ibid para 98.
[143] ibid para 28.
[144] ibid para 98.
[145] ibid para 130.
[146] ibid para 118.

In 1992, the Salvation Army was permitted to register again as a legal entity.[147] Yet in 1999, the Russian government refused an application for re-registration on the grounds that the association was allegedly operating on behalf of a foreign religious organisation. The Russian government's deep suspicion of foreign NGOs and foreign influence in general was a factor in its refusal. The Court found a breach of Articles 11 and 9 of the ECHR since there was nothing to preclude the Salvation Army in Russia from being a 'Russian organisation' – regardless of whether its head office was in London.[148] The ECtHR's role in this regard was, however, controversial due to the political dimensions of the case.

In sum, the jurisprudence of Article 9 of the ECHR permits the following forms of religious accommodation: the formal establishment of a church; financial support for religions organisations and schools even if one religion receives more state resources than others; and state regulation over some religious clergy.[149] Accordingly, a diverse set of arrangements between the state and religions are permissible. This section has merely sketched out some of key principles to illustrate the dimensions of religious organisations and institutional autonomy.

ii. Challenges at the National Level

Modern liberal states have adopted a range of approaches to accommodating religious organisations. This section surveys developments and selects key examples of accommodation. It does not aim to provide a comprehensive or exhaustive account of the role of religious organisations in liberal states. Instead, the examples serve to illustrate the various ways in which religious organisations present a challenge for the liberal state. Following this, some guidelines will be offered as a way to address some of the challenges.

a. Official and Quasi-Official Recognition

The challenge posed by official or quasi-official recognition of religious organisations lies mainly in the fact that legal privileges may be afforded to one religious group over another. There may be historical and cultural reasons to preserve the status quo and ensuring that one religion retains constitutional recognition. For example, in England, 26 Lords Spiritual are members of the House of Lords, but proposals for reform are not a priority. Church establishment, by definition, is the official entrenchment, either in a weak or strong form, of the dominant religion. Other religious groups often seek to obtain the same or similar forms of recognition and its attendant benefits. The liberal state, then, has to ensure that

---

[147] *Moscow Branch of the Salvation Army v Russia* App no 72881/01 (ECtHR, 5 October 2006) para 12.
[148] ibid paras 81–95.
[149] See C Evans and C A Thomas, 'Church-State Relations in the European Court of Human Rights' (2006) *Brigham Young University Law Review* 699, which outlines these in detail.

its institutional and democratic processes are neutral, fair and uphold equality *to some degree.* Thus, there is room for disagreement as to the degree of fairness afforded to different religious organisations and groups.

Representation has been a key problem for some minorities such as Muslim groups in some European states. For example, in Germany, Muslim groups have struggled to obtain forms of official state recognition. Recent attempts by the German government to foster better state–Muslim relations have included the establishment of the German Islam Conference in 2016, which hosted the first 'institutionalised' dialogue between representatives of the government and of Muslim communities in Germany with the purpose of finding practical solutions on issues where there are conflicts between German laws and Islamic practices such as in family law. Tobias Müller comments that 'the [German Islam Conference], as an unprecedented intervention into the regulation of Islamic organizations and individuals in Germany, poses a number of challenges to the self-understanding of the German state as secular'.[150] Active involvement of the state in religious affairs inevitably puts pressure on certain dimensions of state neutrality.

The problem of how to deal with religious organisations has also given rise to controversy in the French context, where attitudes towards new or minority religions have generally been characterised by scepticism. In France, there is a way in which religious organisations can obtain the status of a legal personality. This status can be attained either by registering as an association under the 1901 Law of Association or under the 1905 Law on the Separation of the Churches and State.[151] Although the 1905 Law instituted the principle of strict secularity of the French state and prohibited state funding of religions, there is still room for state funding of religious organisations if, and only if, the purpose of a particular activity is *secular.*[152] This has led to some interesting accommodations of religion where religious purposes have been reinterpreted in secular terms, as in the case of the acquisition and repair of a Church organ;[153] the construction of an elevator in the Basilica of Lyon in the interests of tourism;[154] and, in the context of Islamic Eid festivities, allowing a local slaughterhouse to meet the sanitary requirements in the interests of public safety.[155] Eoin Daly submits that these cases demonstrate that the threshold for public interest has been set quite low, thereby allowing for

---

[150] T Müller, 'Constructing Islam and Secularism in the German Islam Conference' in P Anderson and J Hargreaves (eds), *Muslims in the UK and Europe*, Centre of Islamic Studies, University of Cambridge February 2017, 50.

[151] See J Gunn, 'Religious Freedom and Laicite: A Comparison of the United States and France' (2004) 2 *Brigham Young University Law Review* 419, 977.

[152] E Daly, 'Public Funding of Religions in French Law: The Role of the Council of State in the Politics of Constitutional Secularism' (2014) 3 *Oxford Journal of Law and Religion* 103, 105–09.

[153] Commune de Trélazé, 19 July 2011, no 308544, as cited in Daly (n 152) 103–26.

[154] *Fédération de la libre pensée et de l'action sociale du Rhône*, MP, 19 July 2011, no 308817, as cited in Daly (n 152) 103–26.

[155] *Communauté urbaine du Mans, Le Mans métropole*, 19 July 2011, no 309161, as cited in Daly (n 152) 103–26.

the accommodation of religious activities through public financing.[156] Financial support provided to religious organisations is obviously a significant form of religious accommodation.

b. New Religious Movements and the Recognition of 'New' Religions

Many liberal states are skeptical, if not outright hostile, towards 'new religious movements'. Thus, several approaches towards 'new religious movements' have emerged across liberal states. Part of the question is definitional and normative: what should count as religion? Some states like the UK have generally adopted a wide and relatively generous approach to new religious organisations. For example, the Church of Scientology was recognised as a valid religion, specifically for the purposes of registering marriages. This approach contrasts starkly with the one followed by both the French and German governments, which have treated the Church of Scientology with suspicion.[157]

In Germany, new religious movements or organisations have faced barriers to accommodation because very strict criteria are applied in deciding which religious organisations are eligible to obtain the status of public corporation. In general, religious groups can apply for public corporation status, if 'their constitution and the number of their members offer assurance of their permanency'.[158] However, the accommodation of new religious organisations, in particular of Muslim groups, has proven difficult. There are a number of structural, political and legal reasons for this. In particular, some forms of accommodation such as the establishment of an official place of worship require explicit legal recognition which can be a lengthy process.

Often, a particular request for accommodation engages a range of rights and practices. Some of the complexities vis-à-vis the accommodation of religious organisations in the German context are illustrated by a key case on ritual slaughter. In 1998, the State of Hessen denied a permit for religious slaughter to a Muslim applicant on the grounds that the Quran does not specifically forbid the stunning of animals before slaughter.[159] The Animal Protection Act (*Tierschutzgesetz*) requires that animals for slaughter must be anaesthetised;[160] at the same time, it allows for religious slaughter, if the application for such an exemption is made by members of a religious community whose mandatory rules prohibit the prior stunning of animals.[161] The Federal Administrative Court interpreted the exemption

---

[156] Daly (n 152) 120.
[157] H Seiwert, 'Approaches to Alternative Religions Since 1989' (2003) 64 *Sociology of Religion* 367.
[158] W Heun, *The Constitution of Germany* (Oxford, Hart Publishing, 2011) 224.
[159] 'The Constitutional Court's "Traditional Slaughter" Decision: The Muslims' Freedom of Faith and Germany's Freedom of Conscience' (2002) 3 *German Law Journal*.
[160] *Tierschutzgesetz in der Fassung der Bekanntmachung vom 18 Mai 2006* (BGBl. I S. 1206, 1313), *das zuletzt durch Artikel 141 des Gesetzes vom 29 März 2017* (BGBl. I S. 626) *geändert worden ist.*
[161] See s 32 of the Animal Protection Act (*Tierschutzgesetz*).

for ritual slaughter narrowly and held that Islamic law allows for a departure from the general rule for Muslims in foreign countries on the grounds of feasibility and hardship.[162] Florence Bergeau-Blackler argues that the Court decided for itself that stunning methods are not unlawful in Islam and, accordingly, refused to extend the existing exemption already granted to Jews to the Muslim community.[163] However, the Federal Constitutional Court granted the exemption and also considered the request for an exemption in light of the applicant's constitutional right to practise his occupation. That is to say, the applicant also claimed that his right to occupational freedom was violated since, as a Muslim butcher, his practice had different and specific requirements.[164] Mathias Rohe commented on that case and stated that 'for the first time it was made clear that it is upon the Muslims in Germany alone to decide on their creed and needs'.[165]

New religious movements have not been treated favourably in France either. Fears were stoked by French politicians who alleged that such movements manipulate their followers.[166] In 1996, The International Cult Surveillance Center (L'Observatoire International des Sects) was created whilst in 1998 an Inter-Ministerial Mission for the Fight Against Cults was implemented.[167] The Ministry established a taxonomy for determining what counts as a 'sect' which included the following criteria: the number of adherents; eccentricity; newness; and the existence of an 'external origin'.[168]

Given the possibility of new religious constellations, what constitutes a 'new religion' is continuously open for debate. Do new interpretations of established religions count as a new religious movement? This is an increasingly complex question. For example, the range of Islamic groups within the European context has increased. The spectrum of Islamic organisations comprises perspectives from Islamic Salafi movements to Islamic liberal movements such as those started by the Turkish feminist lawyer, Seyran Ateş, who opened the first 'liberal mosque' in Berlin.[169] The increasing pluralism and 'cross-fertilisation' of religious ideas and the connections made through global and digital networks pose interesting and diffi-cult challenges for the liberal state. The recognition of new religious movements is fraught with definitional and practical problems which makes accommodation

---

[162] *Tierschutzgesetz in der Fassung der Bekanntmachung vom 18. Mai 2006.*

[163] F Bergeau-Blackler, 'New Challenges for Islamic Ritual Slaughter – A European Perspective' (2007) 33 *Journal of Ethnic and Migration Studies* 965.

[164] BVerfG, 1 BvR 1783/99 of 01/15/2002, paragraphs No (1–55).

[165] M Rohe, *Muslim Minorities & the Law in Europe* (Global Media Publications, 2007) 86.

[166] See JJ A Beckford, '"Laïcité," "Dystopia," and the Reaction to New Religious Movements in France' in JT Richardson, *Regulating Religion*, Critical Issues in Social Justice (New York, Kluwer Academic Publishing, 2004).

[167] S Palmer, *The New Heretics of France* (Oxford, Oxford University Press, 2011) 17.

[168] See J Robert, 'Religious Liberty and French Secularism' (2003) 2 *Brigham Young University Law Review* 637, 647–49.

[169] H Sherwood, 'Muslim Feminist plans to Open Liberal Mosque in Britain' *The Guardian* (26 July 2017), available at www.theguardian.com/world/2017/jul/26/seyran-ates-muslim-feminist-liberal-mosque-london-britain.

difficult to manage. The real challenge lies less in finding a permanent legal solution to the accommodation of new religious movements as such, and more in finding pragmatic, medium-term solutions such as enacting specific legislation regulating certain areas (such as charitable status, education, etc).

iii. Religion in Educational and Social Services

Religious organisations fulfil a number of crucial societal roles by providing, for instance, educational, social and charitable services. Official state recognition and state accommodation is necessary to provide some of these services, whilst in some cases it is not necessary depending on the specific laws of a state that regulate the legal status of the religious organisation and the service in question. As education and social services are public goods and support the welfare of society, religious organisations often 'fill in the gap' where the state has withdrawn from its role as service provider.

In the UK, there are large numbers of formal and informal religious organisations affiliated with both the major and minority religions. For example, there are numerous Islamic faith-based organisations, for which the Muslim Council of Britain serves as an umbrella organisation.[170] Campaigns such as 'how much does an imam earn'[171] demonstrate a shift of the priorities of minority religions, from setting up modest mosques to 'professionalising' their religion.

Religious education, whether delivered by secular or religious establishments, enables religious organisations to maintain a degree of social influence. In some states such as Germany, religious education is a mandatory subject. The content of the religious education module as well as the teachers for it are selected by the religious community itself.[172] This autonomy to set the syllabus and appoint teachers in the delivery of official religious education in schools is a concession made by the state to the established Churches. However, parents can request for their children to attend ethics classes as an alternative to religious education.

In Germany, religious and social welfare services are often intertwined. The Churches have considerable influence through the provision of welfare services. The two mainstream providers of social welfare services are the Catholic *Deutscher Caritas Verband*[173] and the Lutheran *Diakonisches Werk der Evangelischen Kirche*.[174] The former performs a range of services including running care centres, nursing homes, playschools and hospitals. It also has a social policy arm with a

---

[170] Muslim Council of Britain, see www.mcb.org.uk/about-mcb/affiliates.
[171] Imams Online, 'Imams Fair Wage Campaign', see www.imamsonline.com/imams-fair-wage-campaign.
[172] H de Wall, 'Religious Education in a Religiously Neutral State: The German Model' in M Hunter-Hénin (ed), *Law, Religious Freedoms and Education in Europe* (Farnham, Ashgate, 2012) 174–76.
[173] See www.caritas-germany.org/aboutus/whatwedo.aspx.
[174] See www.diakonie.de/english.

more activist agenda that seeks to influence government policy and is an employer for over a million people.[175] Similarly, the *Diakonisches Werk der Evangelischen Kirche* works with vulnerable groups and provides care to the elderly and children. Therefore, the significance of religion, and in particular the mainstream Churches in Germany, is evidenced not only by its membership size but also by its extensive provision of social and educational services. Moreover, the main Churches have their own religious education and training programmes that operate beyond state-supported universities. Thus, even if Germany does not have an established Church, religion is very present in the social and public spheres.

The role of faith-based organisations (FBOs) in the UK can be compared to their role in the German context. Göçmen notes that FBOs have always been a part of the UK's civil society. What is changing, however, is the government's direct encouragement of FBOs to provide social welfare and to purchase service contracts.[176] Two of the most successful Christian-based FBOs in the UK are the Salvation Army[177] and World Vision.[178] As in Germany, these FBOs provide key welfare services. According to Julian Rivers, under the New Labour government in the UK, welfare provision came to be treated in the typical 'third way' fashion: it was to be provided privately but regulated publicly so that, even if there was a new openness to faith-based welfare provision, the terms on which it was offered had substantially changed.[179] This is an interesting and subtle development that Rivers calls the 'secularisation of the British Constitution' since the very *terms* on which religion is dealt with by the state have been altered. More specifically, religious bodies or religiously motivated conscientious objections (for example, at the workplace) are now subject to human rights and equality legislation. Rivers argues that the shift in church–state relations is complex: instead of the state regarding religions as providing distinctive public services, in accordance with their own ethos, religious organisations have now been brought within the embrace of the state and are subject to its agenda and values.[180] An example of this is furnished by the case of *Catholic Care (Diocese of Leeds) v Charity Commission for England and Wales* where a Roman Catholic charity was denied an exemption from the requirement to offer its adoption services to homosexual couples.[181] Thus, even if the UK

---

[175] See www.caritas-germany.org/aboutus/socialpolicy.

[176] See I Göçmen, 'The Role of Faith-Based Organizations in Social Welfare Systems: A comparison of France, Germany, Sweden, and the United Kingdom' (2013) 42 *Nonprofit and Voluntary Sector Quarterly* 495, 503 and I-J Sand, 'Globalization and the Transcendence of the Public/Private Divide – What is Public Law under Conditions of Globalization?' in C Mac Amhlaigh et al (eds), *After Public Law* (Oxford, Oxford University Press, 2013) 202.

[177] See www.salvationarmy.org.uk.

[178] See www.worldvision.org.uk/who-we-are/about-world-vision and Göçmen (n 176) 503.

[179] J Rivers, 'The Secularisation of the British Constitution' (2012) 14 *Ecclesiastical Law Journal* 371, 395.

[180] ibid, 396.

[181] *Catholic Care (Diocese of Leeds) v Charity Commission for England and Wales* [2012] UKUT 395 (TCC).

approach to religion has traditionally been fairly liberal and accommodative, there have been important and subtle developments that point to a profound shift. To be precise, the secularisation and regulation of religion limits the autonomy of religious organisations whilst, at the same time, creating a 'market of options' for religious believers. What might appear to be a seemingly accommodative approach has the effect of a regulatory approach in practice. Thus, the different constellations of religious accommodation often present challenges for constitutional law given that the latter often rests on a binary understanding of church–state relations.[182] Currently, religious organisations are regulated in a myriad of ways, and as such, both employees and service-users might make requests for accommodation.

iv. Limits on Religious Organisations

This leads to a final set of arguments. It is arguable that religious accommodation in fact promotes the *regulation* of religion by secular state law. Regulation might lead to more or less autonomy for religions. In fact, it might prompt certain transformations of religious practice through codification by allowing constitutional law to delimit the appropriate boundaries of religion. The jurisdiction of the secular courts enables the multi-culturist approach to be litigated, as has been seen in the UK cases of *Eweida* and *Ladele*.[183] The case studies in France on religious organisations, moreover, demonstrate that religious accommodation takes place at various levels within a 'strict' secular constitutional framework. The case studies in Germany also reveal that the church–state model does not necessarily coincide with the complex realities in practice. In other words, local practices and non-legal solutions concerning the regulation of religion can disclose more about religious accommodation than the bare text of a Constitution or secularism as a constitutional norm. Ultimately, there is a need to put limitations on the accommodation of religious organisations so as to ensure that the secular legitimacy of the liberal state is secure. Central to this is preserving the principle of equality. Anat Scolnicov argues that the individual's rights should trump the rights of religious organisations since participation in religious communal life does not necessarily respect the rights of individuals.[184] Thus, religious organisations ought to be accommodated to the extent that they are consistent with the over-arching legal framework and individual rights. The balance can be difficult to strike and the following guidelines are not comprehensive in the sense that they cover, in detail, all aspects of the scope of religious organisations; rather, they offer a general framework. Moreover, there should be an 'exit' option.[185]

---

[182] O Müller et al, 'The Religious Landscape in Germany' in O Müller et al, *The Social Significance of Religion in the Enlarged Europe* (Farnham, Ashgate, 2012) 98.
[183] *Eweida and others v UK* App nos 48420/10, 59842/10, 51671/10 and 36516/10 [2013] ECHR 37 (ECtHR, 15 January 2013); *Ladele v London Borough of Islington* [2009] EWCA Civ 1357.
[184] Scolnicov (n 85) 220.
[185] See M Malik, *Minority Legal Orders in the UK: Minorities, Pluralism and Law* (London, British Academy, 2012).

The 'right to exit' should exist for every member of a religious organisation. However, it is not possible, nor desirable, for the law to regulate this aspect in detail. Such cases concern 'complex autonomy' where more attention needs to be paid to securing options for individuals.

Guidelines

---

(3) Religious Organisations

- The formal establishment of Church or religion should be subject to the requirements of secularism as a fundamental constitutional norm.
- This means any requests for accommodation that seek to undermine the liberal order will not be accommodated.
- Religious organisations that provide 'core' services should ideally obtain formal recognition so that they can be adequately regulated.
- Religious institutional autonomy should be protected to the extent that it does not harm the autonomy of others outside the organisation. This can be referred to 'internal' autonomy. Internal autonomy might mean that the organisation hires on a particular basis and subjects its employees to certain religious rules that might be contrary to the general equality laws. In this way, internal institutional autonomy constitutes an exemption.
- 'External institutional autonomy' refers to what a religious organisation can reasonably do outside of its internal institutional structure.
- External institutional autonomy should be limited by the implementation of regulatory frameworks that ensure compliance with core human rights obligations.
- Group-based exemptions should be available to a specific class of persons and limited in scope.
- Within a religious organisation, members are able to choose which parts of their autonomy and decision-making they will delegate to others, for example, to a specific religious leader or institution.
- There should be an 'exit' option. The 'right to exit' should exist for every member of a religious organisation. However, it is not possible, nor desirable, for the law to regulate this aspect in detail. Such cases concern 'complex autonomy' where more attention needs to be paid to securing options for individuals.

V. Conclusion

This chapter has addressed the challenge of using 'harm' as a normative guide for resolving the difficult conflicts raised by certain religious claims. Harm is multi-faceted, contextual, and variable. To that end, harm to autonomy might not offer a holistic justification for the non-accommodation of a religious claim. Indeed, in some cases autonomy is not the key principle or value that ought to be protected, as has been demonstrated by the difficult cases discussed in this chapter in the respective contexts of the medical field, children's rights, and religious organisa-tions. Nevertheless, autonomy remains relevant whether it is *the* principle, value or aim that ought to be protected or is merely a subsidiary interest. Moreover, my model can be applied to the 'hard' cases albeit in a modified form. In cases where capacity is partially or fully lacking or where multiple parties are concerned it is important to take into account the complexities of the notion of harm itself. Ultimately, since religious accommodation helps to achieve substantive equal-ity and uphold personal autonomy, hard cases should not deter institutions from implementing standards that are consistent, flexible and practically oriented, such as the guidelines offered in this book.

7

Conclusion

The right to FORB will continue to pose difficult questions for liberal states. As has emerged from the discussion in previous chapters, the right to FORB is complex, contested, and subject to a range of different approaches. Whilst the international, regional and national laws that protect religious freedom set out broad grounds for limitations, there is an urgent need for a principled approach to defining limits to religious freedom. This book has sought to address this need by approaching the question of religious accommodation from the perspective of limitations to religious claims. The justification for non-accommodation of religious claims is a difficult task: on what grounds and how do we limit religious claims of free and equal citizens in a liberal democracy? Perfectionist liberalism offers a promising way forward on the issue of determining the scope of accommodation of religion in a liberal state; it does, however, not provide easy answers to the multi-faceted quandaries posed by religious claims. This book has made a modest contribution to the literature on the relationship between state, law and religion by proposing a model of religious accommodation that focuses on how religious claims can harm the autonomy of others. By proposing a categorisation of different kinds of harm, I have outlined a workable model that can be applied in practice.

*

The book set out to identify the key challenges of the right to FORB and argued that the case for religious accommodation is based on multiple reasons. I offered five arguments in favour of religious accommodation which include the protection of identity, substantive equality, the dignity of the individual, and personal autonomy, as well as its usefulness as a flexible policy tool. One of the challenges of religious accommodation is that it not only presupposes a clear definition of religion – an inherently complex phenomenon – but that possible definitions ultimately depend on the methodological approach adopted. In addition, the debate on whether religion is 'special' does not resolve the problem of when exactly, and on what basis, religious claims ought to be accommodated. Whilst there are different approaches to determining the scope of the right to FORB, current dominant approaches have been problematic. In particular, the principle of neutrality does not pay sufficient attention to deep conceptual problems raised by religion. Neutrality has often been pinpointed as the principle centrally at stake in religious cases. Yet, it has been applied in a rather inconsistent manner by decision-makers in cases on religious freedom. As highlighted recently in the CJEU cases of *Achbita, Bougnaoui* and *IX and MJ v Germany*, neutrality has resulted in limited outcomes for religious believers.[1] This does not mean that neutrality is not relevant to determining the scope of the right to religion or belief, especially since secularism as a constitutional norm is now being regarded as fundamental to the liberal state's legitimacy. However, the existence of different versions of secularism and neutrality calls for conceptual clarity and consistency. Decision-makers, courts and employers across liberal jurisdictions have advanced various arguments about the different kinds of harm that result from different religious claims. This area of law is currently very messy. To somewhat clear up the attendant confusion, my model has sought to systematise the different kinds of harm-based arguments and proposed a general categorisation of four key harms. My model includes the four following categories of harm: dangers to health and safety; limited or blocked access to goods and services; violations of dignity; and excessive practical costs. My model offers practical and effective guidelines that can be applied in various contexts including hard cases. Religious claims require a value judgement to be made. The principle of autonomy should be the guiding principle and normative foundation for religious accommodation in liberal democracies. By supplying normative criteria that could guide decision-making on religious accommodation, the book has argued that religious accommodation can be made more manageable in overall alignment with liberal principles.

* *

The increase of religious diversity and ethical pluralism means that the complexities of the right to FORB will continue to pose serious challenges for liberal states. It is evident that religious freedom is an important right worthy of protection. Yet this does not mean that religion trumps other interests. Raymond Plant's question of whether religion must be adapted in order to be considered acceptable to the liberal state therefore remains a persistently relevant question even for Cecile Laborde's minimal secularism. This is so because Laborde's thesis, similar to Habermas' secular political legitimacy of the state, must grapple with the complexity of what would be deemed illiberal religion. The answer to this conundrum is far from clear, especially as many kinds of religions espouse a conservative morality that is largely at odds with the core principles of the liberal, post-secular state and the latter's increasing tendency to protect the 'right to an open future' and highly personalised fluid identities. Moreover, the political conditions that encourage religion to be perceived as inherently illiberal and

---

[1] Case-157/15 *Samira Achbita and Centrum voor gelijkheid van kansen en voor racismebestrijding v G4S Secure Solutions NV* EU:C:2017:203; Case C-188/15 *Asma Bougnaoui and Association de d fense des droits de l'homme (ADDH) v Micropole SA, formerly Micropole SA* EU:C:2017:204; C-804/18 and C-341/19 *IX v WABE eV and MH Müller Handels GmbH v MJ* EU:C:2021:594, decision handed down on 15 July 2021.

anti-modern are also complex phenomena. The point here is that it would be naïve to assume that liberal states and their institutions, including the constitutional courts, have merely participated in a neutral project of promoting human rights. Human rights are always also political and engender particular political claims against the state. These political questions are intermeshed in complex ways with different versions of secularism, which produce different constitutional interpretations of the right to FORB. This diversity of secularisms and the role of neutrality needs to be accounted for in the case law on religious freedom. The case law often highlights the role of political instrumentalisation of both the religious and secular. How are these concepts used and into whose service are they pressed? When are they invoked and appealed to? What work do they do in practice? These questions are relevant to both understanding and realising the right to religious freedom. Furthermore, these questions are more problematic when considering the specific status of religious organisations. The fear of Islamic fundamentalism overshadows European politics in many ways, but, more often than not, debates avoid, rather than confront, the most difficult challenges raised by religious accommodation. Contemporary scholarly and public debates tend to focus on 'varieties of secularism' and on identifying the appropriate place of religion in the public sphere; at the same time, the important constitutional consequences that follow from multiple conflicting *understandings* of religion and the challenge of post-secularism/post-modernism have been given rather short shrift. As Hervieu-Leger points out, the proliferation of religious groups is best understood as an aspect *of modernity* rather than just a reaction *against* modernity. It is possible that the ruptures of modernity and secularism might be experienced by most religious movements in due course, thereby challenging their foundational claims and goals. The insecurities generated by these new possibilities (of pluralist identities) coupled with the conditions of economic and political uncertainties might mean that some religious groups might not continue to flourish. In light of what Habermas calls the 'post-metaphysical' or 'post-secular age' (that Ratzinger partially cautions against), profound metaphysical questions, which also have direct bearing on the law and state, might require responses beyond the confines of a liberal theory that centralises neutrality. In other words, new ethical dilemmas, such as, in the medical or family context, need to be tackled directly. Thus, modernity should be regarded as an ongoing project that has not yet delivered on all of its promises. Recent far-right populism and religious fundamentalism both alert us to the fact that there are important pockets of reaction against globalisation and liberal modernism. Not everyone has equally benefitted from globalisation or general technological advances. A critical awareness of the instrumentalisation of religious freedom, as discussed by critical religion scholars such as Winnifred Sullivan, is crucial, but it is also important to explore the legal and policy frameworks that enable rights protection. Marie-Bénédicte Dembour argues that 'we must have the intellectual and moral honesty to confront the inherent limitations of the human rights concept and the emancipatory model it purports to embody'.[2] Of course, a generous approach to the right to religion or belief through the implementation of a legal duty or policy approach in favour of religious accommodation is unable to resolve the multitudinous issues that religion raises. Moreover, religious accommodation itself does not *necessarily* make the religious life more fulfilling for claimants. Nor will religious accommodation safeguard others from the excesses and abuses carried out in the name of religion. But it may be one step towards developing a fair, consistent, and transparent approach by implementing my model of religious accommodation in liberal states. A robust liberal solution to the challenges posed by religion in the form of a legal duty or policy in favour of religious accommodation is achievable, as has been demonstrated by my model.

---

[2] M Dembour, *Who Believes in Human Rights?* (Cambridge, Cambridge University Press, 2006) 114.

Appendix: Guidelines on the Limits of Religious Accommodation for Decision-makers

These guidelines are aimed at courts, education providers, employers, and decision makers in order to help them to decide the limits of the right to FORB and to explore how religious accommodation as a duty or policy approach can be realised in practice.

Category 1 Harms to Health and Safety of Others
• (Potential) harm to the health and safety of others is the strongest reason for non-accommodation.
• Harms to the health and safety of others exist on a spectrum.
• Health and safety might be a relevant consideration even if the harm is not readily apparent, for example, if it affects mental wellbeing.
• Harms to the health and safety of others should not be merely abstract.
• Harms must be more than trivial, substantiated by evidence, and balanced against competing interests of autonomy.
• Employers should consider carrying out a risk assessment to determine whether it is possible to eliminate or minimise harm to a negligible degree to the health and safety of others in order to consider seriously whether accommodating a religious claim is possible.
• Public bodies, employers and institutions should justify non-accommodation with well founded and consistent reasons and reference to specific harms and not by appeals to generic health and safety concerns.

Category 2 Harms to the Access to Rights, Goods and Services
• Category 2 harms are concerned with how a religious claim might limit the autonomy of others by preventing or significantly reducing access to rights, goods and services.
• The nature of the right, goods or service is a weighty consideration since protection of access to core rights, goods and services strongly justifies the non-accommodation of a religious claim.

- Where a religious claim would result in the complete prevention of access to core rights, goods and services, it should not be accommodated.
- A religious claim, therefore, should not impede the rights of others to adequate access to a right, good or service.
- Where alternative adequate access to a good exists, there is discretion for the accommodation of a religious practice if the context allows.
- The context will depend on the nature of the right, good or service in question; the feasibility of ensuring safe and efficient services; and whether appropriate and flexible use of discretion is possible.
- Category 2 harms relate to the practical ways in which others are prevented from accessing services because of a religious claim or belief.
- However, restricting access to rights, goods and services might, in some cases, result in dignitarian harm (category 3 harms).

Category 3 Harm to the Dignity of Others

- Religious claims sometimes result in harming the dignity of others.
- Dignity remains an important albeit contested concept.
- Dignity is to be defined as dignity-as-autonomy.
- A harm to dignity is not necessarily the same as unequal treatment, although the two can overlap.
- Dignity is violated if a religious claim undermines:
  - the self-worth of others; or
  - exploits the weaker position of minorities by stigmatising or ostracising them. This is important because stigma, in turn, limits the autonomy of others since it can limit the adequacy of options available to those who are stigmatised.
- Dignity as a harm should not be 'inflated' so as to undermine the right to freedom of expression.
- A contextual approach is necessary since there is always a risk of seepage of social, moral and political biases into the process of identifying what constitutes dignitary harm.

Category 4 Harms caused by Practical Costs

- Category 4 harms arise from the impracticality or cost, financial or otherwise, incurred by accommodating a religious claim.
- Category 4 harms constitute the weakest reasons for non-accommodation because the presumption of the proposed model is in favour of accommodation and, accordingly, practical burdens should generally not be considered weighty reasons for non-accommodation.

- Harm as excessive practical cost is found where an accommodation imposes a high burden on another such as an employer or educational institute.
- Cases that address what might be classified as 'clear direct costs' include harm to economic interests or administrative inconvenience.
- Employers should substantiate the cost or burden of accommodation since employers are generally in a stronger position.

(1) The Medical Context

- Religious accommodation in the medical context is dependent on who makes a religious claim or request for accommodation.
- As a starting point, both healthcare professionals and patients should be able to make requests for accommodation, although different considerations apply in each case.
- Patients reserve the right to refuse a specific course of treatment, and religious reasons might constitute legitimate reasons for the refusal.
- However, where a refusal based on a religious claim is made, healthcare professionals should engage with patients in a non-judgemental and non-confrontational way in order to understand the latter's reasoning, values and wishes and ascertain the extent to which accommodation is possible.
- Healthcare professionals should engage with the families of patients when it is appropriate to do so in order to improve the process of consent and treatment.
- The feasibility of claims should be tested against my model of four categories of harm.
- Claims made by healthcare professionals should be permissible, if:
  - They are consistent with their professional obligations and duties. These duties can be interpreted in light of the four categories of harm where appropriate.
  - The health and safety of others (primarily the patients) is priority and the strongest reason for non-accommodation.
  - Access to health services should not be obstructed by a religious claim.
  - The dignity of patients should be a consideration so that any claims that are accommodated are implemented with sensitivity and discretion.
- Category 4 types of harm are, ideally, to be mitigated by healthcare providers who should consider how they might devise accommodative policies so that certain kinds of exemptions might be granted to healthcare professionals.

(2) Children's Rights

(a) Education

- Full exemptions from school attendance and from state supervision of education should generally not be permitted because they risk harming a child's future autonomy since it is difficult to guarantee a home-schooling education that is holistic and of a high quality.
- Home-schooling should only be permissible if certain strict conditions are met. These should include the following: state supervision; adherence to a standard syllabus; and periodic review and scrutiny of home-schooling practices.
- The education curriculum should be delivered in 'an objective, critical and pluralistic' manner as is required by the jurisprudence of the ECtHR.
- Specific exemptions from classes should be considered on a case-by-case basis and be limited in scope.
- Exemptions from specific classes or topics should not be granted where they would undermine a child's right to a holistic education.
- The child's best interests should be a guiding principle.
- Exemptions from controversial topics such as sex education and evolutionary theory should not be permitted, especially if the exclusion causes harm such as in the case of sex education.

(b) Non-therapeutic Male Circumcision

- Male circumcision is an example where relational autonomy that locates autonomy in its appropriate familial and cultural context is more important than individual autonomy since it usually concerns children whose best interests need to be assessed within their religious, social and cultural context.
- Risks to the health and safety of the child can be minimised if there is an over-arching framework that guides the procedure according to the following two key criteria: (i) the procedure is to be legally regulated; and (ii) it is to be carried out by a suitably qualified medical practitioner.
- A decision to circumcise a male child is inherently one that concerns the autonomy of several parties including the child and both parents.
- Both parents should agree and consent to male circumcision before it is carried out whether it be on the grounds of religious or cultural reasons.
- Male circumcision should always be carried out by a suitable and appropriately qualified medical practitioner.

- The best interests of the child override the interests of parents. This means that other factors aside from religious and cultural factors might need to be taken into consideration in a specific case when determining whether non-therapeutic circumcision should go ahead.
- However, the best interests of the child also include religious and cultural interests.
- The negotiation of competing interests is a preferable option for balancing relevant factors.
- In the case of conflicts between individuals, institutions or rights, mediation should be considered as the first best option as a way to come to an agreeable solution.

(3) Religious Organisations

- The formal establishment of Church or religion should be subject to the requirements of secularism as a fundamental constitutional norm.
- This means any requests for accommodation that seek to undermine the liberal order will not be accommodated.
- Religious organisations that provide 'core' services should ideally obtain formal recognition so that they can be adequately regulated.
- Religious institutional autonomy should be protected to the extent that it does not harm the autonomy of others outside the organisation. This can be referred to 'internal' autonomy. Internal autonomy might mean that the organisation hires on a particular basis and subjects its employees to certain religious rules that might be contrary to the general equality laws. In this way, internal institutional autonomy constitutes an exemption.
- 'External institutional autonomy' refers to what a religious organisation can reasonably do outside of its internal institutional structure.
- External institutional autonomy should be limited by the implementation of regulatory frameworks that ensure compliance with core human rights obligations.
- Group-based exemptions should be available to a specific class of persons and limited in scope.
- Within a religious organisation, members are able to choose which parts of their autonomy and decision-making they will delegate to others, for example, to a specific religious leader or institution.
- There should be an 'exit' option. The 'right to exit' should exist for every member of a religious organisation. However, it is not possible, nor desirable, for the law to regulate this aspect in detail. Such cases concern 'complex autonomy' where more attention needs to be paid to securing options for individuals.

INDEX

Milton Keynes UK
Ingram Content Group UK Ltd.
UKHW031539160224
437875UK00003BA/58